Bible Studies
Judges Ruth Samuel

Second Edition

James Malm

ISBN: 978-1-989208-00-7
copyright © 2016 James Malm
All Rights Reserved
Unless otherwise noted all scripture quotes
are from the KJV

Dedication

This work is dedicated to the Great God whose house is eternity; the Father and Sovereign of all that exists, and the sum of all Truth, Wisdom, Love, Justice and Mercy.
May God's house be filled with children whose chief joy is to be like Him!

Visit Our Website
theshininglight.info

Table of Contents

Judges 7

    Judges 1 8
    Judges 2 14
    Judges 3 19
    Judges 4 25
    Judges 5 30
    Judges 6 36
    Judges 7 42
    Judges 8 47
    Judges 9 52
    Judges 10 59
    Judges 11 62
    Judges 12 68
    Judges 13 70
    Judges 14 74
    Judges 15 78
    Judges 16 81
    Judges 17 87
    Judges 18 89
    True Godliness 95
    Judges 19 103
    Judges 20 107
    Judges 21 113
    Lessons from Judges 116

Ruth 123

    Pentecost and Ruth 124
    Ruth 1 126
    Ruth 2 129
    Ruth 3 133
    Ruth 4 136

First Samuel 139

    1 Samuel 1 140

1 Samuel 2	145
1 Samuel 3	152
1 Samuel 4	156
1 Samuel 5	160
1 Samuel 6	163
1 Samuel 7	167
1 Samuel 8	173
1 Samuel 9	178
1 Samuel 10	182
1 Samuel 11	187
1 Samuel 12	190
1 Samuel 13	194
1 Samuel 14	198
1 Samuel 15	206
1 Samuel 16	213
1 Samuel 17	217
1 Samuel 18	226
1 Samuel 19	232
1 Samuel 20	235
1 Samuel 21	243
1 Samuel 22	246
1 Samuel 23	250
1 Samuel 24	255
1 Samuel 25	258
1 Samuel 26	266
1 Samuel 27	271
1 Samuel 28	273
1 Samuel 29	278
1 Samuel 30	280
1 Samuel 31	285
Second Samuel	**287**
2 Samuel 1	288
2 Samuel 2	292

2 Samuel 3	296
2 Samuel 4	302
2 Samuel 5	304
2 Samuel 6	307
2 Samuel 7	312
2 Samuel 8	321
2 Samuel 9	324
2 Samuel 10	326
2 Samuel 11	331
2 Samuel 12	335
2 Samuel 13	340
2 Samuel 14	347
2 Samuel 15	352
2 Samuel 16	357
2 Samuel 17	361
2 Samuel 18	365
2 Samuel 19	371
2 Samuel 20	377
2 Samuel 21	381
2 Samuel 22	385
2 Samuel 23	390
2 Samuel 24	394

Judges

Judges 1

Deuteronomy is a warning that possession of the promised land is absolutely dependent on people continuing to live by every Word of God, while Joshua is a lesson that it is only through faith and a diligent living by every Word of God that Satan and sin can be conquered.

The books of Judges, Samuel, Kings and Chronicles are a history of what happens when we are zealous to live by every Word of God; and what happens when we fall into idolatry, exalting anyone or anything above the Word of Almighty God.

The first king of Israel, Saul, was the people's choice: God gave them the kind of king they wanted; a worldly kind of political king who catered to the whims of the people and did what he thought was right instead of living by every Word of God.

King Saul was then contrasted by king David who was the real choice of Almighty God, because he tried to live by every Word of God in spite of making occasional errors. The book of Ruth is an introduction to this godly king called David.

The first two chapters of Judges are largely a recap and expansion on the last few chapters of Joshua, explaining the situation in Palestine around the time of the death of Joshua and the transition into the period of the Judges.

During all the days of the leadership of Joshua and the days of those that he had taught; the people followed and lived by every Word of God as Joshua did. Joshua was a godly man and after he and the men he had taught had died, many ungodly men began to lead people away from God in this history, as is also the case in today's Spiritual Ekklesia.

The Canaanites were a type of sin and when Israel failed to drive them out Israel fell into the wicked ways of the Canaanites. This was recorded for our instruction, to teach us to work diligently to drive all sin out of our lives and to follow the whole Word of God, never compromising with or tolerating any sin.

Leaders make a profound impression on the people, and people will largely follow their physical leaders for good or evil. Remember this natural tendency and prove the words of all men by the whole Word of God and follow men only as they follow God (1 Thess 5:21)!

Judges is an historical lesson for us, that when we are zealous for God he will be zealous to deliver us; and when we are lax to follow God and to keep his Word; God will turn away from us.

Judges 1

The tribes of Judah and Simeon go up to occupy the land given to them.

Judges 1:1 Now after the death of Joshua it came to pass, that the children of Israel asked the LORD, saying, Who shall go up for us against the Canaanites first, to fight against them? **1:2** And the LORD said, **Judah shall go up: behold, I have delivered the land into his hand. 1:3** And Judah said unto Simeon his brother, Come up with me into my lot, that we may fight against the Canaanites; and I likewise will go with thee into thy lot. So Simeon went with him.

The Canaanites who lived in the land had become extremely wicked, and were used by God as a type of sin.

Many have said that Egypt was a type of sin and that idea is wrong. Egypt was a type of BONDAGE to Satan and sin. All of the Egyptians were not destroyed; only their first born, their god-king and his army were destroyed as an instructional allegory that Satan himself, the god king of this world and his army of spirits will ultimately be destroyed.

All of the Canaanites were to be utterly destroyed as types of sin and as an example that we, spiritually and physically, must also destroy all sin out of our lives.

1:4 And Judah went up; and the LORD delivered the Canaanites and the Perizzites into their hand: and they slew of them in Bezek ten thousand men. **1:5** And they found Adonibezek in Bezek: and they fought against him, and they slew the Canaanites and the Perizzites. **1:6** But Adonibezek fled; and they pursued after him, and caught him, and cut off his thumbs and his great toes.

Judah and Simeon then did to Adonibezek what he had himself done to seventy kings. This word kings might be better understood today as rulers or leaders, since they ruled over cities and not great nations.

1:7 And **Adonibezek said, Threescore and ten kings, having their thumbs and their great toes cut off, gathered their meat under my table: as I have done, so God hath requited me.** And they brought him to Jerusalem, and there he died.

Jerusalem was defeated but not occupied.

1:8 Now the children of Judah had fought against Jerusalem, and had taken it, and smitten it with the edge of the sword, and set the city on fire.

Judah and Simeon then went south to attack Hebron.

1:9 And afterward the children of Judah went down to fight against the Canaanites, that dwelt in the mountain, and in the south, and in the valley. **1:10** And Judah went against the Canaanites that dwelt in Hebron: (now the name of Hebron before was Kirjatharba:) and they slew Sheshai, and Ahiman, and Talmai.

Caleb's portion

1:11 And from thence he went against the inhabitants of Debir: and the name of Debir before was Kirjathsepher: **1:12** And Caleb said, He that smiteth Kirjathsepher, and taketh it, to him will I give Achsah my daughter to wife.

Kenaz was Caleb's younger brother and his son took the city and was given his cousin Achsah in marriage.

1:13 And Othniel the son of Kenaz, Caleb's younger brother, took it: and he gave him Achsah his daughter to wife.

1:14 And it came to pass, when she came to him, that she moved him to ask of her father a field: and she lighted from off her ass; and Caleb said unto her, What wilt thou? **1:15** And she said unto him, Give me a blessing: for thou hast given me a south land; give me also springs of water. And Caleb gave her the upper springs and the nether springs.

The Kenites who were in-laws of Moses [today called Bedouin] then came and dwelt with Judah in the Negev.

1:16 And **the children** [descendants, family of] **of the Kenite, Moses' father in law,** went up out of the city of palm trees with the children of Judah into the wilderness of Judah, which lieth in the south of Arad; and they went and dwelt among the people.

Judah and Simeon conquered the Negev and all the lands of the Philistines.

1:17 And Judah went with Simeon his brother, and they slew the Canaanites that inhabited Zephath, and utterly destroyed it. And the name of the city was called Hormah. **1:18** Also Judah took Gaza with the coast thereof, and Askelon with the coast thereof, and Ekron with the coast thereof. **1:19** And the LORD was with Judah; and he drave out the inhabitants of the mountain; but could not drive out the inhabitants of the valley, because they had chariots of iron.

If we are zealous to follow and keep the whole Word of God sin will not have dominion over us; but we shall conquer sin through the Might of the God that we follow as he fights for us and gives us the victory through his mighty deliverance!

Caleb the faithful, receives his promised inheritance

1:20 And they gave Hebron unto Caleb, as Moses said: and he expelled thence the three sons of Anak.

Jerusalem which was given to Benjamin remained inhabited by the Jebusites to the day that this was written. Later the city was taken by David the king and made the royal capital city of Israel and the place of the Temple of God.

Events AFTER the death of Joshua and those whom he had taught

1:21 And the children of Benjamin did not drive out the Jebusites that inhabited Jerusalem; but the Jebusites dwell with the children of Benjamin in Jerusalem unto this day [the day this was written].

Judah and Simeon and Joseph and all Israel were victorious as long as they remained faithful to live by every Word of God; it was when they began to turn away from zeal for the Eternal that they ran into trouble.

The same is true of the spiritually called out; as long as we are turned away from the Eternal to do as we think is right in our own eyes we cannot overcome sin; it is only when we are zealous to follow the Eternal and to learn and to live by every Word of God that we will be victorious over sin through the power of our Mighty Deliverer!

1:22 And the house of Joseph, they also went up against Bethel: and the LORD was with them. **1:23** And the house of Joseph sent to descry Bethel. (Now the name of the city before was Luz.)

A man and his family who helped the tribe of Joseph were saved alive and let go.

1:24 And the spies saw a man come forth out of the city, and they said unto him, Shew us, we pray thee, the entrance into the city, and we will shew thee mercy. **1:25** And when he shewed them the entrance into the city, they smote the city with the edge of the sword; but they let go the man and all his family. **1:26** And the man went into the land of the Hittites, and built a city, and called the name thereof Luz: which is the name thereof unto this day [the day that this was written].

After the death of Joshua when Israel had became strong, they began to be filled with pride in their own greatness and began to defy God and they did not drive out the Canaanites but put them under tribute. They did not drive the wicked out as a type of spiritually removing all sin, but began to try to gain advantage from sin.

Jesus Christ then used the Canaanites [a type of sin], to test, try and prove Israel as to their zeal for God. Even so; today, we are also being tested as to our zeal to put out all sin and passionately live by every Word of God!

Just like ancient Israel who did not drive the wicked out of the land, today's Spiritual Ekklesia has not utterly driven out all sin by teaching the brethren to live by every Word of God but has compromised with and allowing unrebuked sin in order to gain members and lucre.

1:27 Neither did Manasseh drive out the inhabitants of Bethshean and her towns, nor Taanach and her towns, nor the inhabitants of Dor and her towns, nor the inhabitants of Ibleam and her towns, nor the inhabitants of Megiddo and her towns: but the Canaanites would dwell in that land. **1:28**

And it came to pass, when Israel was strong, that **they put the Canaanites to tribute, and did not utterly drive them out.**

1:29 Neither did Ephraim drive out the Canaanites that dwelt in Gezer; but the Canaanites dwelt in Gezer among them.

1:30 Neither did Zebulun drive out the inhabitants of Kitron, nor the inhabitants of Nahalol; but **the Canaanites dwelt among them, and became tributaries.**

1:31 Neither did Asher drive out the inhabitants of Accho, nor the inhabitants of Zidon, nor of Ahlab, nor of Achzib, nor of Helbah, nor of Aphik, nor of Rehob: **1:32** But the Asherites dwelt among the Canaanites, the inhabitants of the land: for they did not drive them out.

1:33 Neither did Naphtali drive out the inhabitants of Bethshemesh, nor the inhabitants of Bethanath; but he dwelt among the Canaanites, the inhabitants of the land: nevertheless the inhabitants of Bethshemesh and of Bethanath **became tributaries unto them**.

1:34 And the Amorites forced the children of Dan into the mountain: for they would not suffer them to come down to the valley: **1:35** But the Amorites would dwell in mount Heres in Aijalon, and in Shaalbim: yet the hand of the house of Joseph prevailed, so that **they became tributaries**. **1:36** And the coast of the Amorites was from the going up to Akrabbim, from the rock, and upward.

Judges 2

Because of the wickedness of the people after the death of Joshua, the messenger of God then pronounced sentence on Israel for breaking their covenant to zealously live by every Word of God.

Today's Spiritual Ekklesia as corporate groups have also broken their baptismal covenant and turned away from any zeal for the practical application of the Word of God, into a zeal for their idols of men who teach them contrary to the Word of God. God asks us: **Luke 6:46** And why call ye me, Lord, Lord, and do not the things which I say?

Judges 2:1 And an angel of the LORD came up from Gilgal to Bochim, and said,

The question being asked of physical Israel here is also being asked of the latter day Spiritual Israel: WHY are you zealous for your idols of men, and WHY are you not zealous to destroy all sin out of your midst to live by every Word of God, asks the Eternal?

. . . I made you to go up out of Egypt, and have brought you unto the land which I sware unto your fathers; and I said, I will never break my covenant with you. **2:2** And ye shall make no league with the inhabitants of this land; ye shall throw down their altars: **but ye have not obeyed my voice: why have ye done this?**

Therefore the Canaanites would remain and would be as thorns among Israel to tempt them away from the Eternal.

Today the spiritual Ekklesia commit the same sin by tolerating unrebuked and unrepentant sins in the congregations.

2:3 Wherefore I also said, **I will not drive them out from before you**; but they shall be as thorns in your sides, and their gods shall be a snare unto you.

> Israel's exclusive right to the land was lost through unbelief and rejecting the theocratic rule of God and not keeping the law that God gave them.
>
> The first verses of Judges 3 detail the Canaanite peoples who would remain. "Now these are the nations which the Lord left, to prove Israel by them, even as many of Israel as had not known all the wars of Canaan. Namely, five lords of the Philistines [the Philistines are not Canaanites], and all the Canaanites, and the Sidonians, and the Hivites that dwelt in **mount Lebanon, from mount Baalhermon** [Mount Hermon] **unto the entering in of Hamath.**"
>
> Others like the Hittites also remained in the land for a time. Heth the second son of Canaan was the father of the Hittites. The Hittites lived in Hebron (Gen 23:18-20) until most of whom were driven out of Canaan by invading Assyrians and Babylonians and eventually migrated to Asia Minor, finally founding an empire with the capital city of Troy.
>
> Defeated by the Greeks at Troy they then migrated to northern France, so named because they were called Franks by the Romans; and called their capital city after their king Paris.

Israel repented in words only and not in deeds: Even so we today pay lip service to keeping the Word of God, while in actual deeds we are doing our own ways.

Judges 2:4 And it came to pass, when the angel of the LORD spake these words unto all the children of Israel, that the people lifted up their voice, and wept. **2:5** And they called the name of that place Bochim: and they sacrificed there unto the LORD.

The brief inset about the death of Joshua

Joshua lets the people go and prepares to die

> **2:6** And when Joshua had let the people go, the children of Israel went every man unto his inheritance to possess the land.
>
> **2:7** And the people served the LORD all the days of Joshua, and all the days of the elders that outlived Joshua, who had seen all the great works of the LORD, that he did for Israel.
>
> **2:8 And Joshua the son of Nun, the servant of the LORD, died, being an hundred and ten years old. 2:9** And they buried him in the border of his inheritance in Timnathheres, in the mount of Ephraim, on the north side of the hill Gaash.

The next generation turned from the Eternal into the sins of the Canaanites. The Canaanites had been left in the land with their gods and sins, becoming a temptation to Israel to turn to their sins.

2:10 And also all that generation were gathered unto their fathers: and there arose another generation after them, which knew not the LORD, nor yet the works which he had done for Israel. **2:11 And the children of Israel did evil in the sight of the LORD, and served Baalim: 2:12 And they forsook the LORD God of their fathers, which brought them out of the land of Egypt, and followed other gods, of the gods of the people that were round about them, and bowed themselves unto them, and provoked the LORD to anger.**

2:13 And they forsook the LORD, and served [the sun god] Baal and Ashtaroth [Easter (Semiramis), the consort of Baal].

The God Being who later gave up his God-hood to be made flesh as Jesus Christ then corrected the people who had turned away from him; just as he will correct today's Spiritual Israel for our idols of men and corporate entities, for our tolerating of sin in our midst and for our lack of zeal to learn and live by every Word of God.

Just as Jesus Christ corrected physical Israel, he will also correct spiritual Israel.

2:14 And the anger of the LORD was hot against Israel, and he delivered them into the hands of spoilers that spoiled them, and he sold them into the hands of their enemies round about, so that they could not any longer stand before their enemies. **2:15** Whithersoever they went out, the hand of the

LORD was against them for evil, as the LORD had said, and as the LORD had sworn unto them: and they were greatly distressed.

When they cried out for deliverance Jesus Christ gave them judges [champions] from time to time, who would deliver the people and teach them the Word of God; and yet they continued in their sins, repenting in name and appearance only, while continuing their wicked deeds: Claiming to be righteous while continuing in rebellion against any practical zeal for keeping the whole Word of God.

They proclaimed themselves the people of God, while in their deeds they rebelled against God; just like today's Spiritual Ekklesia.

2:16 Nevertheless the LORD raised up judges, which delivered them out of the hand of those that spoiled them. **2:17** And yet **they would not hearken unto their judges, but they went a whoring after other gods, and bowed themselves unto them: they turned quickly out of the way which their fathers walked in, obeying the commandments of the LORD; but they did not so.**

From time to time Jesus Christ did raise up champions in response to the cries of the people, but the people quickly returned to their sins after the judges were gone.

2:18 And when the LORD raised them up judges, then the LORD was with the judge, and delivered them out of the hand of their enemies all the days of the judge: for it repented the LORD because of their groanings by reason of them that oppressed them and vexed them.

Each time a judge died the people corrupted themselves; just as today most of the Spiritual Ekklesia is largely morally corrupt, rejecting any zeal to live by every Word of God and tolerating sin within their assemblies.

2:19 And it came to pass, when the judge was dead, that they returned, and corrupted themselves more than their fathers, in following other gods to serve them, and to bow down unto them; **they ceased not from their own doings, nor from their stubborn way.**

The anger of Jesus Christ was hot against the rebellious and lukewarm of ancient Israel; just as it is hot against the spiritually lax latter day Spiritual Ekklesia, which he will cast out into the correction of great tribulation (Rev 3:16).

2:20 And the anger of the LORD was hot against Israel; and he said, Because that this people hath transgressed my covenant which I commanded their fathers, and have not hearkened unto my voice; **2:21** I also will not henceforth drive out any from before them of the nations which Joshua left when he died:

Christ used the Canaanites to prove and test the zeal and loyalty of Israel to God the Father and their covenant with him. Jesus Christ is TESTING US TODAY, to prove us, as to whether we will be zealous for our covenant with him to replace the old sinful man with zeal for the righteousness of the whole Word of God!

2:22 That through them I may prove Israel, **whether they will keep the way of the LORD to walk therein, as their fathers did keep it, or not.**

2:23 Therefore the LORD left those nations, without driving them out hastily; neither delivered he them [every Canaanite] into the hand of Joshua.

Judges 3

Today we live in a different dispensation then the period of the Mosaic Covenant. Physical Mosaic Covenant Israel was a national entity with a national religion, while other nations also had their national gods.

Jesus Christ as the God of Israel, was using Israel to demonstrate his might to all peoples, and the history of physical Mosaic Israel was recorded as object lessons for us about the spiritual battle against Satan, sin and death.

The entire history of physical Mosaic Israel in their struggles over physical opposition and sin, is a prophetic allegory of and instructions about the struggle of Spiritual Israel against Satan and sin.

The New Covenant person should understand that our struggle is not against flesh and blood; it against the spiritual powers in high places which manipulate and control men.

We are to condemn the sin, and love the men; forgiving them but not tolerating any sin: collectively with every person acting according to the spiritual gifts and calling that God provides, we are to loudly and openly rebuke all sin.

> **Isaiah 58:1** Cry aloud, spare not, lift up thy voice like a trumpet, and shew my people their transgression, and the house of Jacob their sins.

Judges 3:1 Now these are the nations which the LORD left, to prove Israel by them, even as many of Israel as had not known all the wars of Canaan; **3:2** Only that the generations of the children of Israel might know, to teach them war, at the least such as before knew nothing thereof;

God left five cities of the Philistines and many of the Canaanites and others that dwelt in the promised land remained to test and try the descendants of Israel who were born after the death of Joshua: Just as the spiritually called out are tested concerning our zeal to live by every Word of God.

3:3 Namely, five lords of the Philistines, and all the Canaanites, and the Sidonians, and the Hivites that dwelt in mount Lebanon, from mount Baalhermon unto the entering in of Hamath. **3:4 And they were to prove Israel by them, to know whether they would hearken unto the commandments of the LORD,** which he commanded their fathers by the hand of Moses.

Just as physical Israel fell away from any zeal for God and turned to a zeal for their own ways and the pleasures of sin; today's Spiritual Ekklesia has done the same thing.

3:5 And the children of Israel dwelt among the Canaanites, Hittites, and Amorites, and Perizzites, and Hivites, and Jebusites: **3:6** And they took their [unconverted] daughters to be their wives, and gave their daughters to their [unconverted] sons, **and served their gods.**

Many in today's Spiritual Ekklesia have tried to marry the Word of God with pagan prophecies and teachings, cleaving to many false teachings and rejecting any zeal for the Word of God; some even allowing marriages with the unconverted.

3:7 And the children of Israel did evil in the sight of the LORD, and forgat the LORD their God, and served Baalim and the groves.

In Hebrew, Asherah (of which the plural is Asherim or Asheroth), refers to any idol, and especially refers to either a living tree representing vigorous life, or a tree-like pole, or column set up as an object of worship, being symbolic of the male reproductive organ.

The word is often translated "green trees" or "grove." God forbade all idolatry (Deut. 16: 21; cf. Num. 25: 3; Judg. 2: 11-13; 1 Sam. 7: 3-4; 1 Kgs. 11: 5; Isa. 17: 8; Micah 5: 12).

Groves were mainly upright poles; which were fertility symbols of pagan sun worship based on fertility. In the pagan religion of Baal [worshiped by different names in Egypt, Greece, Rome and other lands] the dragon [cherub aka serpent] Satan was worshiped as the sun god who gave light and fertility to the earth.

Baal [Satan] was worshiped by fertility rites involving eggs, rabbits, evergreen trees [today the Christmas tree supposedly representing eternal life] and poles. Today these "groves" are common through the world as obelisks and steeples.

We are commanded not to gather to worship God near groves [which are steeples, idols [such as crosses, religious pictures, statues or obelisks or any kind of pagan symbol]; **this forbids meeting in any place having these pagan objects and symbols. Let the reader understand!**

This is utterly forbidden by the Word of God; and so is the spiritual idolizing of men and corporate churches as being in authority between men and God.

It was because of the sins of Israel in turning away from any zeal for the Word of God [especially idolatry, Sabbath pollution and marrying the unconverted; which are common sins in today's Spiritual Ekklesia], that they were allowed to fall before their enemies.

Here we have mention of one of the first great and powerful Mesopotamian rulers. God used this king to correct Israel and they were laid under tribute to him for eight years.

This was Jesus Christ correcting physical Israel; how much more will he correct Spiritual Israel who are supposed to have God's Spirit and are supposed to know better than physical Israel?

3:8 Therefore the anger of the LORD was hot against Israel, and **he sold them into the hand of Chushanrishathaim**[interpreted, as "man from Cush"] **king of Mesopotamia:** and the children of Israel served Chushanrishathaim **eight years.**

When the people cried out, God used the nephew of righteous Caleb to deliver them.

3:9 And when the children of Israel cried unto the LORD, the LORD raised up a deliverer to the children of Israel, who delivered them, even Othniel the son of Kenaz, Caleb's younger brother.

Othniel was a faithful man in whom God placed his Spirit: Yes, the Holy Spirit has been given to certain called out people since righteous Abel!

3:10 And **the Spirit of the LORD came upon him**, and he judged Israel, and went out to war: and the LORD delivered Chushanrishathaim king of Mesopotamia into his hand; and his hand prevailed against Chushanrishathaim. **3:11** And the land had rest forty years. And Othniel the son of Kenaz died.

As soon as this righteous leader died Israel fell right back into her sins! Her repentance only being a reaction to the correction, and not genuinely sincere.

This reminds me of fasting in today's assemblies; whenever they feel troubled, desiring a relief from their trouble but are not willing to change their behavior towards a zeal to live by every Word of God they fast. Their fasting's are all about selfishness; me, myself and I, and what we want; and these fasting's have nothing to do with sincere repentance and doing what God teaches us to do.

Moab, Ammon and the Amalekites are then allowed by the God being who later gave u his Godhood to become flesh as Jesus Christ to discomfit and correct Israel.

3:12 And the children of Israel did evil again in the sight of the LORD: and the LORD strengthened Eglon the king of Moab against Israel, because they had done evil in the sight of the LORD. **3:13** And he gathered unto him the children of Ammon and Amalek, and went and smote Israel, and possessed the city of palm trees [by Jericho].

3:14 So the children of Israel served Eglon the king of Moab eighteen years.

Jesus Christ then raised up Ehud who killed Eglon of Moab.

3:15 But when the children of Israel cried unto the LORD, the LORD raised them up a deliverer, **Ehud the son of Gera, a Benjamite, a man lefthanded**: and by him the children of Israel sent a present unto Eglon the king of Moab.

3:16 But Ehud made him a dagger which had two edges, of a cubit length [about 18 inches long from the tip of the blade to the tip of the handle]; and he did gird it under his raiment upon his right thigh. **3:17** And he brought the present unto Eglon king of Moab: and Eglon was a very fat man. **3:18** And when he had made an end to offer the present, he sent away the people that bare the present.

Ehud asks to tell Eglon a secret in privacy; and uses the opportunity to kill him in private.

3:19 But he himself turned again from the quarries that were by Gilgal, and said, I have a secret errand unto thee, O king: who said, Keep silence. And **all that stood by him went out from him.**

Consider the courage of Ehud who stood alone and slew the oppressor alone in his own chambers! Yet he was not alone for Jesus Christ was with him and had called upon him to do this astounding act; just as God the Father has called each of us through Jesus Christ to follow HIM, to trust in HIM and to be strong and of good courage to do whatever God commands.

As Ehud and Joshua were men of COURAGE to destroy sin and to do the will of God; let each of us have the courage to take a stand and keep the Word of God with our all our hearts and minds, by the strength of our Deliverer!

3:20 And Ehud came unto him; and he was sitting in a summer parlour, which he had for himself alone. And **Ehud said, I have a message from God unto thee.** And he arose out of his seat.

3:21 And Ehud put forth his left hand, and took the dagger from his right thigh, and thrust it into his belly: **3:22** And the haft also went in after the blade; and the fat closed upon the blade, so that he could not draw the dagger out of his belly; and the dirt came out.

3:23 Then Ehud went forth through the porch, and shut the doors of the parlour upon him, and locked them. **3:24** When he was gone out, his servants came; and when they saw that, behold, the doors of the parlour were locked, they said, Surely he covereth his feet [relieves himself] in his summer chamber. **3:25** And they tarried till they were ashamed: and, behold, he opened not the doors of the parlour; therefore they took a key, and opened them: and, behold, their lord was fallen down dead on the earth.

3:26 And Ehud escaped while they tarried, and passed beyond the quarries, and escaped unto Seirath.

Ehud then sounded the alarm and call to war; proclaiming that Eglon was dead and that they should rise up and fight to throw off the yoke of bondage.

Even so, today's spiritually called out are to sincerely repent of their idolatry and sin; and rise up and fight valiantly to throw off the yoke of sin; overcoming sin by the Mighty One of Jacob!

3:27 And it came to pass, when he was come, that he blew a trumpet in the mountain of Ephraim, and the children of Israel went down with him from the mount, and he before them.

3:28 And he said unto them, **Follow after me: for the LORD hath delivered your enemies the Moabites into your hand.** And they went down after him, and took the fords of Jordan toward Moab, and suffered not a man to pass over.

3:29 And they slew of Moab at that time about ten thousand men, all lusty [strong courageous young men], and all men of valour; and there escaped not a man. **3:30** So Moab was subdued that day under the hand of Israel. And the land had rest fourscore years.

The next judge was Shamgar the son of Anath

3:31 And after him was Shamgar the son of Anath, which slew of the Philistines six hundred men with an ox goad: and he also delivered Israel.

Judges 4

After Ehud and Shamgar, the people again fell into sin and Jesus afflicted them for their backsliding and covenant breaking by the Canaanite Sisera, until they cried out to God.

Judges 4:1 And the children of **Israel again did evil in the sight of the LORD, when Ehud was dead. 4:2** And **the LORD sold them into the hand of Jabin king of Canaan, that reigned in Hazor; the captain of whose host was Sisera,** which dwelt in Harosheth of the Gentiles.

Israel was then oppressed twenty years under the very heavy yoke of Jabin and Sisera.

4:3 And the children of Israel cried unto the LORD: for he had nine hundred chariots of iron; and twenty years he mightily oppressed the children of Israel.

Deborah a woman who was very zealous for the whole Word of God had become known throughout the nation as a person filled with the wisdom of God and the people looked to her, for God had called her to be a prophetess.

Deborah as a woman, could not be a priest or officiate over sacrifices or over formal commanded assemblies; she could take a Nazarite vow to dedicate herself to serve God; and God could call her as one of his prophets, to declare unto the nation the Word of God and she could teach and judge the people.

God very often calls his prophets from among the lowly [and calls women as prophetesses] to communicate with the brethren and to correct the priests, Levites, elders and leaders because they are not doing their job in teaching a zeal for the Word of God.

The Word of God teaches that a woman may not officiate in solemn assemblies; that does not mean that women cannot be called to the office of prophetesses to communicate the Word of God to the elders and brethren.

Women must not usurp the functions of the priesthood in offering sacrifices, officiating over commanded religious assemblies and formal services. Nevertheless a woman even a prophetess, is always under the authority of her husband as long as he lives. We can therefore say that the husband of Deborah, Lapidoth, was probably also a godly person.

4:4 And Deborah, a prophetess, the wife of Lapidoth, she judged Israel at that time. **4:5** And she dwelt under the palm tree of Deborah between Ramah and Bethel in mount **Ephraim**: and the children of Israel came up to her for judgment.

Jesus Christ sent a message through Deborah to Barak. Notice that Deborah is the messenger; it is Barak who must lead the people and do the job.

4:6 And she sent and called Barak the son of Abinoam out of Kedeshnaphtali, and said unto him, Hath not **the LORD God of Israel commanded, saying, Go and draw toward mount Tabor, and take with thee ten thousand men of the children of Naphtali and of the children of Zebulun?**

Jesus Christ promises that he will draw Sisera out to battle and will go before Barak to destroy Sisera and his army.

4:7 And I will draw unto thee to the river Kishon Sisera, the captain of Jabin's army, with his chariots and his multitude; and I will deliver him into thine hand.

Timid and fearful, Barak then demanded that she go with him; thereby losing any personal acclaim that he might have been given.

4:8 And Barak said unto her, If thou wilt go with me, then I will go: but if thou wilt not go with me, then I will not go. **4:9** And she said, I will surely go with thee: notwithstanding the journey that thou takest shall not be for thine honour; for **the LORD shall sell Sisera into the hand of a woman.** And Deborah arose, and went with Barak to Kedesh.

4:10 And Barak called Zebulun and Naphtali to Kedesh; and he went up with ten thousand men **at his feet** [this phrase means under his authority]: and Deborah went up with him.

Now God uses Heber to bring out the army of Sisera to battle.

4:11 Now Heber the Kenite [A Bedouin was used by God to bring Sisera out to battle.], which was of the children of **Hobab** [Jethro] **the father in law of Moses**, had severed himself from the Kenites, and pitched his tent unto the plain of Zaanaim, which is by Kedesh. **4:12** And they shewed Sisera that Barak the son of Abinoam was gone up to mount Tabor.

Sisera gathered his whole army to battle

4:13 And Sisera gathered together all his chariots, even nine hundred chariots of iron, and all the people that were with him, from Harosheth of the Gentiles unto the river of Kishon.

Deborah delivered Christ's message to Barak to go up to the fight

4:14 And **Deborah said unto Barak, Up; for this is the day in which the LORD hath delivered Sisera into thine hand: is not the LORD gone out before thee?** So Barak went down from mount Tabor, and ten thousand men after him.

Just as the Eternal went before his people in physical battles: If we put our trust in him and follow him the battle to overcome sin: Is the Lord's!

Be not fearful or hesitant to keep the whole Word of God and to follow our Mighty One to overcome sin by HIS might!

4:15 And the LORD discomfited Sisera, and all his chariots, and all his host, with the edge of the sword before Barak; so that Sisera lighted down off his chariot, and fled away on his feet.

Sisera fled and hid while Barak continued to pursue his army and destroy it utterly; figurative of our utterly destroying all sin from ourselves by God's strength.

4:16 But Barak pursued after the chariots, and after the host, unto Harosheth of the Gentiles: and all the host of Sisera fell upon the edge of the sword; and there was not a man left.

Now Sisera while fleeing happens to come by the tent of the very Heber who had warned him that Barak had marshaled an army against him! God had said that he would bring out the army of Sisera and God did so by the word of Heber: And now Sisera was delivered to the tent of Heber, and thinking himself among friends and safe he goes in.

4:17 Howbeit Sisera fled away on his feet to the tent of **Jael the wife of Heber the Kenite**: for **there was peace between Jabin the king of Hazor and the house of Heber the Kenite**.

Jael offers Sisera rest with kind words of peace and encouragement.

4:18 And Jael went out to meet Sisera, and said unto him, Turn in, my lord, turn in to me; fear not. And when he had turned in unto her into the tent, she covered him with a mantle. **4:19** And he said unto her, Give me, I pray thee, a little water to drink; for I am thirsty. And she opened a bottle of milk, and gave him drink, and covered him.

Sisera requests that Jael stand guard over his safety.

4:20 Again he said unto her, Stand in the door of the tent, and it shall be, when any man doth come and enquire of thee, and say, Is there any man here? that thou shalt say, No.

When Sisera was asleep Jael went quietly to him and killed him; for she knew that victorious Barak would surely destroy her and her family for their association with Jabin and Sisera, which doubtless had brought them much gain over the years as collaborators.

4:21 Then Jael Heber's wife took a nail of the tent, and took an hammer in her hand, and went softly unto him, and smote the nail into his temples, and fastened it into the ground: for he was fast asleep and weary. So he died. **4:22** And, behold, as Barak pursued Sisera, Jael came out to meet him, and said unto him, Come, and I will shew thee the man whom thou seekest. And when he came into her tent, behold, Sisera lay dead, and the nail was in his temples.

Just as Deborah had prophesied, Sisera was killed by the hand of a woman: And by Jael's repudiation of Sisera at the end she also saved her own family alive.

Spiritually, this speaks of the fact that it is never too late to repent and turn to zeal for our Deliverer and his Word! It is now time to sincerely repent and turn to zealously learn and live by every Word of God

4:23 So God subdued on that day Jabin the king of Canaan before the children of Israel.

After the defeat of Sisera, Barak continued the fight until king Jabin was totally destroyed.

4:24 And the hand of the children of Israel prospered, and prevailed against Jabin the king of Canaan, until they had destroyed Jabin king of Canaan

Brethren, we must call out to our Great God to deliver us; and we must rise up to battle against the sin that besets us: We must fight the good fight to keep the whole Word of God and internalize the very nature of God, through the power of our Mighty One!

Judges 5

The victory song of Deborah and Barak, praising God for the victory

Judges 5:1 Then sang Deborah and Barak the son of Abinoam on that day, saying, **5:2** Praise ye the LORD for the avenging of Israel, when the people willingly offered themselves. **5:3** Hear, O ye kings; give ear, O ye princes; **I, even I, will sing unto the LORD; I will sing praise to the LORD God of Israel.**

This song picturing God's deliverance of physical Israel from Jabin and Sisera is a prophecy of the coming of Christ to open the graves of the overcomers and to establish God's kingdom over all the earth.

When Christ comes with his chosen elect the earth and its mountains shall SHAKE [this has the meaning of both the physical earth and its governments large and small] at the presence of the Deliverer and after that God's Spirit will be poured out as rain on the earth (Joel 2:28).

5:4 LORD, when thou wentest out of Seir, when thou marchedst out of the field of Edom, the earth trembled, and the heavens dropped, the clouds also dropped water. **5:5** The mountains melted from before the LORD, even that Sinai from before the LORD God of Israel.

Deborah then speaks of the days of the lordship of the Canaanite Jabin over Israel which was symbolic of sin controlling the brethren.

5:6 In the days of Shamgar the son of Anath, in the days of Jael, the highways were unoccupied, and the travellers walked through byways [travelers could not use the main roads and took back roads and trails] . **5:7** The inhabitants of the villages ceased, they ceased in Israel, until that I Deborah arose, that I arose a mother in Israel.

Deborah then rebukes Israel for their sin against God and God's Word.

When Israel turned away from zeal to live by every Word of God to follow their idols of men the Eternal brought then low and humbled them; and when they repented he delivered them. God will do the same with today's Spiritual Ekklesia

Throughout the history of physical Mosaic Covenant Israel the people regularly rebelled against God and were corrected and repented and delivered, and then the next generation went through the same process.

In Spiritual Israel each generation is also tested for their loyalty and zeal for the Eternal and the whole Word of God.

5:8 They chose new gods; then was war in the gates: was there a shield or spear seen among forty thousand in Israel?

Deborah longs for righteous judges [elders] in the land, who would offer themselves willingly to serve the Eternal to teach zeal for the Word of God to all the brethren.

What man ordained the Judges? No man; they were ordained directly by God and they judged and led at the direct calling of God, because the priests and Levites were not doing their jobs!

The situation is the same in today's Ekklesia where the elders are not doing their job of focusing all the brethren on living by every Word of God.

5:9 My heart is toward the governors of Israel, **that offered themselves willingly** [from] **among the people**. Bless ye the LORD.

Deborah calls on the judges and leaders [elders and priests and Levites] of Israel to diligently teach the people to live by every Word of the Great God.

5:10 Speak, ye that ride on white asses [rulers], ye that sit in judgment, and walk by the way.

Let every elder teach the great deeds and righteous acts of the Mighty One of Jacob; and turn the people back from their sins to embrace the Eternal and his Word in true sincere repentance.

Apostate elders and leaders need to return to a zeal for God and the enthusiastic keeping of his Word; then do their jobs and teach the people a passionate uncompromising zeal for God and the learning and keeping of the whole Word of God.

In those days the elders and leaders sat at the gates of the cities so as to be easily found by the people: After Christ comes many people will proclaim the deeds of the Eternal in the public places

5:11 They that are delivered from the noise of archers in the places of drawing water, there shall they rehearse the righteous acts of the LORD, even the righteous acts toward the inhabitants of his villages in Israel: then shall the people of the LORD go down to the gates. .

At his coming Jesus Christ will lead captivity captive and deliver all humanity from bondage to Satan and sin.

Today it is time for the Barak's and the Ehud's and the Deborah's; the Joshua's and Daniel's: To awake and arise and set an example of godliness and courage to take a stand for the Word of our God and teach a passionate zeal for the whole Word of our Mighty God!

5:12 Awake, awake, Deborah: awake, awake, utter a song: arise, Barak, and lead thy captivity captive, thou son of Abinoam.

The faithful and the zealous for the whole Word of God will be resurrected to spirit and made leaders in the Kingdom of God; so that they may teach a passionate zeal for the whole Word of God to all their brethren and to all of humanity!

5:13 Then he made him [the faithful to God] that remaineth have dominion over the nobles among the people: the LORD made me have dominion over the mighty.

At that time there was a revival of righteousness in northern Israel, Barak then fought the Amalekites, and righteous governors were set up and the Word was copied as before by the scribes.

5:14 Out of Ephraim was there a root of them against Amalek; after thee, Benjamin, among thy people; out of Machir came down governors, and out of Zebulun they that handle the pen of the writer.

The leaders of Issachar were with Deborah who asks; why does Reuben remain among the sheep in Bashan [Golan] and not go up to destroy the enemy?

5:15 And the princes of Issachar were with Deborah; even Issachar, and also Barak: he was sent on foot into the valley. For the divisions of Reuben [Reuben refused to help in the battle] there were great thoughts of heart. **5:16** Why abodest thou among the sheepfolds, to hear the bleatings of the flocks? For the divisions of Reuben there were great searchings of heart.

Reuben remained beyond Jordan and part of Dan left in ships, Asher remained by the sea; it was Issachar, Zebulun and Naphtali who fought the oppressor.

5:17 Gilead abode beyond Jordan: and why did Dan remain in ships? Asher continued on the sea shore, and abode in his breaches.

Alone in Israel, Issachar, Zebulun and Naphtali fought the oppressors Jabin and Sisera with the help of their God.

5:18 Zebulun and Naphtali were a people that jeoparded their lives unto the death in the high places of the field.

Then Barak fought the other Canaanite kings who came out against him. The armies of Issachar, Zebulun and Naphtali fought alone with no help from the other tribes, but their God was with them; they fought without wages in enthusiastic zeal for their God!

5:19 The kings came and fought, then fought the kings of Canaan in Taanach by the waters of Megiddo; they [Issachar, Zebulun and Naphtali] took no gain of money.

They fought with the backing of Christ and the enemy was swept away. Even so, WE must fight all sin with a burning zeal to internalize the very nature of our God!

5:20 They fought from heaven; the stars in their courses fought against Sisera. **5:21** The river of Kishon swept them away, that ancient river, the river Kishon. O my soul, thou hast trodden down strength.

The proud strength of sin shall be broken in us by the strength of our Deliverer: if we will only rise up and follow him to fight the good fight and contend with passion for the learning and keeping of every Word of God.

5:22 Then were the horsehoofs broken by the means of the pransings [pride], the pransings [pride] of their mighty ones.

Those who do not stand up in zeal to live by every Word of God are as cursed as the people of Meroz who refused to aid in the fight against the wicked.

5:23 Curse ye Meroz, said the angel of the LORD, curse ye bitterly the inhabitants thereof; because they came not to the help of the LORD, to the help of the LORD against the mighty.

Jael is called blessed because she repented and rose up to destroy the man of sin in her time. Let us also repent of serving sin, following idols of men and from polluting the holy Sabbath day; and turn to serve the whole Word of our God.

5:24 Blessed above women shall Jael the wife of Heber the Kenite be, blessed shall she be above women in the tent. **5:25** He [Sisera] asked water, and she gave him milk; she brought forth butter in a lordly dish. **5:26** She put her hand to the nail, and her right hand to the workmen's hammer; and with the hammer she smote Sisera, she smote off his head, when she had pierced and stricken through his temples.

This wicked oppressor was destroyed by Jael who overcame him; let the spiritually called out destroy sin and turn back to a passionate zeal for our Mighty One.

5:27 At her feet he bowed, he fell, he lay down: at her feet he bowed, he fell: where he bowed, there he fell down dead.

The mother of Sisera bewailed her son and her ladies sought to comfort her with false words. Will we the spiritually called out to the New Covenant who are full of idolatry and sin, be comforted by smooth words when we are in the tribulation of God's righteous correction for our sins?

5:28 The mother of Sisera looked out at a window, and cried through the lattice, Why is his chariot so long in coming? why tarry the wheels of his chariots? **5:29** Her wise ladies answered her, yea, she returned answer to herself, **5:30** Have they not sped? have they not divided the prey; to every man a damsel or two; to Sisera a prey of divers colours, a prey of divers colours of needlework, of divers colours of needlework on both sides, meet for the necks of them that take the spoil?

Let those who love the Eternal enough to be zealous to follow him [alone if necessary] whithersoever he goeth and zealously, passionately learn and keep the whole Word of God: be shining lights of righteousness forever!

Daniel 12:3 And they that be wise [living by every Word of God] shall shine as the brightness of the firmament; and they that turn many to righteousness as the stars for ever and ever.

Judges 5:31 So let all thine enemies perish, O LORD: but let them that love him be as the sun when he goeth forth in his might. And the land had rest forty years.

Judges 6

Israel again fell into sin and was then oppressed by the Midianites for seven years.

Judges 6:1 And the children of Israel did evil in the sight of the LORD: and the LORD delivered them into the hand of Midian seven years.

Because of the severe oppression many of Israel fled into the wilderness.

6:2 And the hand of Midian prevailed against Israel: and because of the Midianites the children of Israel made them the dens which are in the mountains, and caves, and strong holds.

The oppressors took away all the harvest and food out of the land

6:3 And so it was, when Israel had sown, that the Midianites came up, and the Amalekites, and the children of the east, even they came up against them; **6:4** And they encamped against them, and destroyed the increase of the earth, till thou come unto Gaza, and left no sustenance for Israel, neither sheep, nor ox, nor ass. **6:5** For they came up with their cattle and their tents, and they came as grasshoppers for multitude; for both they and their camels were without number: and they entered into the land to destroy it.

Israel then began to repent and to cry out to their Husband, the God Being who later gave up his God-hood to be made flesh as Jesus Christ.

6:6 And Israel was greatly impoverished because of the Midianites; and the children of Israel cried unto the LORD. **6:7** And it came to pass, when the children of Israel cried unto the LORD because of the Midianites,

Just as physical Israel had no zeal to keep the Word of God and fell into idolatry; so the latter day Spiritual Ekklesia has not had a zeal to learn and to keep the whole Word of God and has instead followed their idols of men and false traditions.

Just as physical Israel was delivered out of the bondage of physical Egypt; the called out of Spiritual Israel have been delivered out of bondage to the spiritual Egypt of Satan and sin; yet we have fallen away from Christ our Deliverer, even as physical Israel also fell away.

6:8 That the LORD sent a prophet unto the children of Israel, which said unto them, Thus saith the LORD God of Israel, I brought you up from Egypt, and brought you forth out of the house of bondage; **6:9** And I delivered you out of the hand of the Egyptians, and out of the hand of all that oppressed you, and drave them out from before you, and gave you their land; **6:10** And I said unto you, I am the LORD your God; fear [do not respect foreign gods and the idols of men] not the gods of the Amorites, in whose land ye dwell: **but ye have not obeyed my voice.**

Gideon is called out to deliver a somewhat repentant physical Israel.

Gideon, like Moses, Paul and all the judges and prophets, **was not called or ordained by men**; he was called and ordained to his office by Jesus Christ himself.

6:11 And there came an angel of the LORD, and sat under an oak which was in Ophrah, that pertained unto Joash the Abiezrite: and his son Gideon threshed wheat by the winepress, to hide it from the Midianites.

Gideon is proclaimed a mighty man of valor and zeal for the Eternal and his Word.

6:12 And the angel of the LORD appeared unto him, and said unto him, **The LORD is with thee, thou mighty man of valour.**

Gideon asks: Why have they fallen into such a state if God is with them?

6:13 And Gideon said unto him, Oh my Lord, if the LORD be with us, why then is all this befallen us? and where be all his miracles which our fathers told us of, saying, Did not the LORD bring us up from Egypt? but now the LORD hath forsaken us, and delivered us into the hands of the Midianites.

Gideon is among the poor of Manasseh and asks how he a lowly man can save Israel. God often uses the poor and the lowly to save his people, in fact nearly always; doing so that all will know that the man did not save, but the deliverance was from God.

This is also so that all people may learn that the lowliest and poorest and physically afflicted may conquer all sin through the power of God.

Jesus Christ sent Gideon! Gideon was not ordained to his office by any man, but directly by Jesus Christ.

6:14 And the LORD looked upon him, and said, Go in this thy might [the might of Gideon was his Deliverer, Jesus Christ], and thou shalt save Israel from the hand of the Midianites: **have not I sent thee?**

6:15 And he said unto him, Oh my Lord, wherewith shall I save Israel? behold, my family is poor in Manasseh, and I am the least in my father's house.

Even though God promises to be with him Gideon lacks faith to take a stand to obey and follow God: And so it is today, that very many are lacking the faith to take a stand on the whole Word of God.

6:16 And the LORD said unto him, **Surely I will be with thee, and thou shalt smite the Midianites as one man.**

God would go before them and Gideon and all his men were to act with one accord as one person, to completely destroy the enemy.

6:17 And he said unto him, If now I have found grace in thy sight, then shew me a sign that thou talkest with me. **6:18** Depart not hence, I pray thee, until I come unto thee, and bring forth my present, and set it before thee. And he [Christ] said, I will tarry until thou come again.

Gideon went and prepared a kid to offer to the Eternal; and the Eternal showed Gideon a miracle.

6:19 And Gideon went in, and made ready a kid, and unleavened cakes of an ephah of flour: the flesh he put in a basket, and he put the broth in a pot, and brought it out unto him under the oak, and presented it. **6:20** And the angel of God said unto him, Take the flesh and the unleavened cakes, and lay them upon this rock, and pour out the broth. And he did so. **6:21** Then the angel of the LORD put forth **the end of the staff that was in his hand, and touched the flesh and the unleavened cakes; and there rose up fire**

out of the rock, and consumed the flesh and the unleavened cakes. Then the angel of the LORD departed out of his sight.

Then Gideon was filled with fear; but God comforted him.

6:22 And when Gideon perceived that he was an angel of the LORD, Gideon said, Alas, O LORD God! for because I have seen an angel of the LORD face to face. **6:23** And the LORD said unto him, Peace be unto thee; fear not: thou shalt not die.

6:24 Then Gideon built an altar there unto the LORD, and called it Jehovahshalom: [YHVH's peace] unto this day [the day this was written] it is yet in Ophrah of the Abiezrites.

Jesus then appeared to Gideon and commanded him to destroy the altar of baal and build an altar to the Eternal and sacrifice his father's bullock as a burnt offering on it.

6:25 And it came to pass the same night, that the LORD said unto him, Take thy father's young bullock, even the second bullock of seven years old, and throw down the altar of Baal that thy father hath, and cut down the grove that is by it: **6:26** And build an altar unto the LORD thy God upon the top of this rock, in the ordered place, and take the second bullock, and offer a burnt sacrifice with the wood of the grove which thou shalt cut down.

Gideon obeyed the voice of the Eternal.

6:27 Then Gideon took ten men of his servants, and did as the LORD had said unto him: and so it was, because he feared his father's household, and the men of the city, that he could not do it by day, that he did it by night.

In the morning the people sought to kill Gideon for destroying their idol and building an altar to the Eternal and offering a Burnt Offering on it.

Today the called out to the New Covenant of the later day Ekklesia of God, have many idols; preferring to obey men instead of being zealous to wholeheartedly live by every Word of God.

These idols of men and false traditions that are preferred above zeal for the Word of God need to be totally destroyed just as Gideon destroyed the altar of baal; so that all may become wholeheartedly zealous to learn to live by every Word of God [which wholehearted zeal is symbolized by the whole Burnt Offering].

6:28 And when the men of the city arose early in the morning, behold, the altar of Baal was cast down, and the grove was cut down that was by it, and the second bullock was offered upon the altar that was built. **6:29** And they said one to another, Who hath done this thing? And when they enquired and asked, they said, Gideon the son of Joash hath done this thing.

Those brethren loved their idols and hated the iconoclast in their midst and desired to kill him. It is the same in today's Spiritual Ekklesia.

6:30 Then the men of the city said unto Joash, Bring out thy son, that he may die: because he hath cast down the altar of Baal, and because he hath cut down the grove that was by it.

The father of Gideon then helped him saying; if baal be a god let him come and defend himself!

Even so Jesus Christ will plead with the brethren in the great tribulation saying: You followed these men instead of my Word; now save yourselves if you can!

6:31 And Joash said unto all that stood against him, Will ye plead for Baal? will ye save him? he that will plead for him, let him be put to death whilst it is yet morning: **if he be a god, let him plead for himself, because one hath cast down his altar. 6:32** Therefore on that day he called him because he hath thrown down his altar.

At the time of harvest the enemies came up on the land to take the harvest; and the God who later became flesh as Jesus Christ inspired Gideon to rise up against them.

6:33 Then all the Midianites and the Amalekites and the children of the east were gathered together, and went over, and pitched in the valley of Jezreel.

6:34 But the Spirit of the LORD came upon Gideon, and he blew a trumpet; and Abiezer was gathered after him. **6:35** And he sent messengers throughout all **Manasseh**; who also was gathered after him: and he sent messengers unto **Asher**, and unto **Zebulun**, and unto **Naphtali**; and they came up to meet them.

Gideon then sought reassurance from the Eternal.

6:36 And Gideon said unto God, If thou wilt save Israel by mine hand, as thou hast said, **6:37** Behold, I will put a fleece of wool in the floor; and if the dew be on the fleece only, and it be dry upon all the earth beside, then shall I know that thou wilt save Israel by mine hand, as thou hast said. **6:38**

And it was so: for he rose up early on the morrow, and thrust the fleece together, and wringed the dew out of the fleece, a bowl full of water.

Then Gideon still being unsure, asked for a third test [the first being the kid and the fire].

If we say that Gideon was without faith; remember that Moses also sought reassurance from God.

Remember that we all had very little faith in the beginning and that faith grew as we grew in experience, knowledge and the understanding that comes from DOING the Word of God.

Consider the degree of faith in today's Ekklesia as so many fear to be zealous for the Word of God, afraid of the cost. There are high level elders who know that I speak the truth; yet they are afraid of being ostracized by fellow elders and friends and so they let their fear of men come between them and the Eternal God!

Gideon did not trust in himself, nor did he hide away; rather he sought assurance from God.

If one is unsure, always seek assurance from the Eternal! Today we have a much larger and more complete volume of the Word of God then Gideon had; let us go to it and prove all things by the whole Word of God!

6:39 And Gideon said unto God, Let not thine anger be hot against me, and I will speak but this once: let me prove, I pray thee, but this once with the fleece; let it now be dry only upon the fleece, and upon all the ground let there be dew. **6:40** And God did so that night: for it was dry upon the fleece only, and there was dew on all the ground.

Judges 7

Jesus Christ then told Gideon that the numbers of his army are to be reduced to the point that the people will ascribe the victory to God.

Both physical and spiritual Israel must learn that the victory belongs to the Eternal. Just as physical Israel could not overcome the Canaanites [a type of sin] alone without God; the Spiritual Ekklesia cannot overcome sin on their own and by their own ways.

Judges 7:1 Then Jerubbaal [let baal speak for himself], who is Gideon, and all the people that were with him, rose up early, and pitched beside the well of Harod: so that the host of the Midianites were on the north side of them, by the hill of Moreh, in the valley.

7:2 And the LORD said unto Gideon, The people that are with thee are too many for me to give the Midianites into their hands, **lest Israel vaunt themselves against me, saying, Mine own hand hath saved me.**

God commanded Gideon to let all the fearful go home: This represents that the spiritually fearful cannot overcome sin. To overcome sin we must have the faith to stand on the whole Word of God, no matter what the consequences may be.

7:3 Now therefore go to, proclaim in the ears of the people, saying, **Whosoever is fearful and afraid, let him return and depart early from mount Gilead. And there returned of the people twenty and two thousand; and there remained ten thousand.**

Christ then chooses to reduce the numbers through a test of how they drank water.

7:4 And the LORD said unto Gideon, The people are yet too many; bring them down unto the water, and I will try them for thee there: and it shall be, that of whom I say unto thee, This shall go with thee, the same shall go with thee; and of whomsoever I say unto thee, This shall not go with thee, the same shall not go.

Christ tells Gideon to separate those who lap up water like a dog [lifting up the water in their hands to their mouth, instead of bending down and putting their mouth down to the water to drink like the others]. Who do you suppose inspired these men to do that? Could it be that God had already chosen his men and inspired them to drink like that to fulfill the test?

7:5 So he brought down the people unto the water: and the LORD said unto Gideon, Every one that lappeth of the water with his tongue, as a dog lappeth, him shalt thou set by himself; likewise every one that boweth down upon his knees to drink.

Only three hundred were separated out

7:6 And the number of them that **lapped, putting their hand to their mouth, were three hundred** men: but all **the rest of the people bowed down upon their knees to drink water**.

Jesus Christ then told Gideon to take the three hundred and send the others home. This reduction in the numbers of men was necessary to make it certain that Gideon and all Israel knew that the battle and the victory were the Lord's.

7:7 And the LORD said unto Gideon, By the three hundred men that lapped [lifting water up to their mouth by their hands] will I save you, and deliver the Midianites into thine hand: and let all the other people go every man unto his place.

7:8 So the people took victuals in their hand, and their trumpets: and he sent all the rest of Israel every man unto his tent, and **retained those three hundred men:** and the host of Midian was beneath him in the valley.

Later as the night fell, God instructed Gideon to begin the fight and again sought to encourage Gideon: As we read further we shall see that the Midianites had killed Gideon's brothers, which is why he feared them so much.

7:9 And it came to pass the same night, that the LORD said unto him, Arise, get thee down unto the host; for I have delivered it into thine hand. **7:10** But if thou fear to go down, go thou with Phurah thy servant down to the host: **7:11** And thou shalt hear what they say; and afterward shall thine hands be strengthened to go down unto the host. Then went he [Gideon] down with Phurah his servant unto the outside of the armed men that were in the host.

7:12 And the Midianites and the Amalekites and all the children of the east lay along in the valley like grasshoppers for multitude; and their camels were without number, as the sand by the sea side for multitude.

God inspired the enemy with a dream, the recounting of which was heard by Gideon.

Gideon needed to hear this dream from the mouth of the enemy and understand the fear that God had placed in their hearts to be encouraged to the battle. How often do we need encouragement to take that final step and take a stand for what we know is true?

Today, very many are sitting on the fence fearing the cost of offending their elders, leaders and friends, or the cost of zealously living by every Word of God in their personal lives.

God encouraged Gideon and he will also encourage his called out. Shortly you will see all of the biblical signs of the imminent correction; and then the two servants of God will come in the full power that the scriptures ascribe to them; to encourage you to turn to the Eternal with a wholehearted and sincere zeal for learning and keeping the whole Word of God.

7:13 And when Gideon was come, behold, there was a man that told a dream unto his fellow, and said, Behold, I dreamed a dream, and, lo, a cake of barley bread tumbled into the host of Midian, and came unto a tent, and smote it that it fell, and overturned it, that the tent lay along.

7:14 And **his fellow answered and said, This is nothing else save the sword of Gideon the son of Joash, a man of Israel: for into his hand hath God delivered Midian, and all the host.**

My friends, God will deliver all those who turn to him in sincerity and truth, to be zealous to follow our Lord and keep his Word in passionate zeal.

If we have the courage to stand UP AND FOLLOW HIM; HE WILL GIVE US VICTORY OVER SIN!

7:15 And it was so, when Gideon heard the telling of the dream, and the interpretation thereof, that he worshipped [Gideon was at last impressed and exalted God], and returned into the host of Israel, and said, Arise; for the LORD hath delivered into your hand the host of Midian.

How long will it be before "God's people" are impressed with God and his Word; impressed enough, to love God enough to exalt him and to DO what he has said?

Let us RISE UP, and with the help of our Mighty One join the battle against sin and turn to a zeal to perform every Word of our God!

7:16 And he divided the three hundred men into three companies, and he put a trumpet in every man's hand, with empty pitchers, and lamps within the pitchers. **7:17** And he said unto them, Look on me, and do likewise: and, behold, when I come to the outside of the camp, it shall be that, as I do, so shall ye do.

The order of battle

7:18 When I blow with a trumpet, I and all that are with me, then blow ye the trumpets also on every side of all the camp, and say, The sword of the LORD, and of Gideon.

7:19 So Gideon, and the hundred men that were with him, came unto the outside of the camp in the beginning of the middle watch; and they had but newly set the watch: and they blew the trumpets, and brake the pitchers that were in their hands.

7:20 And the three companies blew the trumpets, and brake the pitchers, and held the lamps in their left hands, and the trumpets in their right hands to blow withal: and they cried, The sword of the LORD, and of Gideon. **7:21** And they stood every man in his place round about the camp; and all the [enemy] host ran, and cried, and fled.

In panic the men of the oppressing army turned on each other

7:22 And the three hundred blew the trumpets, and the LORD set every man's sword against his fellow, even throughout all the host: and the host fled to Bethshittah in Zererath, and to the border of Abelmeholah, unto Tabbath.

Then all the people rose up and pursued the Midianites

7:23 And the men of Israel gathered themselves together out of Naphtali, and out of Asher, and out of all Manasseh, and pursued after the Midianites.

Gideon then called on Manasseh to secure the water sources from the Midianites.

7:24 And Gideon sent messengers throughout all mount Ephraim, saying, come down against the Midianites, and take before them the waters unto Bethbarah and Jordan. Then all the men of Ephraim gathered themselves together, and took the waters unto Bethbarah and Jordan.

The two commanders of the Midianites were taken and killed.

7:25 And they took two princes of the Midianites, Oreb and Zeeb; and they slew Oreb upon the rock Oreb, and Zeeb they slew at the winepress of Zeeb, and pursued Midian, and brought the heads of Oreb and Zeeb to Gideon on the other side Jordan.

Judges 8

Ephraim was offended that they had not been called to partake in such a victory.

Judges 8:1 And the men of Ephraim said unto him, Why hast thou served us thus, that thou calledst us not, when thou wentest to fight with the Midianites? And they did chide with him sharply.

To pacify Ephraim, Gideon then praised Ephraim for their zeal and delivered the princes of Midian into their hands.

8:2 And he said unto them, What have I done now in comparison of you? Is not the gleaning of the grapes of Ephraim better than the vintage of Abiezer? **8:3** God hath delivered into your hands the princes of Midian, Oreb and Zeeb: and what was I able to do in comparison of you? Then their anger was abated toward him, when he had said that.

8:4 And Gideon came to Jordan, and passed over, he, and the three hundred men that were with him, faint, yet pursuing them. **8:5** And he said unto the men of Succoth, Give, I pray you, loaves of bread unto the people that follow me; for they be faint, and I am pursuing after Zebah and Zalmunna, kings of Midian.

Then the leaders of Succoth refused food to Gideon out of their remaining lingering fear of the Midianites.

8:6 And the princes of Succoth said, Are the hands of Zebah and Zalmunna now in thine hand, that we should give bread unto thine army?

Gideon responded that they were helping the enemies of Israel and would face their end as collaborators.

8:7 And Gideon said, Therefore when the LORD hath delivered Zebah and Zalmunna into mine hand, then I will tear your flesh with the thorns of the wilderness and with briers.

The men of Penuel also refused to help Gideon and Israel and Gideon responded that they were helping the enemies of Israel and would also face their end as collaborators.

8:8 And he went up thence to Penuel, and spake unto them likewise: and the men of Penuel answered him as the men of Succoth had answered him. **8:9** And he spake also unto the men of Penuel, saying, When I come again in peace, I will break down this tower.

Gideon then proceeded to finish the destruction of the enemy before returning to Penuel.

8:10 Now Zebah and Zalmunna were in Karkor, and their hosts with them, about fifteen thousand men, all that were left of all the hosts of the children of the east: for there fell an hundred and twenty thousand men that drew sword.

8:11 And Gideon went up by the way of them that dwelt in tents on the east of Nobah and Jogbehah, and smote the host; for the host was [felt] secure.

God and Gideon defeated Midian and took their two rulers

8:12 And when Zebah and Zalmunna fled, he pursued after them, and took the two kings of Midian, Zebah and Zalmunna, and discomfited all the host.

8:13 And Gideon the son of Joash returned from battle before the sun was up, **8:14** And caught a young man of the men of Succoth, and enquired of him: and he described unto him the princes of Succoth, and the elders thereof, even threescore and seventeen men.

Gideon then brought the two rulers of Midian to Succoth and destroyed their seventy-seven elders in the wilderness.

8:15 And he came unto the men of Succoth, and said, Behold Zebah and Zalmunna, with whom ye did upbraid me, saying, Are the hands of Zebah and Zalmunna now in thine hand, that we should give bread unto thy men that are weary? **8:16** And he took the elders of the city, and thorns of the wilderness and briers, and with them he taught the men of Succoth.

8:17 And he beat down the tower of Penuel, and slew the men of the city.

Now a personal element enters in as Gideon declares that these two kings had killed his brothers.

8:18 Then said he unto Zebah and Zalmunna, What manner of men were they whom ye slew at Tabor? And they answered, As thou art, so were they; each one resembled the children of a king. **8:19** And he said, They were my brethren, even the sons of my mother: as the LORD liveth, if ye had saved them alive, I would not slay you.

8:20 And he [Gideon] said unto Jether his firstborn, Up, and slay them. But the youth drew not his sword: for he feared, because he was yet a youth.

8:21 Then Zebah and Zalmunna said, Rise thou, and fall upon us: for as the man is, so is his strength. And Gideon arose, and slew Zebah and Zalmunna, and took away the ornaments that were on their camels' necks.

Then Israel sought to make Gideon their king

8:22 Then the men of Israel said unto Gideon, Rule thou over us, both thou, and thy son, and thy son's son also: for thou hast delivered us from the hand of Midian.

Gideon then gives an answer that we would not hear in most of the Ekklesia today

8:23 And Gideon said unto them, **I will not rule over you, neither shall my son rule over you: the LORD shall rule over you.**

Gideon only asks for the ear rings of the Arabs among the defeated peoples

8:24 And Gideon said unto them, I would desire a request of you, that ye would give me every man the earrings of his prey. (For they had golden earrings, because they were Ishmaelites.) **8:25** And they answered, We will willingly give them. And they spread a garment, and did cast therein every man the earrings of his prey.

8:26 And the weight of the golden earrings that he requested was a thousand and seven hundred shekels of gold; beside ornaments, and collars, and purple raiment that was on the kings of Midian, and beside the chains that were about their camels' necks.

Ephod: A blue priestly garment worn over a white ankle length shirt as an outward sign of office, people would see the ephod and recognize the man as a priest of God. In some cases the ephod became an idol for misguided people.

The ephod was symbolic recognition of the priests who are commanded to deliver the Word of God to the brethren. The ephod of Gideon began to be worshiped itself and became an idol and snare to many.

Today the elders have allowed themselves to become idols of the brethren, instead of teaching the people zeal for every Word of God.

8:27 And Gideon made an ephod thereof, and put it in his city, even in Ophrah: and **all Israel went thither a whoring after it: which thing became a snare unto Gideon, and to his house.**

8:28 Thus was Midian subdued before the children of Israel, so that they lifted up their heads no more. And the country was in quietness forty years in the days of Gideon.

8:29 And Jerubbaal [baal answer for thyself; Gideon] the son of Joash went and dwelt in his own house.

Gideon had 70 sons; having profited from his fame by marrying many wives.

8:30 And Gideon had threescore and ten sons of his body begotten: for he had many wives.

8:31 And his concubine that was in Shechem, she also bare him a son, whose name he called **Abimelech. 8:32** And Gideon the son of Joash died in a good old age, and was buried in the sepulchre of Joash his father, in Ophrah of the Abiezrites.

After the death of Gideon the people quickly turned away from the Eternal back to baal [the sun god representing Satan].

8:33 And it came to pass, as soon as Gideon was dead, that the children of Israel turned again, and went a whoring after Baalim, and made Baalberith their god. **8:34** And the children of Israel remembered not the LORD their God, who had delivered them out of the hands of all their enemies on every side: **8:35** Neither shewed they kindness to the house of Jerubbaal, namely, Gideon, according to all the goodness which he had shewed unto Israel.

Lessons From Gideon

1. When we are called out to fight against sin and serve the Eternal; HE will fight for us and even though the situation may look hopeless we are not to fear what any man can do; for the Eternal is far more powerful then all men together.

2. If we have the courage to take a stand on the Word of God; God the Father and Jesus Christ will give us total victory over sin! Even if we must suffer or die in this life, it is because we are being tested as to our zeal to live by every Word of God, and we are also being formed and molded into the person God wants us to be!

Even if we are not delivered in this life as Gideon and physical Israel were; the faithful and chosen of Spiritual Israel will be raised up to that Promised Land of eternal life at the call of our Lord.

3. When men do what they think is right, even with the best of intentions [as in the case of Gideon's ephod] it will result in bad fruits; ALWAYS seek out the Eternal and his Word to do as the whole Word of God and our Lord commands us.

3. Polygamy appeals to the lusts of men and to the desire of women for helpers at a time without modern machines, but its fruits are very bad. Polygamy like divorce was winked at for a certain time, but neither act was intended by the Creator and both are spiritually sin in the spiritual New Covenant, not being the intention of the Creator.

Judges 9

Gideon's concubine's son in Shechem, Abimelech; rebels against his father seeking a kingdom for himself.

Judges 9:1 And Abimelech the son of Jerubbaal [Gideon] went to Shechem unto his mother's brethren, and communed with them, and with all the family of the house of his mother's father, saying, **9:2** Speak, I pray you, in the ears of all the men of Shechem, Whether is better for you, either that all the sons of Jerubbaal [Gideon], which are threescore and ten persons, reign over you, or that one reign over you? remember also that I am your bone and your flesh. **9:3** And his mother's brethren spake of him in the ears of all the men of Shechem all these words: and their hearts inclined to follow Abimelech; for they said, He is our brother.

This rebellion of Abimelech was backed by the worshipers of baal in Shechem and rose up against the 70 other sons of Gideon, worshipers of God. The term "vain and light persons" is elsewhere termed "sons of Beliel" and refers to persons who had departed from God to baal.

9:4 And they gave him threescore and ten pieces of silver out of the house of Baalberith, wherewith **Abimelech hired vain and light persons, which followed him.**

9:5 And he went unto his father's house at Ophrah, and **slew his brethren the sons of Jerubbaal [Gideon], being threescore and ten persons**, upon one stone: notwithstanding yet **Jotham the youngest son of Jerubbaal was left; for he hid himself.**

The baal worshipers of Shechem made Abimelech their king.

9:6 And all the men of Shechem gathered together, and all the house of Millo, and went, and made Abimelech king, by the plain of the pillar that was in Shechem.

Jotham cried out to these men saying that they had rejected the good and godly to rule over them and had instead chosen the lowly and wicked to be their leader. It is the same today; many have chosen other men to rule over them and have rejected God, his Spirit and his Word.

9:7 And when they told it to Jotham, he went and stood in the top of mount Gerizim, and lifted up his voice, and cried, and said unto them, Hearken unto me, ye men of Shechem, that God may hearken unto you.

In this parable the wicked people of Shechem who exalted baal above God seek someone to rule them, but the godly and righteous refuse to rule over such wicked men.

9:8 The trees went forth on a time to anoint a king over them; and they said unto the olive tree, Reign thou over us. **9:9** But the olive tree said unto them, Should I leave my fatness, wherewith by me they honour God and man, and go to be promoted over the trees?

9:10 And the trees said to the fig tree, Come thou, and reign over us. **9:11** But the fig tree said unto them, Should I forsake my sweetness, and my good fruit, and go to be promoted over the trees? **9:12** Then said the trees unto the vine, Come thou, and reign over us.

The vine also rejected these wicked baal worshipers.

9:13 And the vine said unto them, Should I leave my wine, which cheereth God and man, and go to be promoted over the trees? **9:14** Then said all the trees unto the bramble, Come thou, and reign over us.

Then the wicked Abimelech represented by a bramble weed rose up to lead them.

9:15 And the bramble said unto the trees, If in truth ye anoint me king over you, then come and put your trust in my shadow: and if not, let fire come out of the bramble, and devour the cedars of Lebanon.

The remaining son of Gideon Jotham warned these wicked men that if Abimelech has done righteously by killing Gideon's sons they should trust in Abimelech; but if Abimelech has done wickedly, let them be destroyed for their wickedness. He then rehearses the good that Gideon had done for them and their wickedness against Gideon and his children.

9:16 Now therefore, if ye have done truly and sincerely, in that ye have made Abimelech king, and if ye have dealt well with Jerubbaal [Gideon] and his house, and have done unto him according to the deserving of his hands; **9:17 (For my father fought for you, and adventured his life far, and delivered you out of the hand of Midian: 9:18 And ye are risen up against my father's house this day, and have slain his sons, threescore and ten persons**, upon one stone, and have made Abimelech, the son of his maidservant, king over the men of Shechem, because he is your brother;)

9:19 If ye then have dealt truly and sincerely with Jerubbaal [Gideon] and with his house this day, then rejoice ye in Abimelech, and let him also rejoice in you:

The curse proclaimed against the murderer Abimelech and the men of Milo and Shechem.

9:20 But if not, let fire come out from Abimelech, and devour the men of Shechem, and the house of Millo; and let fire come out from the men of Shechem, and from the house of Millo, and devour Abimelech.

Then Jotham the remaining son of Gideon [besides Abimelech] fled to hide himself for he was alone against the men of Milo and Shechem.

9:21 And Jotham ran away, and fled, and went to Beer, and dwelt there, for fear of Abimelech his brother.

After three years the God Being who later gave up his God-hood to become flesh as Jesus Christ remembered the sin of Abimelech, Milo and Shechem and intervened to cause the curse of Jotham to come to pass.

9:22 When Abimelech had reigned three years over Israel, **9:23** Then God sent an evil spirit between Abimelech and the men of Shechem; and the men of Shechem dealt treacherously with Abimelech: **9:24** That the cruelty done to the threescore and ten sons of Jerubbaal might come, and their blood be laid upon Abimelech their brother, which slew them; and upon the men of Shechem, which aided him in the killing of his brethren.

Then the men of Shechem rebelled against the king they had made and set an ambush for Abimelech

9:25 And the men of Shechem set liers in wait for him in the top of the mountains, and they robbed all that came along that way by them: and it was told Abimelech.

The people rejected Abimelech, setting a new king over themselves.

9:26 And **Gaal the son of Ebed** came with his brethren, and went over to Shechem: and the men of Shechem put their confidence in him. **9:27** And they went out into the fields, and gathered their vineyards, and trode the grapes, and made merry, and went into the house of their god, and did eat and drink, **and cursed Abimelech**.

Abimelech and Gaal join battle

9:28 And Gaal the son of Ebed said, Who is Abimelech, and who is Shechem, that we should serve him? is not he the son of Jerubbaal [Gideon]? and Zebul his officer? serve the men of Hamor the father of Shechem: for why should we serve him? **9:29** And would to God this people were under my hand! then would I remove Abimelech. And he said to Abimelech, Increase thine army, and come out.

Then the governor of the city sent word to Abimelech

9:30 And when Zebul the ruler of the city heard the words of Gaal the son of Ebed, his anger was kindled. **9:31** And he sent messengers unto Abimelech privily, saying, Behold, Gaal the son of Ebed and his brethren be come to Shechem; and, behold, they fortify the city against thee.

Abimelech is advised to hide his men in the fields and attack the people as they come out of the city to work the fields.

9:32 Now therefore up by night, thou and the people that is with thee, and lie in wait in the field: **9:33** And it shall be, that in the morning, as soon as the sun is up, thou shalt rise early, and set upon the city: and, behold, when he and the people that is with him come out against thee, then mayest thou do to them as thou shalt find occasion.

Abimelech heeds the advice

9:34 And Abimelech rose up, and all the people that were with him, by night, and they laid wait against Shechem in four companies.

Abimelech attacks when Gaal opens the city gates in the early morning.

9:35 And Gaal the son of Ebed went out, and stood in the entering of the gate of the city: and Abimelech rose up, and the people that were with him, from lying in wait.

Gaal sees the men running towards him, but his captain says that they are only shadows.

9:36 And when Gaal saw the people, he said to Zebul, Behold, there come people down from the top of the mountains. And Zebul said unto him, Thou seest the shadow of the mountains as if they were men.

Then they are sure and go out to fight instead of closing and barring the gate.

9:37 And Gaal spake again, and said, See there come people down by the middle of the land, and another company come along by the plain of Meonenim.

The captain tells Gaal to fight.

9:38 Then said Zebul unto him, **Where is now thy mouth, wherewith thou saidst, Who is Abimelech, that we should serve him? is not this the people that thou hast despised? go out, I pray now, and fight with them.**

Abimelech defeats Gaal the usurper.

9:39 And Gaal went out before the men of Shechem, and fought with Abimelech. **9:40** And Abimelech chased him, and he fled before him, and many were overthrown and wounded, even unto the entering of the gate.

Abimelech and Gaal then went to other cities and both were rejected by Shechem.

9:41 And **Abimelech dwelt at Arumah**: and **Zebul** [the governor of the city of Shechem] **thrust out Gaal and his brethren**, that they should not dwell in Shechem.

The people of Shechem then told Abimelech that Gaal had been thrust out.

9:42 And it came to pass on the morrow, that the people went out into the field; and they told Abimelech.

Abimelech then attacked Shechem with his loyalists and utterly destroyed the city.

9:43 And he took the people, and divided them into three companies, and laid wait in the field, and looked, and, behold, the people were come forth out of the city; and he rose up against them, and smote them. **9:44** And

Abimelech, and the company that was with him, rushed forward, and stood in the entering of the gate of the city: and the two other companies ran upon all the people that were in the fields, and slew them.

9:45 And Abimelech fought against the city all that day; and he took the city, and slew the people that was therein, and beat down the city, and sowed it with salt.

The remaining men of Shechem gathered themselves into a strong hold, a citadel of baal-berith.

9:46 And when all the men of the tower of Shechem heard that, they entered into an hold of the house of the god Berith. **9:47** And it was told Abimelech, that all the men of the tower of Shechem were gathered together.

Abimelech then burnt them with fire, and the curse against Shechem is fulfilled.

9:48 And Abimelech gat him up to mount Zalmon, he and all the people that were with him; and Abimelech took an axe in his hand, and cut down a bough from the trees, and took it, and laid it on his shoulder, and said unto the people that were with him, What ye have seen me do, make haste, and do as I have done.

9:49 And all the people likewise cut down every man his bough, and followed Abimelech, and put them to the hold, and set the hold on fire upon them; so that all the men of the tower of Shechem died also, about a thousand men and women.

Then Abimelech went to attack another city.

9:50 Then went Abimelech to Thebez, and encamped against Thebez, and took it.

9:51 But there was a strong tower within the city, and thither fled all the men and women, and all they of the city, and shut it to them, and gat them up to the top of the tower. **9:52** And Abimelech came unto the tower, and fought against it, and went hard unto the door of the tower to burn it with fire. **9:53** And a certain woman cast a piece of a millstone upon Abimelech's head, and all to brake his skull. **9:54** Then he called hastily unto the young man his armourbearer, and said unto him, Draw thy sword, and slay me, that men say not of me, A women slew him. And his young man thrust him through, and he died.

Abimelech died, fulfilling the curse against him for his wickedness.

9:55 And when the men of Israel saw that Abimelech was dead, they departed every man unto his place. **9:56** Thus God rendered the wickedness of Abimelech, which he did unto his father, in slaying his seventy brethren: **9:57** And all the evil of the men of Shechem did God render upon their heads: and upon them came the curse of Jotham the son of Jerubbaal [Gideon].

Judges 10

After these things and after Israel had fallen into baalism [idolatry] again; Tola was raised up to judge in Israel for 23 years. These judges were not kings but teachers and keepers of the Word of God who delivered them from their enemies as God commanded them.

Their principle job was to teach a zeal to live by every Word of God after God had demonstrated his power to go before Israel and defeat the Canaanites.

In spiritual terms the Canaanites were a type of sin and the people could not overcome sin on their own and fell into idolatry! It was only when they turned to God and called out to the Eternal in repentance that God delivered them from sin.

This is a lesson for spiritual New Covenant Israel, that we cannot overcome sin on our own!

It is ONLY by being zealous for learning and keeping the whole Word of God and by following our God in all things that sin can be overcome through the power of our God dwelling in us and driving sin out of us. Without a zeal for God we quickly fall into doing what we think is right instead of doing what God says is right, idolizing our own ways and other men; instead of exalting the Word of God.

Judges 10:1 And after Abimelech there arose to defend Israel Tola the son of Puah, the son of Dodo, a man of Issachar; and he dwelt in Shamir in mount Ephraim. **10:2** And he judged Israel twenty and three years, and died, and was buried in Shamir.

Then Jair was called to judge Israel for 22 years.

10:3 And after him arose Jair, a Gileadite, and judged Israel twenty and two years. **10:4** And he had thirty sons that rode on thirty ass colts, and they had thirty cities, which are called Havothjair unto this day, which are in the land of Gilead. **10:5** And Jair died, and was buried in Camon.

The people turned away from any zeal for their God, which then led to their complete falling away into idolatry.

This is an instruction for us, that if we lose our zeal for learning and living by every Word of God we are falling away from the Word of God and into the idolatry of exalting our own ways as idols above the Word of God.

10:6 And the children of Israel did evil again in the sight of the LORD, and served Baalim, and Ashtaroth, and the gods of Syria, and the gods of Zidon, and the gods of Moab, and the gods of the children of Ammon, and the gods of the Philistines, and forsook the LORD, and served not him.

By turning away from any zeal for the Word of God, they angered Christ who sent them into yet another captivity in their own land; which land was promised to them ONLY as long as they were faithful to God.

The same thing is true of today's Spiritual Ekklesia! When we turn away from zeal to keep the whole Word of our God and instead become filled with zeal for idols of men and their ways; God the Father and Jesus Christ are offended and angered and they WILL correct us!

This next oppression expanded to include the Golan.

10:7 And the anger of the LORD was hot against Israel, and he sold them into the hands of the Philistines, and into the hands of the children of Ammon. **10:8** And that year they vexed and oppressed the children of Israel: eighteen years, all the children of Israel that were on the other side Jordan in the land of the Amorites, which is in Gilead. **10:9** Moreover the children of Ammon passed over Jordan to fight also against Judah, and against Benjamin, and against the house of Ephraim; so that Israel was sore distressed.

People only seem to repent when they are suffering correction, and when the next generation comes along it falls back into sin against God.

Very soon now, there will be a final and sincere repentance of both physical and spiritual Israel at the coming of Messiah the Christ as King of kings.

10:10 And the children of Israel cried unto the LORD, saying, We have sinned against thee, both because we have forsaken our God, and also served Baalim.

Once we refuse the warnings from God and insist on our own ways and we fall into great tribulation and cry out for deliverance; God will tell us to cry out to our idols for deliverance! Only when we honestly repent in true sincerity and PROVE that repentance with the works of faithfulness; will we be chosen for the resurrection of the faithful!

10:11 And the LORD said unto the children of Israel, Did not I deliver you from the Egyptians, and from the Amorites, from the children of Ammon, and from the Philistines? **10:12** The Zidonians also, and the Amalekites, and the Maonites, did oppress you; and ye cried to me, and I delivered you out of their hand.

God will correct today's apostate Spiritual Ekklesia just as he corrected those folks in their day.

10:13 Yet ye have forsaken me, and served other gods: wherefore I will deliver you no more. **10:14** Go and cry unto the gods which ye have chosen; let them deliver you in the time of your tribulation.

10:15 And the children of Israel said unto the LORD, We have sinned: do thou unto us whatsoever seemeth good unto thee; deliver us only, we pray thee, this day. **10:16** And they put away the strange gods from among them, and served the LORD: and his soul was grieved for the misery of Israel.

The opposing armies then assembled and Israel sought for a leader

10:17 Then the children of Ammon were gathered together, and encamped in Gilead. And the children of Israel assembled themselves together, and encamped in Mizpeh.

10:18 And the people and princes of Gilead [Manasseh, Reuben and Gad] said one to another, What man is he that will begin to fight against the children of Ammon? he shall be head over all the inhabitants of Gilead [Golan, including Manasseh, Reuben and Gad].

Judges 11

God calls Jephthah to be the next judge of Israel.

Judges 11:1 Now Jephthah the Gileadite [Bashan, Golan; the land of Reuben, Manasseh and Gad east of Jordan] was a mighty man of valour, and he was the son of an harlot: and Gilead begat Jephthah.

Jephthah was despised by his brothers in his father's house.

11:2 And Gilead's wife bare him sons; and his wife's sons grew up, and they thrust out Jephthah, and said unto him, Thou shalt not inherit in our father's house; for thou art the son of a strange woman.

Despised and downtrodden people then gathered around Jephthah, like they would later gather around the rejected David.

11:3 Then Jephthah fled from his brethren, and dwelt in the land of Tob: and there were gathered vain ["empty:" in context; lowly, despised, men who fled from their oppressors in Israel] men to Jephthah, and went out with him.

Then when Ammon came to fight Israel, the elders called Jephthah back to save them. To them he was not good enough to have a share in his father's house, but later he was to become their deliverer.

This reminds us of Jesus Christ who was rejected by his own people and will yet come to deliver them to end the "Time of Jacob's Troubles."

11:4 And it came to pass in process of time, that the children of Ammon made war against Israel. **11:5** And it was so, that when the children of Ammon made war against Israel, the elders of Gilead went to fetch Jephthah out of the land of Tob: **11:6** And they said unto Jephthah, Come, and be our captain, that we may fight with the children of Ammon.

Jephthah asks the elders why they called on him and they answered that they want him to lead them. In context; Jephthah had led his band in the wilderness like David later did, and he was the only one prepared for battle against Ammon.

11:7 And Jephthah said unto the elders of Gilead [Bashan, Golan; the land of Reuben, Manasseh and Gad east of Jordan], Did not ye hate me, and expel me out of my father's house? and why are ye come unto me now when ye are in distress? **11:8** And the elders of Gilead said unto Jephthah, Therefore we turn again to thee now, that thou mayest go with us, and fight against the children of Ammon, and **be our head over all the inhabitants of Gilead**.

The elders covenant with Jephthah that if he delivers them, Jephthah will be their head.

Today Jesus Christ is being rejected by both physical and spiritual Israel as we exalt men and the false traditions of men: Yet during the tribulation, in the near future physical and spiritual Israel will call upon the name of the Mighty One that they have rejected, to come and save them and to be their King.

11:9 And Jephthah said unto the elders of Gilead, If ye bring me home again to fight against the children of Ammon, and the LORD deliver them before me, shall I be your head? **11:10** And the elders of Gilead said unto Jephthah, **The LORD be witness between us, if we do not so according to thy words.**

This covenant between Jephthah and Israel was made in a meeting before God.

11:11 Then Jephthah went with the elders of Gilead, and the people made him head and captain over them: and **Jephthah uttered all his words before the LORD** in Mizpeh.

11:12 And Jephthah sent messengers unto the king of the children of Ammon, saying, What hast thou to do with me, that thou art come against me to fight in my land?

Jephthah inquires why Ammon has come up to fight, and the king of Ammon gives his answer.

11:13 And the king of the children of Ammon answered unto the messengers of Jephthah, **Because Israel took away my land, when they came up out of Egypt, from Arnon even unto Jabbok, and unto Jordan: now therefore restore those lands again peaceably.**

Jephthah then rehearses the history to show that Israel took no land from Moab or Ammon.

11:14 And Jephthah sent messengers again unto the king of the children of Ammon: **11:15** And said unto him, Thus saith Jephthah, Israel took not away the land of Moab, nor the land of the children of Ammon: **11:16** But when Israel came up from Egypt, and walked through the wilderness unto the Red sea, and came to Kadesh; **11:17** Then Israel sent messengers unto the king of Edom, saying, Let me, I pray thee, pass through thy land: but the king of Edom would not hearken thereto. And in like manner they sent unto the king of Moab: but he would not consent: and Israel abode in Kadesh.

11:18 Then they went along through the wilderness, and compassed the land of Edom, and the land of Moab, and came by the east side of the land of Moab, and pitched on the other side of Arnon, but came not within the border of Moab: for Arnon was the border of Moab.

Israel did not fight Edom or Moab, but fought the Amorites. Later Israel did not even attack Moab over the sin of Balaam and Balak but punished only the confederate of Moab Midian.

11:19 And Israel sent messengers unto Sihon king of the Amorites, the king of Heshbon; and Israel said unto him, Let us pass, we pray thee, through thy land into my place. **11:20** But Sihon trusted not Israel to pass through his coast: but Sihon gathered all his people together, and pitched in Jahaz, and fought against Israel. **11:21** And the LORD God of Israel delivered Sihon and all his people into the hand of Israel, and they smote them: so Israel possessed all the land of the Amorites, the inhabitants of that country. **11:22** And they possessed all the coasts of the Amorites, from Arnon even unto Jabbok, and from the wilderness even unto Jordan.

Jephthah declares that the lands Ammon is demanding are the lands of the Amorites in Bashan which were given to Manasseh, Reuben and Gad, and not any land belonging to Ammon; he then asks the king of Ammon why he is demanding the lands of the Amorites for himself.

11:23 So now the LORD God of Israel hath dispossessed the Amorites from before his people Israel, and shouldest thou possess it?

Jephthah then asks the king of Ammon why he is not content with the "land of his god;" saying that Israel should occupy the land that their God had given to them.

11:24 Wilt not thou possess that which Chemosh thy god giveth thee to possess? So whomsoever the LORD our God shall drive out from before us, them will we possess.

Jephthah then asked if the king of Ammon was like Balak who strove with Israel without a cause.

11:25 And now art thou any thing better than Balak the son of Zippor, king of Moab did he ever strive against Israel, or did he ever fight against them

Jephthah then declared that God had given Israel the land of the Golan [Bashan] and that they had dwelt in it for three hundred years; meaning that the king of Ammon was only looking for an excuse to make war to take away the lands given to Israel.

We can see here that Jephthah knew his history and he knew the Word of God, and he gave a reasoned argument in order to try and avoid war with Ammon. Remember that Ammon was of Lot and NOT Canaanites.

11:26 While Israel dwelt in Heshbon and her towns, and in Aroer and her towns, and in all the cities that be along by the coasts of Arnon, three hundred years? why therefore did ye not recover them within that time?

The Eternal had forbidden Israel to attack Moab, Ammon or Edom or to take their lands over three hundred years previously; therefore this attack by the king of Ammon was not right before God.

11:27 Wherefore I have not sinned against thee, **but thou doest me wrong to war against me: the LORD the Judge be judge this day between the children of Israel and the children of Ammon.**

11:28 Howbeit the king of the children of Ammon hearkened not unto the words of Jephthah which he sent him.

Then Jephthah, being rejected by the king of Ammon proceeded to the battle.

11:29 Then the Spirit of the LORD came upon Jephthah, and he passed over Gilead, and Manasseh, and passed over Mizpeh of Gilead, and from Mizpeh of Gilead he passed over unto the children of Ammon.

Then Jephthah makes a rash vow

11:30 And Jephthah vowed a vow unto the LORD, and said, If thou shalt without fail deliver the children of Ammon into mine hands, **11:31** Then it shall be, **that whatsoever cometh forth of the** doors of my house to meet me, when I return in peace from the children of Ammon, shall surely be the LORD's, and I will offer it up for a burnt offering.

The God Being who later was made flesh as Jesus Christ, went before Jephthah and gave him the victory

11:32 So Jephthah passed over unto the children of Ammon to fight against them; and the LORD delivered them into his hands. **11:33** And he smote them from Aroer, even till thou come to Minnith, even twenty cities, and unto the plain of the vineyards, with a very great slaughter. Thus the children of Ammon were subdued before the children of Israel.

Then upon returning home from the victory; his daughter came out to meet him in dances of rejoicing. This must have been crushing to Jephthah. Perhaps this was from God to teach us all a lesson about rash vows?

11:34 And Jephthah came to Mizpeh unto his house, and, behold, his daughter came out to meet him with timbrels and with dances: and she was his only child; beside her he had neither son nor daughter. **11:35** And it came to pass, when he saw her, that he rent his clothes, and said, Alas, my daughter! thou hast brought me very low, and thou art one of them that trouble me: for I have opened my mouth unto the LORD, and I cannot go back.

Jephthah tells his daughter and she accepts the situation with grace and humble obedience. How many of us even keep our baptismal vow of faithfulness to the whole Word of God today by sanctifying the Sabbath Day!

11:36 And she said unto him, My father, if thou hast opened thy mouth unto the LORD, do to me according to that which hath proceeded out of thy mouth; forasmuch as the LORD hath taken vengeance for thee of thine enemies, even of the children of Ammon.

It is to be understood that the Burnt Offering typified whole hearted service to God; and that this lady was not killed and burned [which was forbidden by God's command]; but was to remain an unmarried virgin totally dedicated to the service of God for her lifetime. Hence she bewailed her virginity which was never to be given to any husband.

11:37 And she said unto her father, Let this thing be done for me: let me alone two months, that I may go up and down upon the mountains, and **bewail my virginity**, I and my fellows. **11:38** And he said, Go. And he sent her away for two months: and she went with her companions, and **bewailed her virginity** upon the mountains.

11:39 And it came to pass at the end of two months, that she returned unto her father, who did with her according to his vow which he had vowed: **and she knew no man.** And it was a custom in Israel, **11:40** That the daughters of Israel went yearly to lament the daughter of Jephthah the Gileadite four days in a year.

Judges 12

Ephraim then seeks to have a part in the victory after the battle is already won.

Judges 12:1 And the men of Ephraim gathered themselves together, and went northward, and said unto Jephthah, Wherefore passedst thou over to fight against the children of Ammon, and didst not call us to go with thee? we will burn thine house upon thee with fire.

Jephthah, in jeopardy of his life, then boldly declares that they were called and they did not come.

12:2 And Jephthah said unto them, I and my people were at great strife with the children of Ammon; and when I called you, ye delivered me not out of their hands.

12:3 And when I saw that ye delivered me not, I put my life in my hands, and passed over against the children of Ammon, and the LORD delivered them into my hand: wherefore then are ye come up unto me this day, to fight against me?

Then Ephraim said that these men of Jephthah were wanted men in Ephraim for not including Ephraim in the fight against Ammon. Then war broke out between Ephraim and Jephthah.

12:4 Then Jephthah gathered together all the men of Gilead [Reuben, Gad and the eastern half of Manasseh], and fought with Ephraim: and the men of Gilead smote Ephraim, because they said, Ye Gileadites are fugitives [wanted men] of [by] Ephraim among the Ephraimites, and among the [western half of Manasseh] Manassites.

Then the men of Jephthah from Bashan [Gad, Reuben and the eastern half of Manasseh] defeated Ephraim and were able to take the crossing of Jordan before the fleeing Ephraimites could escape.

12:5 And the Gileadites took the passages of Jordan before the Ephraimites: and it was so, that when those Ephraimites which were escaped said, Let me go over; that the men of Gilead said unto him, Art thou an Ephraimite? If he said, Nay; **12:6** Then said they unto him, Say now Shibboleth: and he said Sibboleth: for he could not frame to pronounce it right. Then they took him, and slew him at the passages of Jordan: and **there fell at that time of the Ephraimites forty and two thousand.**

12:7 And **Jephthah judged Israel six years.** Then died Jephthah the Gileadite, and was buried in one of the cities of Gilead.

12:8 And after him **Ibzan of Bethlehem judged Israel. 12:9** And he had thirty sons, and thirty daughters, whom he sent abroad, and took in thirty daughters from abroad for his sons. And **he judged Israel seven years. 12:10** Then died Ibzan, and was buried at Bethlehem.

12:11 And after him **Elon, a Zebulonite, judged Israel**; and he judged Israel **ten years. 12:12** And Elon the Zebulonite died, and was buried in Aijalon in the country of Zebulun.

12:13 And after him **Abdon the son of Hillel**, a Pirathonite, judged Israel. **12:14** And he had forty sons and thirty nephews, that rode on threescore and ten ass colts: and he **judged Israel eight years. 12:15** And Abdon the son of Hillel the Pirathonite died, and was buried in Pirathon in the land of Ephraim, in the mount of the Amalekites.

Judges 13

We now come to the story of Samson which is full of lessons for us today. Samson was called by God before his birth to be a Nazarite and a Judge in Israel, yet he was a weak man desiring strange [unconverted] wives.

The first lesson is that God has commanded that the converted are NOT to willfully marry unconverted people like Samson and Solomon did, because unconverted spouses are a very strong influence to lead us to compromise with the Word of God.

The second lesson is that God can use a weak person to accomplish his will; for God used Sampson's fascination with Philistine women to diminish the Philistines who were oppressing Israel at that time.

The third lesson is that Jesus Christ does NOT tolerate sin; and just as Moses was corrected for his sin, God allowed his champion Sampson to be corrected for his sins against his calling.

The primary lesson of Judges is that God will NOT tolerate any compromise with his Word and will correct those who allow anything to come between them and God; like marrying unconverted spouses or following corporate idols, or turning away from God to follow idols of men; but God will show mercy to all those who sincerely repent and commit to "go and sin no more!"

God is his marvelous wisdom can still use the sinner to accomplish his will; which does NOT justify the sin and it does not justify us taking part in their sins either. Today spiritual Israel is to be faithful and zealous for our calling to internalize and passionately live by every Word of God in Christ-like zeal.

The circumstances surrounding the birth of Samson

Judges 13:1 And the children of Israel did evil again in the sight of the LORD; and the **LORD delivered them into the hand of the Philistines forty years.**

A barren woman was visited by a spirit and promised a son. Her husband Manoah just like Abraham [father or Isaac], Elkanah [father of Samuel] and Zacharias [father of John Baptist] had barren wives and received promises of sons. These sons were all special gifts of God to barren women and they were all called by God for very special purposes.

13:2 And there was a certain man of Zorah, of the family of the Danites, whose name was Manoah; and his wife was barren, and bare not.

The angel gives the promise of a son and then reveals that this son was from God and called by God from before his conception; and gives instructions to the woman to keep herself from any unclean thing. The woman is herself forbidden to take any wine or alcohol [strong drink] during her pregnancy, for the child was to be kept pure from very conception.

Notice the detailed instructions for the purity and holiness of this man in sharp contrast to his own personal behavior in adulthood.

13:3 And the angel of the LORD appeared unto the woman, and said unto her, Behold now, thou art barren, and bearest not: but thou shalt conceive, and bear a son. **13:4** Now therefore beware, I pray thee, and drink not wine nor strong drink, and eat not any unclean thing:

Samson is called to be a Nazarite from his very conception.

13:5 For, lo, thou shalt conceive, and bear a son; and no razor shall come on his head: for **the child shall be a Nazarite unto God from the womb**: and he shall **begin** to deliver Israel out of the hand of the Philistines.

The woman then tells her husband these things.

13:6 Then the woman came and told her husband, saying, A man of God came unto me, and his countenance was like the countenance of an angel of God, very terrible: but I asked him not whence he was, neither told he me his name: **13:7** But he said unto me, Behold, thou shalt conceive, and bear a son; and now drink no wine nor strong drink, neither eat any unclean thing: for the child shall be a Nazarite to God from the womb to the day of his death.

The husband believed his wife, and full of faith asks God for instructions regarding the child. Notice that Manoah, Abraham [father or Isaac], Elkanah [father of Samuel] and Zacharias [father of John Baptist] were all godly men of faith, full of the works of faith.

13:8 Then Manoah intreated the LORD, and said, O my Lord, let the man of God which thou didst send come again unto us, and **teach us what we shall do unto the child** that shall be born. **13:9** And God hearkened to the voice of Manoah; and the angel of God came again unto the woman as she sat in the field: but Manoah her husband was not with her. **13:10** And the woman made haste, and ran, and shewed her husband, and said unto him, Behold, the man hath appeared unto me, that came unto me the other day.

Manoah asks for instructions about raising the child

13:11 And Manoah arose, and went after his wife, and came to the man, and said unto him, Art thou the man that spakest unto the woman? And he said, I am. **13:12** And Manoah said, Now let thy words come to pass. **How shall we order** [teach and raise] **the child, and how shall we do unto him?**

The angel then repeats his instructions concerning the woman during her pregnancy.

13:13 And the angel of the LORD said unto Manoah, Of all that I said unto the woman let her beware. **13:14** She may not eat of any thing that cometh of the vine, neither let her drink wine or strong drink, nor eat any unclean thing: all that I commanded her let her observe.

Manoah offers the angel food; which the angel rejects and instructs them that a Burnt Offering be made to YHVH. The Burnt Offering being entirely burned was a symbol of wholehearted service to God.

13:15 And Manoah said unto the angel of the LORD, I pray thee, let us detain thee, until we shall have made **ready a kid for thee. 13:16** And the angel of the LORD said unto Manoah, Though thou detain me, I will not eat of thy bread [food]: and if thou wilt offer a burnt offering, **thou must offer it unto the LORD.** For Manoah knew not that he was an angel of the LORD.

Manoah asks the angel his name and the angel refuses him an answer; must assuredly because all honor should be given to God.

13:17 And Manoah said unto the angel of the LORD, What is thy name, that when thy sayings come to pass we may do thee honour? **13:18** And the angel of the LORD said unto him, Why askest thou thus after my name, seeing it is secret?

The angel then ascended into heaven in the fire of the offering.

13:19 So Manoah took a kid with a meat offering, and offered it upon a rock unto the LORD: and the angel did wonderously; and Manoah and his wife looked on. **13:20** For it came to pass, when the flame went up toward heaven from off the altar, that the angel of the LORD ascended in the flame of the altar. And Manoah and his wife looked on it, and fell on their faces to the ground.

13:21 But the angel of the LORD did no more appear to Manoah and to his wife. Then Manoah knew that he was an angel of the LORD.

Manoah then feared, and was consoled by his wife.

13:22 And Manoah said unto his wife, We shall surely die, because we have seen God. **13:23** But his wife said unto him, If the LORD were pleased to kill us, he would not have received a burnt offering and a meat [unleavened bread] offering at our hands, neither would he have shewed us all these things, nor would as at this time have told us such things as these.

13:24 And the woman bare a son, and called his name Samson: and the child grew, and the LORD blessed him.

Samson seems to have lived in the section of Dan that was on the coast near Philistia.

13:25 And the Spirit of the LORD began to move him at times in **the camp of Dan between Zorah and Eshtaol.**

Judges 14

Samson now a young man feeling his need, saw and desired a Philistine woman.

Judges 14:1 And Samson went down to Timnath, and saw a woman in Timnath of **the daughters of the Philistines.**

Samson asks his parents to get this woman for his wife; it being the custom for parents to provide wives for their sons after the example of Abraham.

14:2 And he came up, and told his father and his mother, and said, I have seen a woman in Timnath of the daughters of the Philistines: now therefore get her for me to wife.

Samson's parents objected but Samson insists.

14:3 Then his father and his mother said unto him, Is there never a woman among the daughters of thy brethren, or among all my people, that thou goest to take a wife of the uncircumcised Philistines? And Samson said unto his father, Get her for me; for she pleaseth me well.

Samson's parents were greatly grieved.

14:4 But his father and his mother knew not that it was of the LORD, that he sought an occasion against the Philistines: for at that time the Philistines had dominion over Israel.

Samson then began to exhibit the gift of God's strength.

14:5 Then went Samson down, and his father and his mother, to Timnath, and came to the vineyards of Timnath: and, behold, a young lion roared against him. **14:6** And **the Spirit of the LORD came mightily upon him**, and he rent [killed the lion with his hands] him as he would have rent a kid, and he had nothing in his hand: but he told not his father or his mother what he had done. **14:7** And he went down, and talked with the woman; and she pleased Samson well.

After speaking with the lady he left and later returned on the appointed day.

14:8 And after a time he returned to take her, and he turned aside to see the carcase of the lion: and, behold, there was a swarm of bees and honey in the carcase of the lion.

Samson now eats honey, telling NO ONE of the lion and the source of the honey.

14:9 And he took thereof in his hands, and went on eating, and came to his father and mother, and he gave them, and they did eat: but **he told not them that he had taken the honey out of the carcase of the lion**.

Samson and his father went to take the bride and a wedding feast was held.

14:10 So his father went down unto the woman: and Samson made there a [wedding] feast; for so used the young men to do. **14:11** And it came to pass, when they saw him, that they brought thirty companions to be with him.

Samson then challenges his thirty Philistine "friends".

14:12 And Samson said unto them, I will now put forth a riddle unto you: if ye can certainly declare it me within the seven days of the feast, and find it out, then I will give you thirty sheets and thirty change of garments: **14:13** But if ye cannot declare it me, then shall ye give me thirty sheets and thirty change of garments. And they said unto him, Put forth thy riddle, that we may hear it.

The riddle

14:14 And he said unto them, Out of the eater came forth meat [food], and out of the strong came forth sweetness. And they **could not in three days** expound the riddle.

After three days they asked the lady to entice her husband to reveal the answer, and on the seventh day they threatened to burn her and her family alive if she failed.

14:15 And it came to pass on the seventh day, that they said unto Samson's wife, Entice thy husband, that he may declare unto us the riddle, lest we burn thee and thy father's house with fire: have ye called us to take that we have? is it not so?

14:16 And Samson's wife wept before him, and said, Thou dost but hate me, and lovest me not: thou hast put forth a riddle unto the children of my people, and hast not told it me. And he said unto her, Behold, I have not told it my father nor my mother, and shall I tell it thee? **14:17** And she wept before him the [on the seventh day, fearing the threat and having no faith in God and in Samson to protect them] seven days, while their feast lasted: and it came to pass on the seventh day, that he told her, because she lay sore upon him: and she told the riddle to the children of her people.

The sun going down [sunset] ended the day and the Philistines answered the riddle before the seventh day ended, and Samson immediately knew that the only one he had ever told the matter to was his bride.

14:18 And the men of the city said unto him on the seventh day **before the sun went down** [before the seventh day ended], What is sweeter than honey? And what is stronger than a lion? and he said unto them, If ye had not plowed with my heifer, ye had not found out my riddle.

In has fury Samson killed thirty Philistines of Ashkelon and gave their clothes to pay off his wager. Then Samson was angry with his bride and returned to his father's house.

Just so, Jesus Christ will be furious with us for our betrayal of him to follow idols of men and corporate entities, or if we lose faith and turn aside from him for ANY REASON!

If we turn aside from absolute loyalty to God and faith in God to deliver us; We will be rejected by Almighty God the Father and Jesus Christ our espoused Husband.

14:19 And the Spirit of the LORD came upon him, and he went down to Ashkelon, and slew thirty men of them, and took their spoil, and gave change of garments unto them which expounded the riddle. And his anger was kindled, and he went up to his father's house.

The woman's father then thinking that she had been abandoned, gave her to a Philistine, the friend of Samson.

14:20 But Samson's wife was given to his companion, whom he had used as his friend.

Judges 15

After his anger cooled Samson went back to take his wife around Pentecost.

Judges 15:1 But it came to pass within a while after, in **the time of wheat harvest**, that Samson visited his wife with a kid; and he said, I will go in to my wife into the chamber. But her father would not suffer him to go in.

The woman's father explains what he has done and offers Samson her younger sister to make things right, but Samson is again enraged for he had loved his bride.

15:2 And her father said, I verily thought that thou hadst utterly hated her; therefore I gave her to thy companion: is not her younger sister fairer than she? take her, I pray thee, instead of her. **15:3** And Samson said concerning them, Now shall I be more blameless than the Philistines, though I do them a displeasure.

Then Samson burns the fields of the Philistines which were ripe and dry.

15:4 And Samson went and caught three hundred foxes, and took firebrands, and turned tail to tail, and put a firebrand in the midst between two tails.

15:5 And when he had set the brands on fire, he let them go into the standing corn [standing grain; referring to the wheat ready for harvest] of the Philistines, and **burnt up both the shocks, and also the standing corn** [wheat]**, with the vineyards and olives.**

The Philistines then burned Samson's wife and her father in revenge.

15:6 Then the Philistines said, Who hath done this? And they answered, Samson, the son in law of the Timnite, because he had taken his wife, and given her to his companion. And the Philistines came up, and burnt her and her father with fire.

Samson then attacks the Philistines because they had murdered his wife and her father.

15:7 And Samson said unto them, Though ye have done this, yet will I be avenged of you, and after that I will cease. **15:8** And he smote them hip and thigh with a great slaughter: and he went down and dwelt in the top of the rock Etam.

Then the Philistines went out to get rid of Samson.

15:9 Then the Philistines went up, and pitched in Judah, and spread themselves in Lehi. **15:10** And the men of Judah said, Why are ye come up against us? And they answered, To bind Samson are we come up, to do to him as he hath done to us.

Judah then goes to bind Samson and turn him over to their masters the Philistines.

15:11 Then **three thousand men of Judah** went to the top of the rock Etam, and said to Samson, Knowest thou not that **the Philistines are rulers over us**? what is this that thou hast done unto us? And he said unto them, As they did unto me, so have I done unto them.

Samson permits the Jews to bind him.

15:12 And they said unto him, We are come down to bind thee, that we may deliver thee into the hand of the Philistines. And Samson said unto them, **Swear unto me, that ye will not fall upon me yourselves. 15:13 And they spake unto him, saying, No; but we will bind thee fast, and deliver thee into their hand: but surely we will not kill thee.** And they bound him with two new cords, and brought him up from the rock.

The strength of Samson was by the Spirit of God, revealing lesson four from Samson; that our own strength is nothing compared to the strength of God.

Spiritually, it is by the strength of God the Father and Jesus Christ IN US; that we overcome sin; not by trying to fight the battle alone.

15:14 And when he came unto Lehi, the Philistines shouted against him: and the Spirit of the LORD came mightily upon him, and the cords that were upon his arms became as flax that was burnt with fire, and his bands loosed from off his hands.

15:15 And he found a new jawbone of an ass, and put forth his hand, and took it, and slew a thousand men therewith. **15:16** And Samson said, With the jawbone of an ass, heaps upon heaps, with the jaw of an ass have I slain a thousand men.

15:17 And it came to pass, when he had made an end of speaking, that he cast away the jawbone out of his hand, and called that place Ramathlehi.

15:18 And he was sore athirst, and called on the LORD, and said, Thou hast given this great deliverance into the hand of thy servant: and now shall I die for thirst, and fall into the hand of the uncircumcised?

God brings water from the jaw of the ass

15:19 But God clave an hollow place that was in the jaw, and there came water thereout; and when he had drunk, his spirit came again, and he revived: wherefore he called the name thereof Enhakkore, which is in Lehi unto this day.

15:20 And **he judged Israel in the days of the Philistines twenty years.**

Judges 16

The Philistines supposed that they had surrounded and trapped Samson in a harlot's house and that he would remain there until morning. Visiting harlot's is not the act of a righteous man, but God used the weakness of Samson to help deliver Israel from the Philistines.

Samson made many mistakes but he ultimately overcame in the end.

Judges 16:1 Then went Samson to Gaza, and saw there an harlot, and went in unto her. **16:2** And it was told the Gazites, saying, Samson is come hither. And they compassed him in, and laid wait for him all night in the gate of the city, and were quiet all the night, saying, In the morning, when it is day, we shall kill him.

Samson arises at midnight and removes the strong and very heavy city gates to a far hill top. This exploit would have astonished the Philistines and convinced them of his strength.

16:3 And Samson lay till midnight, and arose at midnight, and took the doors of the gate of the city, and the two posts, and went away with them, bar and all, and put them upon his shoulders, and carried them up to the top of an hill that is before Hebron.

Samson still finds pleasure in foreign women.

16:4 And it came to pass afterward, that he loved a woman in the valley of Sorek, whose name was Delilah.

Delilah is offered a huge irresistible price for finding out the secret of Samson's strength,

16:5 And the lords of the Philistines came up unto her, and said unto her, Entice him, and see wherein his great strength lieth, and by what means we may prevail against him, that we may bind him to afflict him; and we will give thee every one of us eleven hundred pieces of silver.

Delilah seeks the secret from Samson but he toys with her.

16:6 And Delilah said to Samson, Tell me, I pray thee, wherein thy great strength lieth, and wherewith thou mightest be bound to afflict thee. **16:7** And Samson said unto her, If they bind me with seven green withs that were never dried, then shall I be weak, and be as another man.

Delilah then tests out what Samson has said, delivering him to the Philistines. Samson is still distracted by her charms and does not reject her for betraying him.

16:8 Then the lords of the Philistines brought up to her seven green withs which had not been dried, and she bound him with them. **16:9** Now there were men lying in wait, abiding with her in the chamber. And she said unto him, The Philistines be upon thee, Samson. And he brake the withs, as a thread of tow is broken when it toucheth the fire. So his strength was not known.

Delilah quickly uses her influence to get the secret of Samson's strength before he can come to his senses and reject her.

16:10 And Delilah said unto Samson, Behold, thou hast mocked me, and told me lies: now tell me, I pray thee, wherewith thou mightest be bound.

Samson again deceives her, not willing to reveal his secret.

16:11 And he said unto her, If they bind me fast with new ropes that never were occupied, then shall I be weak, and be as another man. **16:12** Delilah therefore took new ropes, and bound him therewith, and said unto him, The Philistines be upon thee, Samson. And there were liers in wait abiding in the chamber. And he brake them from off his arms like a thread.

Again she betrays Samson and again he cleaves to this traitorous woman, and again they play their little game.

16:13 And Delilah said unto Samson, Hitherto thou hast mocked me, and told me lies: tell me wherewith thou mightest be bound. And he said unto her, If thou weavest the seven locks of my head with the web.

Delilah wove his hair and fastened it to a main beam of the house, yet he rose up and carried the beam away.

16:14 And she fastened it with the pin, and said unto him, The Philistines be upon thee, Samson. And he awaked out of his sleep, and went away with the pin of the beam, and with the web.

Again the game is played by Delilah and one wonders at Samson and his blind passion for her.

16:15 And she said unto him, How canst thou say, I love thee, when thine heart is not with me? thou hast mocked me these three times, and hast not told me wherein thy great strength lieth.

Finally even though she has betrayed him many times, Samson is foolish enough to tell this traitorous woman his secret.

16:16 And it came to pass, when she pressed him daily with her words, and urged him, so that his soul was vexed unto death; **16:17** That he told her all his heart, and said unto her, There hath not come a razor upon mine head; for I have been a Nazarite unto God from my mother's womb: if I be shaven, then my strength will go from me, and I shall become weak, and be like any other man.

Delilah then caused Samson to lie down with his head on her knees so that the Philistines could easily cut his hair while he slept.

16:18 And when Delilah saw that he had told her all his heart, she sent and called for the lords of the Philistines, saying, Come up this once, for he hath shewed me all his heart. Then the lords of the Philistines came up unto her, and brought money in their hand. **16:19** And she made him sleep upon her knees; and she called for a man, and she caused him to shave off the seven locks of his head; and she began to afflict him, and his strength went from him.

16:20 And she said, The Philistines be upon thee, Samson. And he awoke out of his sleep, and said, I will go out as at other times before, and shake myself. And he wist not that the LORD was departed from him.

Samson was then taken by the Philistines and his eyes blinded; he was then made to grind the grain like a bullock pulling the wheel.

16:21 But the Philistines took him, and put out his eyes, and brought him down to Gaza, and bound him with fetters of brass; and **he did grind in the prison house.**

16:22 Howbeit the hair of his head began to grow again after he was shaven.

16:23 Then the lords of the Philistines gathered them together for to offer a great sacrifice unto Dagon their god, and to rejoice: for they said, Our god hath delivered Samson our enemy into our hand. **16:24** And when the people saw him, they praised their god: for they said, Our god hath delivered into our hands our enemy, and the destroyer of our country, which slew many of us.

The Philistines held a victory feast for their god Dagon the fish god, an ancient fertility god. Fish are NOT Christian, as wrongly thought by many today. The papal crown is a Dagon hat, and depictions of fish for religious purposes are Dagon worship.

16:25 And it came to pass, when their hearts were merry, that they said, Call for Samson, that he may make us sport. And they called for Samson out of the prison house; and he made them sport: and they set him between the pillars.

They made sport and mocked Samson rejoicing, for they supposed that Dagon had power over Samson and the God of Israel.

16:26 And Samson said unto the lad that held him by the hand, Suffer me that I may feel the pillars whereupon the house standeth, that I may lean upon them.

16:27 Now the house was full of men and women; and all the lords of the Philistines were there; and there were upon the roof about three thousand men and women, that beheld while Samson made sport.

Then Samson called on the Eternal to strengthen him one last time.

16:28 And Samson called unto the LORD, and said, O Lord God, remember me, I pray thee, and strengthen me, I pray thee, only this once, O God, that I may be at once avenged of the Philistines for my two eyes. **16:29** And Samson took hold of the two middle pillars upon which the house stood, and on which it was borne up, of the one with his right hand, and of the other with his left.

16:30 And Samson said, Let me die with the Philistines. And he bowed himself with all his might; and the house fell upon the lords, and upon all the people that were therein. So the dead which he slew at his death were more than they which he slew in his life.

16:31 Then his brethren and all the house of his father came down, and took him, and brought him up, and buried him between Zorah and Eshtaol in the buryingplace of Manoah his father. And he **judged Israel twenty years.**

The story of Samson was recorded for our instruction.

His mother and father were instructed to maintain the holiness of avoiding all uncleanness from the moment of conception, yet Samson loved an unconverted women and did not hesitate to engage in whoring.

Yet in spite of his weakness, God used him to perform God's will. Samson was an example of how NOT to live, when called out to God! Yet Samson was also used by God to demonstrate to us that God's will, will be done regardless of the actions of men.

We have been called to a zeal to learn and to keep the whole Word of God; a zeal which Samson did not initially have. His love for the unconverted is a type of the modern day spiritually called out brethren's love for worldliness and their idols of men; for in scripture the great false religion and her daughters are painted as a great whore.

We are to love the Lord our God with all our hearts; and we are not to marry unconverted spouses; or associate with false doctrines and false religions.

God will judge all people based on what they do or do not do, with what they have been given.

Samson had many things going for him including a set of virtuous parents who scrupulously followed God's instructions regarding Samson's rearing. Yet in the end it was Samson and no one else, who determined what he would do with the special calling God had granted him.

Many of us are familiar with the biblical teaching: **Proverbs. 22:6** "Train up a child in the way he should go: and when he is old, he will not depart from it." We also know that Paul was inspired of God to write: **I Corinthians 7:14** "For the unbelieving husband is sanctified by the wife, and the unbelieving wife is sanctified by the husband: else were your children unclean; but now are they holy.

Many converted parents model God's way for their children in their example and they teach them to live by every Word of God. Yet when some of these youth reach the age of personal accountability, parents sometimes have their hearts broken by seeing their children turn their backs on God and the teachings and examples of their parents. With the possible exception of having to bury a child, there is no greater heartache for a parent than to witness such a spectacle in the lives of their own child or children.

They then wonder: What did I forget to do? What did I do wrong? How did I fail my child? I am sure that Samson's parents must have wondered these same things as they watched their beloved son make such serious mistakes.

Sometimes the answer is that the parents did nothing wrong and that the children simply did not understand.

Finally the really big lessons from Samson, are that being called of God does not mean one has it made or that the way will be easy; there are many sorrows to work through and it is written that many are called and few will be chosen (Mat 22:14). Sampson despite his several failures did overcome in the end (Hebrews 11), while Saul and others did fail to persevere.

We are called to a life of growing, overcoming and living by every Word of God. It is not the calling to God or an office that saves; it is our response to God's calling to live by every Word of God, or to go our own way; which determines our final end.

Baptism and or ordination itself means absolutely nothing if we do not live by every Word of God!

Judges 17

How part of Dan migrated north to get a new city and new gods

Micah of Ephraim stole eleven hundred shekels of silver from his mother; and later repented restoring it.

Judges 17:1 And there was a man of mount **Ephraim**, whose name was Micah. **17:2** And he said unto his mother, The eleven hundred shekels of silver that were taken from thee, about which thou cursedst, and spakest of also in mine ears, behold, the silver is with me; I took it. And his mother said, Blessed be thou of the LORD, my son.

His mother tells him that she had dedicated her silver to make an idol for him.

17:3 And when he had restored the eleven hundred shekels of silver to his mother, his mother said, I had wholly dedicated the silver unto the LORD from my hand for my son, **to make a graven image and a molten image:** now therefore I will restore it unto thee.

Micah's mother made him an idol.

17:4 Yet he restored the money unto his mother; and his mother took two hundred shekels of silver, and gave them to the founder, who made thereof a graven image and a molten image: and they were in the house of Micah.

Micah had many idol gods just like today's Ekklesia has idols of men and false traditions.

17:5 And the man Micah had an house of gods, and made an ephod [priestly vestment], and teraphim [idols], and consecrated one of his sons, who became his priest [from Ephraim and NOT of Aaron, therefore a false priest of false gods].

17:6 In those days there was no king [ruler or Judge] in Israel, but every man did that which was right in his own eyes.

A Levite came to Ephraim from Bethlehem of Judah.

17:7 And there was a young man out of Bethlehemjudah of the family of Judah, who was a Levite, and he sojourned there.

The Levite traveled from Bethlehem of Judah looking for a place to start his synagogue [school], to teach.

17:8 And the man departed out of the city from Bethlehemjudah to sojourn where he could find a place: and he came to mount Ephraim to the house of Micah, as he journeyed.

Micah met the Levite and invited the Levite to come and be the "priest" of his gods.

17:9 And Micah said unto him, Whence comest thou? And he said unto him, I am a Levite of Bethlehemjudah, and I go to sojourn where I may find a place. **17:10** And Micah said unto him, Dwell with me, and be unto me a father and a priest, and I will give thee ten shekels of silver by the year, and a suit of apparel, and thy victuals. So the Levite went in.

This Micah was no respecter of gods and worshiped all gods; and added an apostate Levite in his collection of priests and gods.

17:11 And the Levite was content to dwell with the man; and the young man was unto him as one of his sons. **17:12** And Micah consecrated the Levite; and the young man became his priest, and was in the house of Micah.

17:13 Then said Micah, Now know I that the LORD will do me good, seeing I have a Levite to my priest.

Judges 18

The area east of Lake Hulah including Dan was given to but not occupied by Naphtali when Israel divided the land under Joshua. The original land given to Dan by Joshua was by the central sea coast.

Judges 17-19 covers the taking of the northern territory by part of the tribe of Dan. Dan had been given land on the coast and considered that land too small for them, and so sought out another place; and thus Dan became divided between a part on the coast and a landlocked part in the north belonging to but not occupied by Naphtali.

Later the coastal seafaring Dan went by sea to Spain and then on to Ireland; and when God gave the northern ten tribes to Assyria, northern Dan was taken to Mesopotamia and then migrated to Denmark.

It was prophesied that [Northern] Dan would leap from Bashan [Golan] and that is what Dan did.

Dan is still divided with two nations [Ireland and Denmark] today.

Judges 18:1 In those days there was no king in Israel: and in those days the tribe of **the Danites sought them an inheritance to dwell in**; for unto that day **all their inheritance had not fallen unto them** among the tribes of Israel.

Dan sent out reconnaissance to find more land, and the five men came and found rest with Micah the worshiper of many gods of chapter 17.

18:2 And the children of Dan sent of their family five men from their coasts, men of valour, from Zorah, and from Eshtaol, to spy out the land, and to search it; and they said unto them, Go, search the land: who when they came to mount Ephraim, to the house of Micah, they lodged there.

Spies from Dan recognized the voice of the Levite as someone they knew and asked him his story.

18:3 When they were by the house of Micah, they knew the voice of the young man the Levite: and they turned in thither, and said unto him, Who brought thee hither? and what makest thou in this place? and what hast thou here?

The whole situation in the area is one of gross idolatry and attempts to call idolatry and false priests as godly. These idols and foreign gods separated these folks from the Eternal God. Today many false leaders have infiltrated the Spiritual Ekklesia and have led the brethren to exalt and follow them away from any zeal for the Word of God; which is idolatry as well!

18:4 And he said unto them, Thus and thus dealeth Micah with me, and hath hired me, and I am his priest.

18:5 And they [the spies from Dan] said unto him, Ask counsel, we pray thee, of God, that we may know whether our way which we go shall be prosperous.

This false priest told these men that God was with them. The same lie is told to the brethren today, as the false leaders and elders feign to be of God in order to lead men to follow themselves away from any zeal to live by every Word of God; as Jesus himself warned us would happen in Matthew 24.

You shall know the godly from the ungodly by their fruits, Matthew 7.

Are your leaders zealous for every Word of God to learn it and to keep it? Or do they teach the brethren to relax any zeal to live by every Word of God and instead follow themselves?

18:6 And the priest said unto them, Go in peace: before the LORD is your way wherein ye go.

The spies scouted the land and came to Laish east of the northern lake and rivers, and found it undefended and a rich land.

18:7 Then the five men departed, and came to Laish, and saw the people that were therein, how they dwelt careless, after the manner of the Zidonians, quiet and secure; and there was no magistrate in the land, that might put them to shame in any thing; and they were far from the Zidonians, and had no business with any man.

The five spies reported back to their cities.

18:8 And they came unto their brethren to [in] Zorah and Eshtaol: and their brethren said unto them, What say ye? **18:9** And they said, Arise, that we may go up against them: for we have seen the land, and, behold, it is very good: and are ye still? be not slothful to go, and to enter to possess the land. **18:10** When ye go, ye shall come unto a people secure, and to a large land: for God hath given it into your hands; a place where there is no want of any thing that is in the earth.

An army of 600 was sent to take the city, and they camped at the house of Micah to seek a blessing from the "priest."

18:11 And there went from thence of the family of the Danites, out of Zorah and out of Eshtaol, six hundred men appointed with weapons of war. **18:12** And they went up, and pitched in Kirjathjearim, in Judah: wherefore they called that place Mahanehdan unto this day: behold, it is behind Kirjathjearim. **18:13** And they passed thence unto mount Ephraim, and came unto the house of Micah.

The five men had also told the 600 about the priest and the house of Micah.

18:14 Then answered the five men that went to spy out the country of Laish, and said unto their brethren, Do ye know that there is in these houses an ephod, and teraphim, and a graven image, and a molten image? now therefore consider what ye have to do.

The 600 went to the home of Micah and his "priest," and waited at the gate as the five men went inside.

18:15 And they turned thitherward, and came to the house of the young man the Levite, even unto the house of Micah, and saluted him. **18:16** And the six hundred men appointed with their weapons of war, which were of the children of Dan, stood by the entering of the gate.

As the "priest " spoke with the 600 the five went and stole the priestly raiment and the gods of Micah.

18:17 And the five men that went to spy out the land went up, and came in thither, and took the graven image, and the ephod, and the teraphim, and the molten image: and the priest stood in the entering of the gate with the six hundred men that were appointed with weapons of war. **18:18** And these [the five men] went into Micah's house, and fetched the carved image, the ephod, and the teraphim, and the molten image. Then said the priest unto them, What do ye?

When the "priest" saw this he demanded to know what they were doing in taking away the gods.

The men then offered the man an opportunity to be the "priest" of the 600 instead of a priest of only one family; and the priest left for the better job, stealing the gods of his benefactor!

How like many elders today who reject any zeal to live by every Word of God and sell themselves to follow idols of men.

18:19 And they said unto him, Hold thy peace, lay thine hand upon thy mouth, and go with us, and be to us a father and a priest: is it better for thee to be a priest unto the house of one man, or that thou be a priest unto a tribe and a family in Israel? **18:20** And the priest's heart was glad, and he took the ephod, and the teraphim, and the graven image, and went in the midst of the people.

The 600 men and their animals and families moved on towards the north, and Micah called on his neighbors and friends to pursue them.

18:21 So they turned and departed, and put the little ones and the cattle and the carriage before them. **18:22** And when they were a good way from the house of Micah, the men that were in the houses near to Micah's house were gathered together, and overtook the children of Dan.

Micah demands the return of the gods that he had made.

18:23 And they cried unto the children of Dan. And they turned their faces, and said unto Micah, What aileth thee, that thou comest with such a company? **18:24** And he said, Ye have taken away my gods which I made, and the priest, and ye are gone away: and what have I more? and what is this that ye say unto me, What aileth thee?

Then the people of Dan replied that they had 600 men of war and told Micah to be content to let go of his "priest" and gods, lest he die.

18:25 And the children of Dan said unto him, Let not thy voice be heard among us, lest angry fellows run upon thee, and thou lose thy life, with the lives of thy household. **18:26** And the children of Dan went their way: and when Micah saw that they were too strong for him, he turned and went back unto his house.

Dan then smote Laish a city at peace with Israel; and named it Dan.

18:27 And they took the things which Micah had made, and the priest which he had, and came unto Laish, unto a people that were at quiet and secure: and they smote them with the edge of the sword, and burnt the city with fire. **18:28** And there was no deliverer, because it was far from Zidon, and they had no business with any man; and it was in the valley that lieth by Bethrehob. And they built a city, and dwelt therein.

18:29 And they called the name of the city Dan, after the name of Dan their father, who was born unto Israel: howbeit the name of the city was Laish at the first.

Northern Dan then set up false priests not of Aaron, and worshiped idols through history. Even today it is recorded of Dan that they shall have no part in the 12,000 called out of each tribe of Israel at the end of the tribulation (Rev 7).

18:30 And the children of Dan set up the graven image: and Jonathan, the son of Gershom, the son of Manasseh, he and his sons were priests to the tribe of Dan until the day of the captivity of the land [the removal of the ten tribes by the Assyrians].

18:31 And they set them up Micah's graven image [in northern Dan], which he made, all the time that the house of God was in Shiloh.

Brethren, in the Mosaic Covenant a true priest of God was a son of Aaron who was called to that office; to teach zeal for the whole Word of God, to officiate over the offerings and to turn the people to God.

In the New Covenant Jesus Christ commanded us to judge who we are willing to follow by their fruits of godliness.

An elder who is not called of God to that office and does not live and teach others to zealously live by every Word of God; is not a true elder!

A man who was ordained for his talents and organizational loyalty, is not ordained of God; ONLY a person who is called and ordained to his office by God the Father, and who has the fruits of that calling by their zeal for God and his Word to keep it and to teach it; is a true elder and minister of Jesus Christ.

Just as John baptized only those who had proved their repentance by their fruits: We are to baptize and ordain only those who have the full fruits of repentance to godliness, evidenced by their uncompromising zeal to learn, keep and teach the whole Word of God, and to fearlessly rebuke all sin!

Just as Micah's false "priest" was ordained of men; to our great shame we have also ordained false elders who are content to close their eyes to idolizing men and corporate entities and false teachings, and encouraging lukewarmness for keeping the Word of God; for a reward of wages.

Not every priest or elder is of God! Prove all things, hold fast that which is good and consistent with the whole Word of God (1 Thess 5:20-22).

True Godliness

Serve God with all your hearts and do good to others; that is the will of God.

Matthew 7:13 Enter ye in at the strait gate: for wide is the gate, and broad is the way, that leadeth to destruction, and many there be which go in threat: **7:14** Because strait is the gate, and narrow is the way, which leadeth unto life, and few there be that find it.

Few have the dedication to follow through with enduring and overcoming to become part of the chosen. God wants Kings and Priests for offices of responsibility for all eternity. He must be certain of our fidelity to him; therefore let us put him and his Kingdom FIRST at all times, and be passionate to live by every Word of God so that we may have a part in the bride of Christ!

Like a marriage salvation is a dual effort. God the Father must call people to himself through the Son and open our minds to Him and his Word; yet WE must respond! Jesus Christ as the espoused Husband leads and enables, but those who want a part in the collective bride must FOLLOW HIM!

We MUST sincerely repent and we MUST commit to keeping God's Word; to "go and sin NO more!"

We MUST make every possible effort to overcome; and we MUST diligently seek God's help!

We are called to God the Father through a Marriage Covenant with Jesus Christ: A marriage is a TEAM effort; two uniting as one. Those called to become a part of the collective bride of Christ MUST do their part and that part is to follow Christ and obey God the Father; and we NEED their help to accomplish that!

We overcome through the power of Christ living in us through the indwelling of God's Spirit; we must be willing to follow Christ and God's Spirit as it leads us to live by every Word of God.

The big problem in religion today is that people do not follow Christ and do not diligently live by every Word of God, instead they do what is right in their own eyes.

We have become righteous in our own eyes, but we are wicked in the eyes of Almighty God; doing what we think is right instead of doing what God says is right!

Our part is NOT to do what WE think is right! Our part is to do what God SAYS is right!

We are to seek to grow in knowledge and understanding of God's ways; we are to seek to become like God the Father with ALL our hearts minds and strength; but not ALONE! We are also to seek God's help, diligently and consistently; for we ultimately can overcome ONLY by God's power.

Just like God delivered Israel out of Egypt, he can and will deliver us out of bondage of sin!

Jesus Christ overcame this world, he WILL overcome this world living in us! Even in ancient physical Egypt Israel had to follow God out of bondage! So we must be willing to follow God in whatever he commands; that is our part.

Matthew 22:37 Jesus said unto him, Thou shalt love the Lord thy God with all thy heart, and with all thy soul, and with all thy mind. 22:38 This is the first and great commandment.

IF we loved God: We would DO what God says!

We must be willing followers of Jesus Christ and willing DOERS of every Word of God the Father; for the sacrifice of Jesus Christ the very Lamb of God will ONLY be applied to the repentant who are committed DOERS of God's Word [Acts 5:32)!

Romans 2:13 (For not the hearers of the law are just before God, but the doers of the law shall be justified.

Yes we have our part; we MUST be willing DOERS of the law! We must diligently seek out God with all our hearts and we MUST serve God ONLY; not serving idols of men with their false traditions!

When we are tempted to compromise with God's Word we must boldly declare in the name of Jesus Christ: **Matthew 4:10** Then saith Jesus unto him, GET THEE HENCE, SATAN: for it is written, Thou shalt worship the Lord thy God, and him only shalt thou serve.

Yes we do have our part, yet we cannot do it alone!

We MUST seek our God with all our might, follow him in all things, trust and obey him alone and serve him with passionate enthusiastic love! We must ASK for his Spirit of Power to overcome, we MUST diligently seek knowledge of his ways and apply what we learn as we learn.

We must reject temptation the second it rears its ugly head and we must hide ourselves in the armor of God.

We must fight the good fight, but if we rely on our Mighty One we are not alone in that fight against temptation, compromise and sin!

Alone we will fail for we are no match for Satan the god-king of this world, but TOGETHER with our Awesome Beloved Father and his Son; the god-king of this world is NO match for us!

Ephesians 6:10 Finally, my brethren, be strong in the Lord, and in the power of his might.

It is our FAITH in our Great God, married to the action of faithfully FOLLOWING Him and living by every Word of God that makes us strong! It is our faithful service to our God which brings deliverance for us!

The whole armor of God is there for us; but we MUST put it on: We must USE it!

Ephesians 6:11 Put on the whole armour of God, that ye may be able to stand against the wiles of the devil. **6:12** For we wrestle not against flesh and blood, but against principalities, against powers, against the rulers of the darkness of this world, against spiritual wickedness in high places.

We MUST fight the good fight against the wickedness warring against us, USING all the help and strength that God provides!

Ephesians 6:13 Wherefore take unto you the whole armour of God, that ye may be able to withstand in the evil day, and having done all, to stand.

We MUST fight to overcome and we shall overcome by the power and righteousness of God the Father and Jesus Christ dwelling in and strengthening us through the Spirit of God!

Ephesians 6:14 Stand therefore, having your loins girt about with truth, and having on the breastplate of righteousness;

Righteousness IS the keeping of every Word of God! We MUST live in and by the truth of God, which is every WORD of God.

Ephesians 6:15 And your feet shod with the preparation of the gospel of peace;

The Gospel of peace between God and man, is the Gospel of repentance and reconciliation to God.

It is sincere repentance, an unshakable commitment to faithful obedience and the gift of atonement, reconciliation through the application of the sacrifice of the Lamb of God; which brings empowerment with God's Spirit of power and a sound mind enabling us to overcome.

We MUST DO our part and God will DO his!

Ephesians 6:16 Above all, taking the shield of faith, wherewith ye shall be able to quench all the fiery darts of the wicked.

If we are filled with faith in the strength of our God; and we depend and put our TRUST in our God and His Word, rejecting any temptation to compromise with God's Word; God WILL deliver us.

Brethren, it is this lack of faith which has caused us to compromise with God's Word and turn the Gospel message of warning and repentance into a lukewarm business model inoffensive message. This in turn offends Jesus Christ and we will be rejected by him until we repent.

Each year at Passover time we study the mighty miracles that Christ performed for his people; and then we go and compromise with God's ways out of fear of persecution or lust for mammon!

2 Timothy 3:5 Having a form of godliness, but denying the power thereof: from such turn away.

Ephesians 5:17 And take the helmet of salvation, and the sword of the Spirit, which is the word of God:

Let us cover ourselves with the gift of salvation, given to the sincerely repentant who are diligent to live by every Word of God; let us fight the good fight, wielding the TRUTH, the WORD of God; which is the sword of the Spirit; for God is truth and his Spirit shall: **John 16:13** Howbeit when he, the Spirit of truth, is come, he will guide you into all truth:

Yes we MUST DO our part, yet we NEED God's HELP! We cannot overcome ALONE!

Ephesians 6:18 Praying always with all prayer and supplication in the Spirit, and watching thereunto with all perseverance and supplication for all saints;

Matthew 7:15 Beware of false prophets, which come to you in sheep's clothing, but inwardly they are ravening wolves.

A wolf feeds himself first, and ravages the flock.

Ezekiel 34 the entire chapter is about those shepherds in BOTH physical and spiritual Israel who are wolves and feed themselves with all the good things of the flock while neglecting to feed the flock with the truth is due season.

Those who are political and seek the chief seats, who seek self-aggrandizement and personal advantage; are the wolves hiding among the sheep. Today there are very many wolves who do not feed the sheep the true Gospel of: warning, repentance, and diligent faithful obedience to God and salvation: Which is the way of life and the way to salvation.

Ezekiel 34:1 And the word of the LORD came unto me, saying, 34:2 Son of man, prophesy against the shepherds of Israel, prophesy, and say unto them, Thus saith the Lord GOD unto the shepherds; Woe be to the shepherds of Israel that do feed themselves! should not the shepherds feed the flocks?

Matthew 7:16 Ye shall know them by their fruits. Do men gather grapes of thorns, or figs of thistles? **7:17** Even so every good tree bringeth forth good fruit; but a corrupt tree bringeth forth evil fruit.

If any man teaches tolerance for sin out of a phony false love; if any elder tolerates sin [the breaking of God's Word, not the breaking of some organizational edict] without rebuke; if any organization does not preach a message of warning and repentance to the world: They are corrupt branches that will be pruned away!

The True Good Shepherd feeds the flock with the words of truth; with the teachings that lead to salvation; strongly rebuking all sin. We are to follow that true Good Shepherd with the diligent KEEPING of the whole Word of God, so that the whole flock internalizes God the Father and the Son; growing into a full spiritual unity with God!

John 15:1 I am the true vine, and my Father is the husbandman.

15:2 Every branch in me that beareth not fruit he taketh away: and every branch that beareth fruit, he purgeth it, that it may bring forth more fruit.

15:3 Now ye are clean through the word which I have spoken unto you.

15:4 Abide in me, and I in you. As the branch cannot bear fruit of itself, except it abide in the vine; no more can ye, except ye abide in me.

15:5 I am the vine, ye are the branches: He that abideth in me, and I in him, the same bringeth forth much fruit: for without me ye can do nothing.

15:6 If a man abide not in me, he is cast forth as a branch, and is withered; and men gather them, and cast them into the fire, and they are burned.

Matthew 7:18 A good tree cannot bring forth evil fruit, neither can a corrupt tree bring forth good fruit.

The good tree is that Good Shepherd who is working to bring the whole flock into a fullness of unity with Jesus Christ and God the Father! We are to follow that Good Shepherd who gave his all, his very life for the Father's flock; and did not seek his own.

We are to follow that example that was set for us and faithfully serve the Father by feeding his flock with the very Word of God, the very nature of God without fear or compromise; regardless of what men think or do.

There are some good shepherds among you even now, who teach the true way of salvation and are alert watchmen discerning the signs of the times. They may be kept down, ridiculed and even persecuted by others, yet God the Father will reward them.

Luke 12:42 And the Lord said, Who then is that faithful and wise steward, whom his lord shall make ruler over his household, to give them their portion of meat in due season?

12:43 Blessed is that servant, whom his lord when he cometh shall find so doing.

12:44 Of a truth I say unto you, that he will make him ruler over all that he hath.

Matthew 7:19 Every tree that bringeth not forth good fruit is hewn down, and cast into the fire.

The evil servant

Luke 12:45 But and if that servant say in his heart, My lord delayeth his coming; and shall begin to beat the menservants and maidens, and to eat and drink, and to be drunken;

Abusing others and seeking our own pleasures

12:46 The lord of that servant will come in a day when he looketh not for him, and at an hour when he is not aware, and will cut him in sunder, and will appoint him his portion with the unbelievers.

12:47 And that servant, which knew his lord's will, and prepared not himself, neither did according to his will, shall be beaten with many stripes.

12:48 But he that knew not, and did commit things worthy of stripes, shall be beaten with few stripes. For unto whomsoever much is given, of him shall be much required: and to whom men have committed much, of him they will ask the more.

Matthew 7:20 Wherefore by their fruits ye shall know them.

You shall know the good shepherds by their love of God and their diligent keeping and teaching of every Word of God and by their diligence to do the will of HIM who called them.

Matthew 23:11 But he that is greatest among you shall be your servant. **23:12** And whosoever shall exalt himself shall be abased; and he that shall humble himself shall be exalted.

Matthew 7:21 Not every one that saith unto me, Lord, Lord, shall enter into the kingdom of heaven; **but he that doeth the will of my Father which is in heaven.**

7:22 Many will say to me in that day, Lord, Lord, have we not prophesied in thy name? and in thy name have cast out devils? and in thy name done many wonderful works? **7:23** And then will I profess unto them, I never knew you: depart from me, ye that work iniquity.

7:24 Therefore whosoever heareth these sayings of mine, and doeth them, I will liken him unto a wise man, which built his house upon a rock [the Might Rock of our Salvation, the whole Word of God and Messiah the Christ]: **7:25** And the rain descended, and the floods came, and the winds blew, and beat upon that house; and it fell not: for it was founded upon a rock.

Those who internalize the nature of God the Father and Jesus Christ; who become one with them in total spiritual unity, through a deep love for God and all the things of God, those who love the passionate keeping of every Word of God and who set a good example of godliness and FEED THE FLOCK with the good pasture of the Word, watering them with the Spirit of Godliness, are building on the foundation of the Word of God: Which shall NEVER be moved.

Ephesians 2:20 And are built upon the foundation of the apostles and prophets, Jesus Christ himself being the chief corner stone;

Matthew 7:26 And every one that heareth these sayings of mine, **and doeth them not,** shall be likened unto a foolish man, which built his house upon the sand: **7:27** And the rain descended, and the floods came, and the winds blew, and beat upon that house; and it fell: and great was the fall of it.

The words of Christ are not taught today, because they are NOT KEPT in today's assemblies! This is because the Word of God exposes the many false shepherds among us! It is because the Word of God cuts sharply into the very heart and spirit of our organizations and convicts us of our sins and egocentric complacency; and our lack of Christ centeredness; exposing our almost total lack of Christ-like zeal for God the Father's will and ways!

Jesus Christ stands at the door of each of those called to God the Father through him; knocking (Rev 3), calling us to repent of our self-righteous idolizing of our own ways; calling us to a diligent dedicated passionate obedience to every Word of God; calling us to a zeal for the keeping of God's Word and instructions; calling us to sincerely repent of our self-seeking embracing of worldliness.

Judges 19

Benjamin almost destroyed for gross wickedness

A concubine was a woman having a lower standing than a legal wife, usually an maidservant. In cases of infidelity a concubine was considered as belonging to a man, in the same sense as a wife.

Judges 19:1 And it came to pass in those days, when there was no king in Israel, that there was a certain Levite sojourning on the side of mount Ephraim, who took to him a concubine out of Bethlehemjudah.

This concubine was unfaithful to the man and went [perhaps out of fear of an angry master] back to her father's house.

19:2 And his concubine played the whore against him, and went away from him unto her father's house to Bethlehemjudah, and was there four whole months.

After four months the man cooled down and went to take her back.

19:3 And her husband arose, and went after her, to speak friendly unto her, and to bring her again, having his servant with him, and a couple of asses: and she brought him into her father's house: and when the father of the damsel saw him, he rejoiced to meet him.

The father in law rejoiced at the reconciliation.

19:4 And his father in law, the damsel's father, retained him; and he abode with him three days: so they did eat and drink, and lodged there.

When the man desired to return to his home the father in law tried to delay their departure.

19:5 And it came to pass on the fourth day, when they arose early in the morning, that he rose up to depart: and the damsel's father said unto his son in law, Comfort thine heart with a morsel of bread, and afterward go your way. **19:6** And they sat down, and did eat and drink both of them together: for the damsel's father had said unto the man, Be content, I pray thee, and tarry all night, and let thine heart be merry. **19:7** And when the man rose up to depart, his father in law urged him: therefore he lodged there again.

19:8 And he arose early in the morning on the fifth day to depart; and the damsel's father said, Comfort thine heart, I pray thee. And they tarried until afternoon, and they did eat both of them. **19:9** And when the man rose up to depart, he, and his concubine, and his servant, his father in law, the damsel's father, said unto him, Behold, now the day draweth toward evening, I pray you tarry all night: behold, the day groweth to an end, lodge here, that thine heart may be merry; and to morrow get you early on your way, that thou mayest go home.

Finally on the fifth day of this delaying; the man refused to delay any longer and took his servant and the lady, departing to go to his own home much too late in the day.

19:10 But the man would not tarry that night, but he rose up and departed, and came over against Jebus, which is Jerusalem; and there were with him two asses saddled, his concubine also was with him.

The man felt safer and more comfortable in a city of Israel.

19:11 And when they were by Jebus [Jerusalem], the day was far spent; and the servant said unto his master, Come, I pray thee, and let us turn in into this city of the Jebusites, and lodge in it. **19:12** And his master said unto him, We will not turn aside hither into the city of a stranger, that is not of the children of Israel; we will pass over to Gibeah.

They made it to Gibeah of Benjamin as the sun set.

19:13 And he said unto his servant, Come, and let us draw near to one of these places to lodge all night, in Gibeah, or in Ramah. **19:14** And they passed on and went their way; and the sun went down upon them when they were by Gibeah, which belongeth to Benjamin.

19:15 And they turned aside thither, to go in and to lodge in Gibeah: and when he went in, he sat him down in a street of the city: for there was no man that took them into his house to lodging.

19:16 And, behold, there came an old man from his work out of the field at even, which was also of mount Ephraim; and he sojourned in Gibeah: but the men of the place were Benjamites.

19:17 And when he had lifted up his eyes, he saw a wayfaring man in the street of the city: and the old man said, Whither goest thou? and whence comest thou? **19:18** And he said unto him, We are passing from Bethlehemjudah toward the side of mount Ephraim; from thence am I: and I went to Bethlehemjudah, but I am now going to

the house of the LORD [at Shiloh]; and there is no man that receiveth me to house.

The old man of Ephraim who dwelled among Benjamin was hospitable, while the Benjamites were not.

19:19 Yet there is both straw and provender for our asses; and there is bread and wine also for me, and for thy handmaid, and for the young man which is with thy servants: there is no want of any thing. **19:20** And the old man said, Peace be with thee; howsoever let all thy wants lie upon me; only lodge not in the street. **19:21** So he brought him into his house, and gave provender unto the asses: and they washed their feet, and did eat and drink.

As they were eating and drinking wicked men came to the door and demanded sexual satisfaction from the man.

19:22 Now as they were making their hearts merry, behold, the men of the city, certain sons of Belial [wickedness], beset the house round about, and beat at the door, and spake to the master of the house, the old man, saying, Bring forth the man that came into thine house, that we may know him.

19:23 And the man, the master of the house, went out unto them, and said unto them, Nay, my brethren, nay, I pray you, do not so wickedly; seeing that this man is come into mine house, do not this folly.

This Levite then protested but then instead of trusting in God he tried to deal with the situation on his own by offering his own daughter to these despicable people.

19:24 Behold, here is my daughter a maiden, and his concubine; them I will bring out now, and humble ye them, and do with them what seemeth good unto you: but unto this man do not so vile a thing.

Then the husband of the concubine brought her out himself.

There is no excuse for trying to save ourselves by ethical and moral compromise; for when we face such severe tests we are to RUN TO OUR GOD for his help and we are not to sin against our Mighty One!

19:25 But the men would not hearken to him: so the man took his concubine, and brought her forth unto them; and they knew her, and abused her all the night until the morning: and when the day began to spring, they let her go.

The woman was finally let go and she sought out her lord, dying on his door step.

19:26 Then came the woman in the dawning of the day, and fell down at the door of the man's house where her lord was, till it was light. **19:27** And her lord rose up in the morning, and opened the doors of the house, and went out to go his way: and, behold, the woman his concubine was fallen down at the door of the house, and her hands were upon the threshold.

The woman died at his threshold

19:28 And he said unto her, Up, and let us be going. But none answered.

The Levite then took her to his home and cut her into twelve pieces to send one piece to every tribe in Israel, calling on them to take action against this wicked city.

Then the man took her up upon an ass, and the man rose up, and gat him unto his place. **19:29** And when he was come into his house, he took a knife, and laid hold on his concubine, and divided her, together with her bones, into twelve pieces, and sent her into all the coasts of Israel.

The Levite managed to shock Israel into action.

19:30 And it was so, that all that saw it said, There was no such deed done nor seen from the day that the children of Israel came up out of the land of Egypt unto this day: consider of it, take advice, and speak your minds.

Judges 20

All Israel gathered before God at the place of the covenant between Laban and Jacob; the pillar in Mizpeh.

Judges 20:1 Then all the children of Israel went out, and the congregation was gathered together as one man, from Dan even to Beersheba, with the land of Gilead, unto the LORD in Mizpeh.

400,000 men gathered themselves at Mizpeh.

20:2 And the chief of all the people, even of all the tribes of Israel, presented themselves in the assembly of the people of God, four hundred thousand footmen that drew sword.

Israel then demanded an explanation for the actions of the Levite in cutting up the woman and calling them together.

20:3 (Now the children of Benjamin heard that the children of Israel were gone up to Mizpeh.) Then said the children of Israel, Tell us, how was this wickedness?

20:4 And the Levite, the husband of the woman that was slain, answered and said, I came into Gibeah that belongeth to Benjamin, I and my concubine, to lodge. **20:5** And the men of Gibeah rose against me, and beset the house round about upon me by night, and thought to have slain me: and my concubine have they forced, that she is dead. **20:6** And I took my concubine, and cut her in pieces, and sent her throughout all the country of the inheritance of Israel: for they have committed lewdness and folly in Israel.

The Levite then pleads his case and asks for a decision of the people.

20:7 Behold, ye are all children of Israel; give here your advice and counsel.

The people decided to take 10% of the men as workers to supply the rest; and the remainder would go up to destroy Gibeah.

20:8 And all the people arose as one man, saying, We will not any of us go to his tent, neither will we any of us turn into his house. **20:9** But now this shall be the thing which we will do to Gibeah; we will go up by lot against it; **20:10** And we will take ten men of an hundred throughout all the tribes of Israel, and an hundred of a thousand, and a thousand out of ten thousand, to fetch victual for the people, that they may do, when they come to Gibeah of Benjamin, according to all the folly that they have wrought in Israel.

20:11 So all the men of Israel were gathered against the city, knit together as one man.

Then Israel demanded that Benjamin deliver up the wicked men, but Benjamin would not deliver them.

This is a lesson for us that today's Ekklesia will also be sternly corrected and almost destroyed for not rejecting wickedness from among us.

20:12 And the tribes of Israel sent men through all the tribe of Benjamin, saying, What wickedness is this that is done among you? **20:13** Now therefore deliver us the men, the children of Belial, which are in Gibeah, that we may put them to death, and put away evil from Israel. But the children of Benjamin would not hearken to the voice of their brethren the children of Israel.

Benjamin sought to join battle in defense of the wicked.

20:14 But the children of Benjamin gathered themselves together out of the cities unto Gibeah, to go out to battle against the children of Israel. **20:15** And the children of Benjamin were numbered at that time out of the cities **twenty and six thousand men** that drew sword, beside the inhabitants of Gibeah, which were numbered **seven hundred chosen men.**

20:16 Among all this people there were seven hundred chosen men lefthanded; every one could sling stones at an hair breadth, and not miss.

Benjamin with 26,700, sought to defend the wicked against the 400,000 of Israel

20:17 And the men of Israel, beside Benjamin, were numbered four hundred thousand men that drew sword: all these were men of war.

God commanded that Judah go up to the battle first.

20:18 And the children of Israel arose, and went up to the house of God [at Shiloh], and asked counsel of God, and said, Which of us shall go up first to the battle against the children of Benjamin? And **the LORD said, Judah shall go up first.**

Benjamin wins the day's battle, killing 22,000 of Israel; most would have been from Judah who led the attack. God seems to be trying to teach Israel a lesson with these defeats by the obviously wicked.

20:19 And the children of Israel rose up in the morning, and encamped against Gibeah. **20:20** And the men of Israel went out to battle against Benjamin; and the men of Israel put themselves in array to fight against them at Gibeah. **20:21** And the children of Benjamin came forth out of Gibeah, and **destroyed down to the ground of the Israelites that day twenty and two thousand** men.

Israel seeks to encourage themselves and asks God if they should go up to battle or leave off; and God said "go up and fight."

20:22 And the people the men of Israel encouraged themselves, and set their battle again in array in the place where they put themselves in array the first day. **20:23** (And the children of Israel **went up and wept before the LORD until even, and asked counsel of the LORD**, saying, Shall I go up again to battle against the children of Benjamin my brother? **And the LORD said, Go up against him.**) **20:24** And the children of Israel came near against the children of Benjamin the second day.

Benjamin again wins the day's battle, killing 18,000 of Israel with no mention of casualties in Benjamin.

20:25 And Benjamin went forth against them out of Gibeah the second day, and **destroyed down to the ground of the children of Israel again eighteen thousand men**; all these drew the sword.

Israel did not lose faith but fasted and gave offerings to the Eternal. This should be a lesson for us that even if we have many trials we must still trust in God and persevere in godliness.

20:26 Then all the children of Israel, and all the people, went up, and came unto the house of God, and wept, and sat there before the LORD, and fasted that day until even, and offered burnt offerings and peace offerings before the LORD.

At this point the Eternal said; go up to the battle and promised Israel victory.

20:27 And the children of Israel enquired of the LORD, (for the ark of the covenant of God was there in those days, **20:28** And Phinehas, the son of Eleazar, the son of Aaron, stood before it in those days,) saying, Shall I yet again go out to battle against the children of Benjamin my brother, or shall I cease? **And the LORD said, Go up; for to morrow I will deliver them into thine hand.**

Israel now uses a strategy, drawing the now over confident Benjamin out into an ambush.

20:29 And Israel set liers in wait round about Gibeah. **20:30** And the children of Israel went up against the children of Benjamin on the third day, and put themselves in array against Gibeah, as at other times.

Israel drew Benjamin out of their place and fell back before them.

20:31 And the children of Benjamin went out against the people, and were drawn away from the city; and they began to smite of the people, and kill, as at other times, in the highways, of which one goeth up to the house of God, and the other to Gibeah in the field, about thirty men of Israel. **20:32** And the children of Benjamin said, They are smitten down before us, as at the first. But the children of Israel said, Let us flee, and draw them from the city unto the highways.

Israel fled only so far and then turned back upon Benjamin; while others of Israel rose up out of their hiding place and sacked the city of Gibeon.

20:33 And all the men of Israel rose up out of their place, and put themselves in array at Baaltamar: and the liers in wait of Israel came forth out of their places, even out of the meadows of Gibeah. 20:34 And there came against Gibeah ten thousand chosen men out of all Israel, and the battle was sore: but they knew not that evil was near them.

Then the God Being who later gave up his God-hood to become flesh as Jesus Christ, went out before Israel and Israel destroyed 25,100 men of Benjamin that day.

20:35 And the LORD smote Benjamin before Israel: and the children of Israel **destroyed of the Benjamites that day twenty and five thousand and an hundred men**: all these drew the sword.

Israel trusted in the ambush and fled drawing Benjamin away from the city.

20:36 So the children of Benjamin saw that they were smitten: for the men of Israel gave place to the Benjamites, **because they trusted unto the liers in wait which they had set beside Gibeah**.

After Israel fell back drawing Benjamin after them, the hidden 10,000 of Israel were able to rise up and take the city.

20:37 And the liers in wait hasted, and rushed upon Gibeah; and the liers in wait drew themselves along, and smote all the city with the edge of the sword.

When the flames began to rise from the city; it was the appointed sign for those fleeing to turn back on their pursuers.

20:38 Now there was an appointed sign between the men of Israel and the liers in wait, that they should make a great flame with smoke rise up out of the city. **20:39** And when the men of Israel retired [were fleeing] in the battle, Benjamin began to smite and kill of the men of Israel about thirty persons: for they said, Surely they are smitten down before us, as in the first battle.

Then when Benjamin looked back and saw their city in flames Benjamin was taken by surprise and Israel turned back to fight them; in shock they were overwhelmed by Israel.

20:40 But when the flame began to arise up out of the city with a pillar of smoke, the Benjamites looked behind them, and, behold, the flame of the city ascended up to heaven. **20:41** And when the men of Israel turned again, the men of Benjamin were amazed: for they saw that evil was come upon them. **20:42** Therefore they turned their backs before the men of Israel unto the way of the wilderness; but the battle overtook them; and them which came out of the cities they destroyed in the midst of them. **20:43** Thus they inclosed the Benjamites round about, and chased them, and trode them down with ease over against Gibeah toward the sunrising.

Thus was Benjamin destroyed almost to the loss of a whole tribe of Israel.

20:44 And there **fell of Benjamin eighteen thousand men;** all these were men of valour. **20:45** And they turned and fled toward the wilderness unto the rock of Rimmon: and they gleaned of them in the highways five thousand men [Israel killed 5,000 more of Benjamin in the highways]; and pursued hard after them unto Gidom, and slew [another] two thousand men of them.

20:46 So that all which fell that day of Benjamin were twenty and five thousand men that drew the sword; all these were men of valour.

Israel then went and destroyed all Benjamin, but 600 men escaped and hid in the wilderness.

20:47 But six hundred men turned and fled to the wilderness unto the rock Rimmon, and abode in the rock Rimmon four months. **20:48** And **the men of Israel turned again upon the children of Benjamin, and smote them with the edge of the sword, as well the men of every city, as the beast, and all that came to hand: also they set on fire all the cities that they came to.**

Judges 21

Judges 21:1 Now the men of Israel had sworn in Mizpeh, saying, **There shall not any of us give his daughter unto Benjamin to wife.**

Then the people realized the magnitude of their rash oath and the deed of destroying Benjamin and cried out to God.

21:2 And the people came to the house of God, and abode there till even before God, and lifted up their voices, and wept sore; **21:3** And said, O LORD God of Israel, why is this come to pass in Israel, that there should be to day one tribe lacking in Israel? **21:4** And it came to pass on the morrow, that the people rose early, and built there an altar, and offered burnt offerings and peace offerings.

The people then sought for those who had not made a vow to withhold their daughters from Benjamin in marriage so that the surviving men of Benjamin might have wives, and that Benjamin might not perish out of Israel.

21:5 And the children of Israel said, Who is there among all the tribes of Israel that came not up with the congregation unto the LORD? For they had made a great oath concerning him that came not up to the LORD to Mizpeh, saying, He shall surely be put to death.

The people repented dearly for Benjamin, but were forced to keep their vow; therefore they sought out any who had not made the vow.

21:6 And the children of Israel repented them for Benjamin their brother, and said, There is one tribe cut off from Israel this day. **21:7** How shall we do for wives for them that remain, seeing we have sworn by the LORD that we will not give them of our daughters to wives?

They found one city that had not made a vow not to give their daughters to Benjamin.

21:8 And they said, What one is there of the tribes of Israel that came not up to Mizpeh to the LORD? And, behold, **there came none to the camp from Jabeshgilead to the assembly. 21:9** For the people were numbered, and, behold, there were none of the inhabitants of Jabeshgilead there.

Israel then destroyed the males that did not come up to fight against the wickedness of Benjamin and took their virgins for the remaining men of Benjamin. This a lesson that those who tolerate open sin among us will also be destroyed from among the people of God.

21:10 And the congregation sent thither twelve thousand men of the valiantest, and commanded them, saying, **Go and smite the inhabitants of Jabeshgilead with the edge of the sword, with the women and the children. 21:11** And this is the thing that ye shall do, **Ye shall utterly destroy every male, and every woman that hath lain by man.**

21:12 And they found among the inhabitants of Jabeshgilead four hundred young virgins, that had known no man by lying with any male: and they brought them unto the camp to Shiloh, which is in the land of Canaan. **21:13** And the whole congregation sent some to speak to the children of Benjamin that were in the rock Rimmon, and to call peaceably unto them. **21:14** And **Benjamin came again at that time; and they gave them wives which they had saved alive of the women of Jabeshgilead: and yet so they sufficed them not.**

Israel repented and sought more wives for the remainder of Benjamin.

21:15 And the people repented them for Benjamin, because that the LORD had made a breach in the tribes of Israel. **21:16** Then the elders of the congregation said, How shall we do for wives for them that remain, **seeing the women are destroyed out of Benjamin? 21:17** And they said, There must be an inheritance for them that be escaped of Benjamin, that a tribe be not destroyed out of Israel. **21:18 Howbeit we may not give them wives of our daughters: for the children of Israel have sworn, saying, Cursed be he that giveth a wife to Benjamin.**

They then decided on a stratagem so that they would not give wives to Benjamin, but neither would they fight if Benjamin kidnapped wives away for themselves.

21:19 Then they said, Behold, there is a feast of the LORD in Shiloh yearly in a place which is on the north side of Bethel, on the east side of the highway that goeth up from Bethel to Shechem, and on the south of Lebonah.

The elders of Israel therefore told the men of Benjamin to kidnap wives of the daughter of Shiloh for themselves.

21:20 Therefore they commanded the children of Benjamin, saying, Go and lie in wait in the vineyards; **21:21** And see, and, behold, **if the daughters of Shiloh come out to dance in dances, then come ye out of the vineyards, and catch you every man his wife of the daughters of Shiloh, and go to the land of Benjamin.**

The leaders of Israel promised to aid Benjamin by reasoning with the men of Shiloh; saying that because they did not "give" their daughters voluntarily they did not break their vow.

21:22 And it shall be, when their fathers or their brethren come unto us to complain, that we will say unto them, Be favourable unto them for our sakes: because we reserved not to each man his wife in the war: **for ye did not give unto them at this time, that ye should be guilty**.

Thus was the problem of wives for Benjamin solved

21:23 And the children of Benjamin did so, and took them wives, according to their number, of them that danced, whom they caught: and they went and returned unto their inheritance, and repaired the cities, and dwelt in them. **21:24** And the children of Israel departed thence at that time, every man to his tribe and to his family, and they went out from thence every man to his inheritance.

The book of Ruth comes next and is appointed to be read on the Feast of Pentecost. Ruth is in the later Judges period, setting the background for the rise of the dynasty of the house of David.

In Judges God raised up occasional Judges [strong men or rulers], it was not until David that God established a dynastic covenant to create a dynasty of kings.

21:25 In those days there was no king in Israel: every man did that which was right in his own eyes.

Lessons from Judges

The story of the book of Judges and Israel's continual cycle of apostasy, correction and repentance, is an allegory of our need to fight the spiritual good fight against all sin and that whenever we may inadvertently slip we should quickly repent and get back up with God's help to continue our personal struggle to overcome all sin in our lives.

Today, most are no different than Mosaic Israel was during the period of the Judges.

The vast majority of today's Spiritual Ekklesia have fallen away from any zeal to follow God the Father and Jesus Christ and have fallen away from any zeal to learn and gain more understanding of and to live by every Word of God.

Whatever the specific sins during the period of the Judges; the main overriding core and foundational sin was: to turn away from any zeal to learn and to live by every Word of God!

It is because they fell away from their covenant to be zealous to live by every Word of God; that they fell into all of these sins and evil situations.

The situation is exactly the same today!

It is because today's Ekklesia has fallen away from the New Covenant of zeal to learn and to live by every Word of God and have followed our own ways, exalting ourselves and our leaders and corporate entities above any zeal for the Word of God; that we have fallen into many sins with each one doing what is right in his own eyes, instead of doing what is right in the eyes of God!

Because we are full of zeal for our own ways and have no zeal for advancing in the knowledge of God or for keeping the Word of God: We have been judged and found wanting by our espoused Husband Jesus Christ and we are in grave danger of being fully rejected by him into the correction of the furnace of affliction so that through the afflicting of the flesh the spirit might possibly be saved.

Revelation 3:14 And unto the angel of the church of the Laodiceans write; These things saith the Amen, the faithful and true witness, the beginning of the creation of God;

Laodicea is spiritually lukewarm, professing godliness while keeping the commandments according to their own imaginations instead of living by every Word of God

We pay lip service to godliness without any zeal to learn and live by every Word of God. Our zeal is for our own ways and what we think, it is for our own past false traditions and our idols of men; and not for what God says. We stand on false past traditions and proudly think we know it all; refusing any spiritual growth we are stagnant or even falling backward in our spiritual condition.

We are hot for our own traditions, and for the teachings of our idols of men about the Word of God, and we are cold for zealously keeping the whole Word as God, as God has commanded us. This mixture of hot for our idols of men and corporate entities, and a cold, lack of zeal to keep the Word of God makes us lukewarm and revolting to God the Father and Jesus Christ.

We are idolaters of men and the false traditions of men; proud, thinking that we know it all spiritually and therefore we refuse correction from God or man; we reject the Word of God for our own ways and we reject any growth in truth and refuse to turn from error, going deeper and deeper into error and sin.

Because we have rejected living by every Word of God to follow our idols of men, we will be rejected into the correction of great tribulation, in the hope that through the correction of the flesh the spirit may be saved.

Revelation 3:15 I know thy works, that thou art neither cold nor hot: I would thou wert cold or hot. **3:16** So then because thou art lukewarm, and neither cold nor hot, **I will spue thee out of my mouth** [we will be rejected by God the Father and Jesus Christ into severe correction]**.**

The vast majority today think they know it all, because we trust in our own ways; and we have no idea of how spiritually wretched and blind we really are.

Proud and self-willed, we think we are spiritually rich and know it all, having no need of spiritual growth, and we reject the increase in spiritual knowledge and understanding promised for the last days (Dan 12).

We reject any part of scripture that we do not want to follow, saying it is for others or that it is not reliable and we are so proud we have no idea how spiritually wretched, miserable and poor we really are.

We are wilfully blind to our own condition and to the things of God that disprove our false ways; We lack the garments of righteousness and are naked before God, our many sins are exposed to him; beginning with the sins of pride, stubborn self-will, self-justification and self-approval.

3:17 Because thou sayest, I am rich [spiritually], and increased with goods [spiritual knowledge], and have need of nothing [no one not even Jesus Christ (the Word of God) can tell them anything]; and knowest not that thou art [spiritually] wretched, and miserable, and [spiritually] poor [knowing almost nothing of God as they ought to know it], and blind [wilfully blind to their wretched spiritual state], and naked [naked of any true godly righteousness, not being zealous to keep the Word of God]:

Seek the gold of the Word of God in the fire of affliction so that we may become spiritually rich. Seek the clothing of the righteousness of the Word of God so that the shame of our sinful ways is covered by the righteousness of the ways of God. Seek after the eye salve of the Spirit of God through zeal for all the things of God that our spiritual blindness may be healed.

Christ counsels those with the Laodicean attitude to buy spiritual gold in the fire of tribulation; so that they may become spiritually rich.

They are bidden to sincerely repent of their prideful sins so that the nakedness of their wickedness may be covered by the application of the sacrifice of Christ; so that they may receive God's Holy Spirit and the white raiment of the righteousness of the zealous keeping of the whole Word of God.

They are commanded to anoint their eyes and open them to see themselves as God sees them, and to sincerely repent from their pride and false ways and to turn away from their idols of men and false traditions to follow the Spirit of God into all truth; rejecting all error and sin to embrace godly truth that they might be saved.

3:18 I counsel thee to buy of me [spiritual knowledge] gold tried in the fire [during the period of our correction in the fire of tribulation], that thou mayest be [become spiritually rich] rich; and white raiment [the righteousness of zealously keeping the whole Word of God], that thou mayest be clothed, and that the shame of thy nakedness [that our sins might be covered by the righteousness of God] do not appear; and anoint thine eyes with eyesalve, that thou mayest see [open our eyes to see ourselves as God sees us, to see ourselves as we really are so that we can repent and be saved].

Jesus reminds these folks that he rebukes them only because he truly loves them and is not willing that they should perish. They are rejected only because they first rejected Christ, refusing to live by every Word of God, refusing to follow God the Father and Jesus Christ and refusing to live by every Word of God in Christ-like zeal.

Jesus Christ tells those of the Laodicean attitude, which is the overwhelming attitude in the Ekklesia today; to REPENT of their pride and self-righteousness and to REPENT of trusting in idols of men and false traditions.

Jesus Christ tells us to turn to live by every Word of God, to learn it and to keep it; to turn from our false idols of men and false traditions and to become zealous to remove error and embrace the truth of God!

3:19 As many as I love, I rebuke and chasten: be zealous therefore, and repent.

Jesus is warning and calling each one of God's straying sheep; He wants us to reject idols and to follow him to God the Father, to be zealous to remove sin and embrace God's righteous truth, to internalize the solid meat of the Word of God in fellowship with Christ.

We have an open invitation from Jesus Christ who is gladly willing to accept us, if we would only open up our eyes and turn to God!

3:20 Behold, I stand at the door, and knock: if any man hear my voice, and open the door, I will come in to him, and will sup [eat; internalize the Word of God] with him, and he with me.

Only those who overcome this Laodicean attitude of pride and self-centeredness will be resurrected to spirit. Only those who sincerely repent of the sins of Laodicea will be in the resurrection to eternal life and have a place in the eternal government of God.

3:21 To him that overcometh will I grant to sit with me in my throne, even as I also overcame, and am set down with my Father in his throne.

3:22 He that hath an ear, let him hear what the Spirit saith unto the churches.

As the seventh and last assembly, Laodicea has all of the problems of the other churches.

That is because pride is the chief cause of most of the various problems.

Today professing Christianity and the Brotherhood are full of pride and idolatry, rejecting any biblical thing they do not agree with as unreliable or applying only to others.

They think of themselves as the repository of all wisdom and truth, and refuse any zeal to keep the whole Word of God, in order to follow their corporate idols, idols of men and their own false traditions.

Today the Organizations call the Sabbath and High Days, Holy; and then walk all over them while claiming that the commandments not to cook or buy food on Sabbath somehow apply to others and not to themselves. They insist on following the apostate Rabbinic Calendar and refuse to keep the Biblical Calendar of God; even though the proofs are overwhelming.

They have almost no understanding of the Festivals, rejecting the true meanings of the Festivals; even claiming that the seven day Feast of Tabernacles somehow represents only one thousand years.

They reject any zeal for living by every Word of God, and insist on a zeal for the corporate idols, idols of men and past false traditions, insisting that people should obey them above the Word of God.

Jesus Christ loves God's people, therefore he will correct us, so that through afflicting the flesh the spirit may be saved.

If we continue to exalt our own ways above any zeal to learn and to keep the whole Word of God: We SHALL be chastised in the furnace of affliction. We have the promise of Jesus Christ that he will do that for us, to save us from ourselves!

I will not lie to you brethren. Only a few scattered here and there, are truly pillars standing on the solid foundation of the whole Word of God.

The vast majority of the people are enthusiastically following their own ways and lacking in any zeal to grow in understanding, or in any zeal to keep the whole Word of God with enthusiastic joy.

Ruth

Pentecost and Ruth

When Ezra canonized the Hebrew Scriptures the book of Ruth was appointed to be read on the Feast of Pentecost.

After the preamble, the setting of the book in Bethlehem begins in the period of the spring harvest; beginning with the barley harvest at Wave Offering Sunday and continuing through the wheat harvest right up to Pentecost.

Ruth appears to have been written by Samuel. The names used have considerable meaning and may be aliases used for the story.

> Elimelech means "God is King".
>
> Naomi: "Well favored, A delight to God and Man,"
>
> Orpah means "stubborn and stiff necked,"
>
> Chilion: "pining away".
>
> Ruth: "A friend and companion"
>
> Mahlon: "sickly"
>
> Boaz: "In God is Strength;" which is also the name of one of the two pillars beside the entry into the Temple Inner Court.

The first part gives the background to the situation, with the real heart of the story beginning with Ruth accepting the God of Israel and her loyalty to her adopted family.

The book of Ruth shows the Covenant being extended to Ruth, a Gentile; by her being grafted into Israel through her marriage to Boaz.

This is an allegory of and prophesies of the New Covenant calling of both Jew and Gentile, into a kind of spiritual Israel which is to come in its fullness at the coming of Messiah and the pouring out of God's Spirit on all flesh on a future Feast of Pentecost. (Joel 2:28, Acts 2)

Ruth in its ultimate type, prophesies the calling out of all mankind and espousing all people then living to Jesus Christ (with the potential to overcome and be changed into spirit, and being added to His bride), and grafted into the New Covenant; which will be extended to all flesh then living, at the establishment of the Kingdom of God on Pentecost when God's Spirit is poured out on all flesh (Joel 2:28).

The book of Ruth pictures a future Pentecost when all who are still alive including Israelites [today being spiritually Gentiles not yet having been called into the spiritual New Covenant of espousal to Christ] and Gentiles; being called into the New Covenant at the establishment of the Kingdom of God over all the earth.

Ruth is a type of the first fruits of this world; with Boaz as a type of Christ: The book is a type of Christ's love for his bride, and her love and faithfulness to the God she had dedicated herself to.

The harvest gleaning is a type of our diligent personal effort at seeking the Bread of Life, and Christ rewarding us and helping us in that effort just as Boaz helped Ruth.

Ruth 1

Ruth 1:1 Now it came to pass in the days when the judges ruled, that there was a famine in the land. And a certain man of Bethlehemjudah went to sojourn in the country of Moab, he, and his wife, and his two sons. **1:2** And the name of the man was Elimelech, and the name of his wife Naomi, and the name of his two sons Mahlon and Chilion, Ephrathites of Bethlehemjudah. And they came into the country of Moab, and continued there. **1:3** And Elimelech Naomi's husband died; and she was left, and her two sons.

1:4 And they took them wives of the women of Moab; the name of the one was Orpah, and the name of the other Ruth: and they dwelled there about ten years. **1:5** And Mahlon and Chilion died also both of them; and the woman was left of her two sons and her husband.

1:6 Then she arose with her daughters in law, that she might return from the country of Moab: for she had heard in the country of Moab how that the LORD had visited his people in giving them bread. **1:7** Wherefore she went forth out of the place where she was, and her two daughters in law with her; and they went on the way to return unto the land of Judah.

1:8 And Naomi said unto her two daughters in law, Go, return each to her mother's house: the LORD deal kindly with you, as ye have dealt with the dead, and with me. **1:9** The LORD grant you that ye may find rest, each of you in the house of her husband. Then she kissed them; and they lifted up their voice, and wept.

1:10 And they said unto her, Surely we will return with thee unto thy people.

This is a graphic lesson on the difference between mere words and deeds, for Orpah professed loyalty and quickly returned to her own ways and gods; While Ruth professed allegiance to God and her marriage family and she WAS faithful.

That is a lesson for us today.

1:11 And Naomi said, Turn again, my daughters: why will ye go with me? are there yet any more sons in my womb, that they may be your husbands? **1:12** Turn again, my daughters, go your way; for I am too old to have an husband. If I should say, I have hope, if I should have an husband also to night, and should also bear sons;

Now Naomi knew of the levirate law and that the next of kin of her husband or his next of kin should marry the widow yet she was testing her daughters in law; that she would be sure of their loyalty; even as God tests his people to see if they will make a worthy part of the bride of Christ.

1:13 Would ye tarry for them till they were grown? would ye stay for them from having husbands? nay, my daughters; for it grieveth me much for your sakes that the hand of the LORD is gone out against me. **1:14** And they lifted up their voice, and wept again: and Orpah kissed her mother in law; but Ruth clave unto her.

Orpah kissed he mother in law goodbye, and went back to her family and her gods.

1:15 And she [Naomi] said, Behold, thy sister in law is gone back unto her people, and unto her gods: return thou after thy sister in law.

Ruth however pledged her loyalty to God and to Naomi in the most thorough and loving manner; as we should also pledge our love and loyalty to our God our Father and to our espoused Husband Jesus Christ.

1:16 And Ruth said, Intreat me not to leave thee, or to return from following after thee: for whither thou goest, I will go; and where thou lodgest, I will lodge: thy people shall be my people, and thy God my God: 1:17 Where thou diest, will I die, and there will I be buried: the

LORD do so to me, and more also, if ought but death part thee and me.

Thereupon Naomi KNEW her daughter in law was diligently faithful and left off from testing her.

1:18 When she saw that she was stedfastly minded to go with her, then she left speaking unto her.

1:19 So they two went until they came to Bethlehem. And it came to pass, when they were come to Bethlehem, that all the city was moved about them, and they said, Is this Naomi? **1:20** And she said unto them, Call me not Naomi, call me Mara: for the Almighty hath dealt very bitterly with me.

1:21 I went out full and the LORD hath brought me home again empty: why then call ye me Naomi, seeing the LORD hath testified against me, and the Almighty hath afflicted me? **1:22** So Naomi returned, and Ruth the Moabitess, her daughter in law, with her, which returned out of the country of Moab: and they came to Bethlehem in the beginning of barley harvest.

Naomi and Ruth come to Bethlehem where Elimelech owned a field. Elimelech having died, his son Mahlon inherited the field, but he and his brother died childless, now Ruth had control of the field until she bore an heir to her husband Mahlon by his next of kin. If Ruth also died childless the land would then be inherited by the nearest next of kin.

Naomi must have been aware of the natures of the two closest next of kin and she directed Ruth to seek Boaz, rather than to seek out the other. Ruth hearing about Boaz from Naomi then sought him out to glean in his field; for Naomi must have spoken of him as a close kinsman who was of a generous mind.

Ruth 2

Ruth 2:1 And Naomi had a kinsman of her husband's, a mighty man of wealth, of the family of Elimelech; and his name was Boaz. **2:2** And Ruth the Moabitess said unto Naomi, Let me now go to the field, and glean ears of corn [grain, in this case barley] after him in whose sight I shall find grace.

And she said unto her, Go, my daughter. **2:3** And she went, and came, and gleaned in the field after the reapers: and her hap was to light on a part of the field belonging unto Boaz, who was of the kindred of Elimelech.

Boaz coming to his field to visit his laborers, notices Ruth and inquires about her, and then speaks to her.

2:4 And, behold, Boaz came from Bethlehem, and said unto the reapers, The LORD be with you. And they answered him, The LORD bless thee.

2:5 Then said Boaz unto his servant that was set over the reapers, Whose damsel is this? **2:6** And the servant that was set over the reapers answered and said, It is the Moabitish damsel that came back with Naomi out of the country of Moab: **2:7** And she said, I pray you, let me glean and gather after the reapers among the sheaves: so she came, and hath continued even from the morning until now, that she tarried a little in the house.

Ruth later takes a rest in the house [laborers rest shack] and was again inquired about by Boaz, who hearing of her good reputation and her loyalty to God and her adopted family, is willing to give her a blessing.

2:8 Then said Boaz unto Ruth, Hearest thou not, my daughter? Go not to glean in another field, neither go from hence, but abide here fast by my maidens: **2:9** Let thine eyes be on the field that they do reap, and go thou after them: have I not charged the young men that they shall not touch thee? and when thou art athirst, go unto the vessels, and drink of that which the young men have drawn.

2:10 Then she fell on her face, and bowed herself to the ground, and said unto him, Why have I found grace in thine eyes, that thou shouldest take knowledge of me, seeing I am a stranger? **2:11** And Boaz answered and said unto her, It hath fully been shewed me, all that thou hast done unto thy mother in law since the death of thine husband: and how thou hast left thy father and thy mother, and the land of thy nativity, and art come unto a people which thou knewest not heretofore.

2:12 The LORD recompense thy work, and a full reward be given thee of the LORD God of Israel, under whose wings thou art come to trust.

Brethren, this is an allegory of the love of Christ for those that God the Father has called to him; who are faithful and of good reputation; who love God the Father and Jesus Christ to whom they are called to espousal.

This story speaks of how those who are faithful to God and all his ways, finding favor with Christ and finally, will be united in marriage to Christ at the Wedding Feast at the marriage of the Lamb in heaven (Rev 15, Rev 19).

2:13 Then she said, Let me find favour in thy sight, my lord; for that thou hast comforted me, and for that thou hast spoken friendly unto thine handmaid, though I be not like unto one of thine handmaidens.

2:14 And Boaz said unto her, At mealtime come thou hither, and eat of the bread, and dip thy morsel in the vinegar. And she sat beside the reapers: and he reached her parched corn, and she did eat, and was sufficed, and left. **2:15** And when she was risen up to glean, Boaz commanded his young men, saying, Let her glean even among the sheaves, and reproach her not: **2:16** And let fall also some of the handfuls of purpose for her, and leave them, that she may glean them, and rebuke her not.

This gleaning of grain is about our quest for spiritual food from the "Bread of Life" Jesus Christ; and how if we work hard and diligently glean out the words of truth; in his mercy and love our espoused Husband will instruct his angels to give us much increase.

Just as Ruth worked hard to find food, we are to work hard and diligently, to seek out that spiritual food of the Word of God; diligently seeking to gather into ourselves: the Word, commandments and very nature of God the father and our espoused Husband Jesus Christ.

2:17 So she gleaned in the field until even, and beat out that she had gleaned: and it was about an ephah of barley. **2:18** And she took it up, and went into the city: and her mother in law saw what she had gleaned: and she brought forth, and gave to her that she had reserved after she was sufficed.

2:19 And her mother in law said unto her, Where hast thou gleaned to day? and where wroughtest thou? blessed be he that did take knowledge of thee. And she shewed her mother in law with whom she had wrought, and said, The man's name with whom I wrought to day is Boaz.

Now Naomi when she saw the grain that Ruth brought, knew that the man felt strongly for Ruth to do her such a service, and remarked that he was a near kinsman; this too being part of the analogy, for Jesus Christ is near kinsman to all humans by virtue of being our Creator, and was of Judah and is therefore a near kinsman to physical AND Spiritual Israel, as Boaz was near kinsman through the husband of Ruth..

2:20 And Naomi said unto her daughter in law, Blessed be he of the LORD, who hath not left off his kindness to the living and to the dead. And Naomi said unto her, The man is near of kin unto us, one of our next kinsmen.

2:21 And Ruth the Moabitess said, He said unto me also, Thou shalt keep fast by my young men, until they have ended all my harvest. **2:22** And Naomi said unto Ruth her daughter in law, It is good, my daughter, that thou go out with his maidens, that they meet thee not in any other field.

Boaz entreats Ruth to come to his field only, and Naomi tells Ruth that it would be good for her to go to Boaz only; so that she would not be seen by potential suitors.

We can see the thoughts of love in the mind of Boaz and that he wanted her for himself, and in the mind of Naomi that she also preferred Boaz over the other near kinsmen.

This is analogous to the love of Christ for those called to him by God the Father; and his jealousy that we should come to him alone.

As Ruth was called by God to come forth from Moab to the field of Boaz; many are called out of this world to come to the field of Christ, there to learn of him by partaking of the Bread of Life the Word of God; which is Jesus Christ in print.

This gleaning period is a period of testing as is our espousal to Christ; Ruth was tested and courted by Boaz; being blessed by him and no doubt conversing with him during the harvest. In the same manner we are to be absolutely faithful through all our testing's and to be in constant communication with God the Father

2:23 So she kept fast by the maidens of Boaz to glean unto the end of barley harvest and of wheat harvest; and dwelt with her mother in law.

In the larger area of Israel, the wheat harvest continued past Pentecost for a few weeks, however in the area by Bethlehem the barley harvest progressed into the wheat harvest which ended by Pentecost.

It is near Pentecost that Naomi advises Ruth to seek marriage with Boaz.

Ruth 3

Ruth 3:1 Then Naomi her mother in law said unto her, My daughter, shall I not seek rest for thee, that it may be well with thee? **3:2** And now is not Boaz of our kindred, with whose maidens thou wast? Behold, he winnoweth barley to night in the threshingfloor.

3:3 Wash thyself therefore, and anoint thee, and put thy raiment upon thee, and get thee down to the floor: but make not thyself known unto the man, until he shall have done eating and drinking. **3:4** And it shall be, when he lieth down, that thou shalt mark the place where he shall lie, and thou shalt go in, and uncover his feet, and lay thee down; and he will tell thee what thou shalt do.

3:5 And she said unto her, All that thou sayest unto me I will do.

Ruth was advised to make herself ready, to cleanse herself and put on her best; and to seek out Boaz and ask him to cover her with his garment. This is similar to God's instructions to make ourselves ready for the coming of our Lord husband by cleansing ourselves from all blemishes of uncleanness and sin; so that he might cover us with the garment of His Righteousness.

Boaz had been "winnowing barley" on "the threshing floor." He slept there in order to guard "the heap of grain" which he had been unable to transport into his granary.

She laid down at his feet and covered herself with his blanket, which was symbolic of her accepting him as her husband, and accepting him as an authority over her.

Boaz had commended Ruth for taking refuge under the "wings" of the Lord, the God of Israel." Now she asked her kinsman to let her find safety under his "wings." The expression "to spread a skirt over or to cover a woman" meant, to take her in marriage (Ezekiel 16:8; Deuteronomy 22:30).

3:6 And she went down unto the floor, and did according to all that her mother in law bade her.

3:7 And when Boaz had eaten and drunk, and his heart was merry, he went to lie down at the end of the heap of corn: and she came softly, and uncovered his feet, and laid her down. **3:8** And it came to pass at midnight, that the man was afraid, and turned himself: and, behold, a woman lay at his feet.

3:9 And he said, Who art thou? And she answered, I am Ruth thine handmaid: spread therefore thy skirt over thine handmaid; for thou art a near kinsman. **3:10** And he said, Blessed be thou of the LORD, my daughter: for thou hast shewed more kindness in the latter end than at the beginning, inasmuch as thou followedst not young men, whether poor or rich.

3:11 And now, my daughter, fear not; I will do to thee all that thou requirest: for all the city of my people doth know that thou art a virtuous woman.

Boaz then accepts Ruth to be his wife, but there is another who has first claim on her. It is the very same with us today for sin has its claim on us and that claim must be paid. We must be redeemed from our near kinsman in sin, Satan; by the payment of our debt of sin.

Our Lord loved us so very much that he laid down his life for us in payment to redeem us from our debt of sincerely repented past sin:

> **1 Corinthians 6:19** What? know ye not that your body is the temple of the Holy Ghost which is in you, which ye have of God, and ye are

not your own? 20 For ye are bought with a price: therefore glorify God in your body, and in your spirit, which are God's.

3:12 And now it is true that I am thy near kinsman: howbeit there is a kinsman nearer than I.

3:13 Tarry this night, and it shall be in the morning, that if he will perform unto thee the part of a kinsman, well; let him do the kinsman's part: but if he will not do the part of a kinsman to thee, then will I do the part of a kinsman to thee, as the LORD liveth: lie down until the morning.

3:14 And she lay at his feet until the morning: and she rose up before one could know another. And he said, Let it not be known that a woman came into the floor.

3:15 Also he said, Bring the vail that thou hast upon thee, and hold it. And when she held it, he measured six measures of barley, and laid it on her: and she went into the city.

3:16 And when she came to her mother in law, she said, Who art thou, my daughter? And she told her all that the man had done to her. **3:17** And she said, These six measures of barley gave he me; for he said to me, Go not empty unto thy mother in law.

3:18 Then said she, Sit still, my daughter, until thou know how the matter will fall: for the man will not be in rest, until he have finished the thing this day.

Boaz acting quickly then goes to the near kinsman before the witnesses of the elders at the city gate, and asks the man about his intentions.

Ruth 4

Ruth 4:1 Then went Boaz up to the gate, and sat him down there: and, behold, the kinsman of whom Boaz spake came by; unto whom he said, Ho, such a one! turn aside, sit down here. And he turned aside, and sat down.

4:2 And he took ten men of the elders of the city, and said, Sit ye down here. And they sat down.

4:3 And he said unto the kinsman, Naomi, that is come again out of the country of Moab, selleth a parcel of land, which was our brother Elimelech's: **4:4** And I thought to advertise thee, saying, Buy it before the inhabitants, and before the elders of my people. If thou wilt redeem it, redeem it: but if thou wilt not redeem it, then tell me, that I may know: for there is none to redeem it beside thee; and I am after thee. And he said, I will redeem it.

4:5 Then said Boaz, What day thou buyest the field of the hand of Naomi, thou must buy it also of Ruth the Moabitess, the wife of the dead, to raise up the name of the dead upon his inheritance. **4:6** And the kinsman said, I cannot redeem it for myself, lest I mar mine own inheritance: redeem thou my right to thyself; for I cannot redeem it.

This man knew that if he produced a child for Ruth, that child would carry on in the name of Mahlon, and not his own name; and would inherit all that was Elimelech's; which if Ruth had no son he would inherit being the nearest kinsman.

4:7 Now this was the manner in former time in Israel concerning redeeming and concerning changing, for to confirm all things; a man plucked off his shoe, and gave it to his neighbour: and this was a testimony in Israel. **4:8** Therefore the kinsman said unto Boaz, Buy it for thee. So he drew off his shoe.

4:9 And Boaz said unto the elders, and unto all the people, Ye are witnesses this day, that I have bought all that was Elimelech's, and all that was Chilion's and Mahlon's, of the hand of Naomi.

4:10 Moreover Ruth the Moabitess, the wife of Mahlon, have I purchased to be my wife, to raise up the name of the dead upon his inheritance, that the name of the dead be not cut off from among his brethren, and from the gate of his place: ye are witnesses this day.

4:11 And all the people that were in the gate, and the elders, said, We are witnesses. The LORD make the woman that is come into thine house like Rachel and like Leah, which two did build the house of Israel: and do thou worthily in Ephratah, and be famous in Bethlehem: **4:12** And let thy house be like the house of Pharez, whom Tamar bare unto Judah, of the seed which the LORD shall give thee of this young woman.

4:13 So Boaz took Ruth, and she was his wife: and when he went in unto her, the LORD gave her conception, and she bare a son.

4:14 And the women said unto Naomi, Blessed be the LORD, which hath not left thee this day without a kinsman, that his name may be famous in Israel.

4:15 And he shall be unto thee a restorer of thy life, and a nourisher of thine old age: for thy daughter in law, which loveth thee, which is better to thee than seven sons, hath born him.

4:16 And Naomi took the child, and laid it in her bosom, and became nurse unto it.

4:17 And the women her neighbours gave it a name, saying, There is a son born to Naomi; and they called his name Obed: he is the father of Jesse, the father of David.

4:18 Now these are the generations of Pharez: Pharez begat Hezron, **4:19** And Hezron begat Ram, and Ram begat Amminadab, **4:20** And Amminadab begat Nahshon, and Nahshon begat Salmon, **4:21** And

Salmon begat Boaz, and Boaz begat Obed, **4:22** And Obed begat Jesse, and Jesse begat David.

Now Obed inherited all the land and wealth of Elimelech by the levirate law; and he also inherited all the land and wealth of Boaz. Becoming the head of a very wealthy and powerful family, out of which came David the king and into which family Jesus the Christ the King of kings was born.

First Samuel

1 Samuel 1

The last Judge of Israel, Samuel

First and Second Samuel were originally (and still are in some Jewish Bibles) a single book, but the Septuagint [LXX] translation, produced in the centuries immediately before Christ, divided Samuel into two books and this dividing of Samuel was adopted by other translators.

The ever faithful, ever enduring Samuel is an example of steadfast faithful righteousness which is too often overlooked in comparison to the fascinating deeds of others.

Samuel was the last Judge before the establishment of the permanent line of kings in Israel; and as the transitional Judge, Samuel is given his own Book and a special place in the scriptures.

The first two chapters of 1 Samuel cover the circumstances surrounding his birth and introduction to Eli.

> According to the genealogical tables in Chronicles, Elkanah was a Levitical priest of Kohath - a fact not mentioned in the books of Samuel. The fact that Elkanah, a Levitical priest, was denominated an Ephraimite meant that he lived in a Levitical city belonging to Judah (1 Chronicles 6:16-30).

Samuel [Shemuel] the priest prophet had a son Joel, and Heman has grandson was a Levitical singer. **1 Chronicles 6:33** And these are they that waited with their children. Of the sons of the Kohathites: Heman a singer, the son of Joel, the son of Shemuel,

Who wrote Samuel? There is a problem with the idea that this book was written by Samuel, since Samuel died in 1 Samuel 25 and there is the whole of second Samuel left. Samuel likely dictated at least some of the first part and the remainder may well have been written or dictated by the high priest or the prophets during the life of David.

1 Samuel 1:1 Now there was a certain man of Ramathaimzophim, of mount Ephraim, and his name was Elkanah, the son of Jeroham, the son of Elihu, the son of Tohu, the son of Zuph, an Ephrathite: **1:2** And he had two wives; the name of the one was Hannah, and the name of the other Peninnah: and **Peninnah had children, but Hannah had no children.**

This is likely a reference to one of the three annual pilgrim feasts

1:3 And this man went up out of his city **yearly to worship and to sacrifice unto the LORD of hosts in Shiloh.** And the two sons of Eli, Hophni and Phinehas, the priests of the LORD, were there.

Humanly Elkanah might have given more to Peninnh than Hannah because Paninnh was the mother of his children, yet Hannah's husband was generous to her at the Feast for the very reason that she was childless and yet greatly beloved of her husband. The implication here is that Elkanah was a fair and righteous man who deeply loved his wives and knowing Hannah's sadness he sought to be extra kind to her.

1:4 And when the time was that Elkanah offered, he gave to Peninnah his wife, and to all her sons and her daughters, portions: **1:5** But **unto Hannah he gave a worthy portion; for he loved Hannah**: but the LORD had shut up her womb.

It seems that Peninnah belittled Hannah because Hannah was childless; much like Hagar mocked Sarah and the rivalries between the wives of Jacob.

These kinds of rivalries where wives compete for their husband's affections and the often jealousies of this type of relationship are a few of the potential evils of polygamy, which often included frustrated polygamous wives being driven to lesbianism with the other wives and tempted to engage in adultery with other men.

1:6 And her adversary also provoked her sore, for to make her fret, because the LORD had shut up her womb.

Hannah could not eat because of her upset over the provocations of Peninnah and her grief over her childlessness. The situation was one of extreme sorrow, shame and upset for Hannah.

1:7 And as he did so year by year, when she went up to the house of the LORD, so she provoked her; therefore she wept, and did not eat [was so distraught that she could not rejoice at the Feast].

Then Elkanah her husband tried to comfort Hannah; being very kind to her and loving her more than many sons.

1:8 Then said Elkanah her husband to her, Hannah, why weepest thou? and why eatest thou not? and why is thy heart grieved? am not I better to thee than ten sons?

Hannah was very tortured in spirit for her situation and desired a son more than anything in the world.

1:9 So Hannah rose up after they had eaten in Shiloh, and after they had drunk. Now Eli the priest sat upon a seat by a post of the temple of the LORD. **1:10** And she was in bitterness of soul, and prayed unto the LORD, and wept sore.

Hannah then promised God that she would dedicate her son to be a Nazarite to serve God all his days; if God would only give her a son.

Hannah's trial can be seen as typical of the trials of the spiritually called out person who suffers much in this world and is often filled with many sorrows; yet will ultimately be delivered if we are faithful and put our trust in the Lord to faithfully live by every Word of God.

1:11 And she vowed a vow, and said, O LORD of hosts, if thou wilt indeed look on the affliction of thine handmaid, and remember me, and not forget thine handmaid, but wilt give unto thine handmaid a man child, then I will give him unto the LORD all the days of his life, and there shall no razor come upon his head.

Hannah spoke quietly and privately before God.

1:12 And it came to pass, as she continued praying before the LORD, that Eli marked her mouth. **1:13** Now Hannah, she spake in her heart; only her lips moved, but her voice was not heard: therefore Eli thought she had been drunken.

Eli rebuked her for drunkenness not realizing the situation and the depth of Hannah's despair.

1:14 And Eli said unto her, How long wilt thou be drunken? put away thy wine from thee. **1:15** And Hannah answered and said, No, my lord, I am a woman of a sorrowful spirit: I have drunk neither wine nor strong drink, but have poured out my soul before the LORD.

She explains herself and Eli sends her away with a blessing that God might grant her request.

1:16 Count not thine handmaid for a daughter of Belial: for out of the abundance of my complaint and grief have I spoken hitherto. **1:17** Then Eli answered and said, Go in peace: and the God of Israel grant thee thy petition that thou hast asked of him.

Hannah was encouraged and her spirit was revived.

1:18 And she said, Let thine handmaid find grace in thy sight. So the woman went her way, and did eat, and her countenance was no more sad.

They returned home and Hannah became pregnant.

1:19 And they rose up in the morning early, and worshipped before the LORD, and returned, and came to their house to Ramah: and Elkanah knew Hannah his wife; and the LORD remembered her.

Samuel is translated as "Heard by God" or "God has heard" (from 'shama', "heard," and 'El', God)

1:20 Wherefore it came to pass, when the time was come about after Hannah had conceived, that she bare a son, and **called his name Samuel, saying, Because I have asked him of the LORD.**

1:21 And the man Elkanah, and all his house, **went up to offer unto the LORD the yearly sacrifice, and his vow.**

Hannah remained at home until the child was weaned [natural weaning usually begins late in the first year and is completed at the age of approximately three years old]. The term "yearly sacrifice" pins this down as the Passover, to be offered annually since no other sacrifice was commanded to be offered annually by individuals in scripture. All other festival sacrifices were to be offered by the priesthood on behalf of the whole nation; only the Passover was a commanded personal annual "Feast of the Lord" sacrifice to be eaten by the people.

1:22 But Hannah went not up; for she said unto her husband, I will not go up until the child be weaned, and then I will bring him, that he may appear before the LORD, and there abide for ever.

His character was such that Elkanah not only allowed her to remain home and blessed her and the child, but he approved of her vow to give his son to lifelong service to the priests as a Nazarite.

1:23 And Elkanah her husband said unto her, **Do what seemeth thee good; tarry until thou have weaned him; only the LORD establish his word.** So the woman abode, and gave her son suck until she weaned him.

When the child was fully weaned he was taken to the tabernacle with a sacrifice by his family.

1:24 And when she had weaned him, she took him up with her, with three bullocks, and one ephah of flour, and a bottle of wine, and brought him unto the house of the LORD in Shiloh: and the child was young. **1:25** And they slew a bullock, and brought the child to Eli.

Samuel was then presented to Eli

Consider the righteousness of Hannah that she kept her vow and gave up the son of her barrenness to Eli and the Eternal; and consider the righteousness and love of her husband that he initially approved of her vow and then gave up his son by his beloved Hannah.

1:26 And she said, Oh my lord [Eli], as thy soul liveth, my lord, I am the woman that stood by thee here, praying unto the LORD. **1:27** For this child I prayed; and the LORD hath given me my petition which I asked of him: **1:28** Therefore also I have lent him to the LORD; as long as he liveth he shall be lent to the LORD. And he worshipped the LORD there.

1 Samuel 2

Hannah's prayer of rejoicing for Samuel the gift of God

This could be the prayer of EVERY person who is faithful to keep the whole Word of God! Almighty God will deliver his zealous faithful followers, while correcting those who turn away from their zeal for his Word!

1 Samuel 2:1 And Hannah prayed, and said, My heart rejoiceth in the LORD, mine horn is exalted in the LORD: my mouth [my words are fulfilled before my enemies] is enlarged over mine enemies;

because I rejoice in thy salvation.

Eternal Salvation is the gift of God to all those who follow and obey HIM!

2:2 There is none [as] holy as the LORD: for there is none beside thee: neither is there any rock like our God.

Let us repent of our proud arrogance of doing what we think is right in our own eyes; and turn to do what God teaches in his Word.

2:3 Talk no more so exceeding proudly; let not arrogancy come out of your mouth: for the LORD is a God of knowledge, and by him [all deeds are judged] actions are weighed.

2:4 The bows of the mighty men [enemy warriors; spiritually Satan and sin] are broken, and they [the faithful to God who stumble] that stumbled are girded with strength. **2:5** They that were full [the physically rich, who are spiritually poor; are driven to beg bread] have hired out themselves for bread; and they that were hungry ceased [the spiritually hungry are filled by our Mighty God]: so that the barren [we may think we are alone, but our faithfulness to the Eternal will bear much fruit] hath born seven; and she that hath many children is waxed feeble.

ONLY the Eternal has the power to give eternal life.

2:6 The LORD killeth, and maketh alive: he bringeth down to the grave, and bringeth up. **2:7** The LORD maketh poor, and maketh rich: he bringeth low, and lifteth up. **2:8** He raiseth up the poor out of the dust, and lifteth up the beggar from the dunghill, to set them among princes, and to make them inherit the throne of glory: for the pillars of the earth are the LORD's, [the earth will be given to the spiritual pillars that stand firm on the solid foundation of the whole Word of God] and he hath set the world upon them.

Man cannot prevail by his own ways or by his own strength.

2:9 He will keep the feet of his saints, and the wicked shall be silent in darkness [the unrepentant shall see eternal death]; for by strength shall no man prevail.

Those who condemn the zealous and who will not keep the Word of God faithfully, who are permissive and compromising and lukewarm for keeping the whole Word of God; have become his adversaries and they shall be corrected and their pride crushed to contrition.

2:10 The adversaries of the LORD shall be broken to pieces; out of heaven shall he thunder upon them: the LORD shall judge the ends of the earth; and he [God the Father] shall give strength unto his king [Messiah the king], and exalt the horn [the authority and power of Jesus Christ the Messiah the king] of his anointed.

These people knew of God by the family name of YHVH; they did not know of the difference between the Father and Son; and Judah does not understand that to this day.

Samuel was given to Eli to be taught the things of God, and to serve the Eternal.

2:11 And Elkanah went to Ramah to his house. And the child did minister unto the LORD before Eli the priest.

Eli had two sons who were wicked and selfish men: Like many church leaders of today, they lusted after the very best for themselves and abused the brethren.

2:12 Now the sons of Eli were sons of Belial; they knew not the LORD.

These priests took for themselves the most and the best.

2:13 And the priest's custom with the people was, that, when any man offered sacrifice, the priest's servant came, while the flesh was in seething, with a fleshhook of three teeth in his hand; **2:14** And he struck it into the pan, or kettle, or caldron, or pot; all that the fleshhook brought up the priest took for himself. So they did in Shiloh unto all the Israelites that came thither.

2:15 Also before they burnt the fat, the priest's servant came, and said to the man that sacrificed, Give flesh to roast for the priest; for he will not have sodden flesh of thee, but raw.

Those apostate priests and many of today's elders insist that they must be obeyed instead of God, and today the faithful for God are often forced out of the assemblies [Synagogue].

2:16 And if any man said unto him, Let them not fail to burn the fat presently [as God commanded], and then take as much as thy soul desireth; then he would answer him, **Nay; but thou shalt give it me now: and if not, I will take it by force.**

These two priests abhorred to offer to the Eternal what was God's and instead took of the offerings for themselves in their greed, instead of doing what God had commanded.

The same sin of greedily seeking the very best and exalting themselves, is committed wholesale in today's Ekklesia.

2:17 Wherefore the sin of the young men was very great before the LORD: for men abhorred [The sins of these priests caused many to leave off giving offerings to God.] the offering of the LORD.

Samuel was faithful in serving the Eternal.

Consider that God may have inspired that whole situation surrounding the birth of Samuel, and that Hannah may have been barren and conceived Samuel by her supplication according to the plan and will of God!

2:18 But Samuel ministered before the LORD, being a child, girded with a linen ephod. **2:19** Moreover his mother made him a little coat, and brought it to him from year to year, when she came up with her husband to offer the yearly sacrifice.

Eli blessed Hannah for giving Samuel in service to God; implying that Samuel was a good and faithful lad. Here we see that despite any hardships in this life, if we overcome and are diligently faithful to keep the whole Word of God we shall ultimately be blessed.

2:20 And Eli blessed Elkanah and his wife, and said, The LORD give thee seed of this woman for the loan which is lent to the LORD. And they went unto their own home. **2:21** And the LORD visited Hannah, so that she conceived, and bare three sons and two daughters. And the child Samuel grew before the LORD.

Eli waxed old and he heard of the evils of his sons and how they refused to obey the instructions of God and lusted after the chief seats and the best things, and that they took advantage of the women.

Without doubt many today compromise with the Word of God teaching many false things and seeking the best things and chief seats for themselves; and exalting personal gain above obedience to the whole Word of God.

2:22 Now Eli was very old, and heard all that his sons did unto all Israel; and how they lay with the women that assembled at the door of the tabernacle of the congregation.

Eli then called his sons to account.

2:23 And he said unto them, Why do ye such things? for I hear of your evil dealings by all this people. **2:24** Nay, my sons; for it is no good report that I hear: ye make the LORD's people to transgress.

Then because they would not listen to their father and repent; YHVH who later became Jesus Christ judged them for their wickedness.

It is no different today and very many elders and leaders of today will be rejected by Christ, because we have rejected living by every Word of God for our own evil ways.

When we fall into the correction of Almighty God: Who can deliver us?

2:25 If one man sin against another, the judge shall judge him: but **if a man sin against the LORD, who shall intreat for him?**

Notwithstanding they hearkened not unto the voice of their father, because [of which] the LORD would slay them.

Samuel grew up faithful to the whole Word of God in sharp contrast to the two sons of Eli; and because of that difference in behavior there must have also been conflict between these wicked older men and the faithful young Samuel.

They must have made his life miserable; yet Samuel remained faithful to the Word of God.

2:26 And the child Samuel grew on, and was in favour both with the LORD, and also with men.

God sent a prophet to Eli the priest

2:27 And there came a man of God unto Eli, and said unto him,

Thus saith the LORD, Did I plainly appear unto the house of thy father [speaking of Eli as a descendant of Aaron], when they were in Egypt in Pharaoh's house? **2:28** And did I choose him [Aaron] out of all the tribes of Israel to be my priest, to offer upon mine altar, to burn incense, to wear an ephod [priestly garment] before me? and did I give unto the house of thy father all the offerings made by fire of the children of Israel?

Eli is rebuked for allowing his sons to reject his criticism and for allowing them to continue to exercise the office of priests. Jesus Christ asks Eli why he honors his sons and does not honor God.

The leaders and elders of today's spiritual Israel are also being warned; and they are rejecting the warnings to do what they think is right and to exalt themselves above what Almighty Gad said is right in his Word.

2:29 Wherefore kick ye at my sacrifice and at mine offering, which I have commanded in my habitation; and **honourest thy sons above me, to make yourselves fat with the chiefest of all the offerings of Israel my people?**

Jesus Christ condemns those who are not faithful to God and do whatever they want instead of living by every Word of God.

2:30 Wherefore the LORD God of Israel saith, I said indeed that thy house, and the house of thy father [Aaron], should walk before me [as my priests] for ever: but now the LORD saith, Be it far from me [that the wicked should be called God's priests and elders]; **for them that honour me I will honour, and they that despise me shall be lightly esteemed.**

Jesus Christ issues his judgment that Eli's descendants would be cut off from the altar of the Lord forever.

This is also a spiritual judgment that all those in spiritual Israel who are not zealous and faithful to learn, keep and teach the whole Word of God; will have NO PART in the resurrection to eternal life as part of the collective bride of Christ.

Make NO mistake, all those who seek the chief seats and are willing to willfully compromise with the Word of God: Are cut off from Almighty God and the resurrection to eternal life.

2:31 Behold, the days come, that I will cut off thine arm, and the arm of thy father's house, that there shall not be an old man in thine house.

All those who teach against a passionate zeal to learn and to live by every Word of God are cut off from God!

2:32 And thou [speaking to Eli who would not rebuke sin, and to all wicked men] shalt see an enemy in my habitation, in all the wealth which God shall give Israel: and there shall not be an old man [Eli's descendants will all dies young.] in thine house for ever. **2:33** And the man of thine, whom I shall not cut off from mine altar, shall be to consume thine eyes, and to grieve thine heart: and **all the increase of thine house shall die in the flower of their age.**

The judgment of Jesus Christ against today's elders who do not strongly rebuke sin and cast out willful sinners is that they are cut off from inheriting eternal life.

The two sons of Eli are condemned to die on the same day

2:34 And this shall be a sign unto thee, that shall come upon thy two sons, on Hophni and Phinehas; in one day they shall die both of them.

Here God prophesies of the resurrection of the zealously faithful, into the eternal priesthood of Melchizedek.

2:35 And I will raise me up a faithful priest [Jesus the Messiah and High Priest of our salvation after the order of Melchizedek], that shall do according to that which is in mine heart and in my mind: and I will build him a sure house; and he shall walk before mine anointed **for ever.**

After Messiah the Christ comes the physical descendants of Aaron will repent and beg to be reinstated into the physical priesthood; and the faithful sons of Zadok will yet serve in the Ezekiel Temple.

2:36 And it shall come to pass, that every one that is left in thine house shall come and crouch to him for a piece of silver and a morsel of bread, and shall say, Put me, I pray thee, into one of the priests' offices, that I may eat a piece of bread.

1 Samuel 3

The Eternal departed from among the people because they rejected living by every Word of God; this is precisely what is happening in today's Spiritual Ekklesia.

1 Samuel 3:1 And the child Samuel ministered unto the LORD before Eli. And the word of the LORD was precious [very scarce] in those days; there was no open vision.

Just like today there was no vision among God's people because of their sins. Then when Eli grew old and feeble and began to fall sleep in the early evening; YHVH spoke to Samuel in the night.

3:2 And it came to pass at that time, when Eli was laid down in his place, and his eyes began to wax dim, that he could not see; **3:3** And ere the lamp of God went out in the temple of the LORD, where the ark of God was, and Samuel was laid down to sleep;

Samuel heard a voice calling him, and he ran to Eli supposing that Eli had called him.

3:4 That the LORD called Samuel: and he answered, Here am I. **3:5** And he ran unto Eli, and said, Here am I; for thou calledst me. And he said, **I called not; lie down again. And he went and lay down.**

Samuel was called a second time and again he ran to Eli only to be told that he had not been called by Eli.

3:6 And the LORD called yet again, Samuel. And Samuel arose and went to Eli, and said, Here am I; for thou didst call me. And he answered, I called not, my son; lie down again.

The young Samuel did not know that God might call to him.

3:7 Now Samuel did not yet know the LORD, neither was the word of the LORD yet revealed unto him.

YHVH called to Samuel the third time and then Eli understood that God had called him.

God sometimes honors and speaks to those that are his and faithful to him in dreams and visions, sometimes by inspiration and sometime in a still small voice. God does not do this lightly, but does so for his own good purpose.

3:8 And the LORD called Samuel again the third time. And he arose and went to Eli, and said, Here am I; for thou didst call me. And Eli perceived that the LORD had called the child.

Eli then instructed Samuel how to respond to God.

3:9 Therefore Eli said unto Samuel, Go, lie down: and it shall be, if he call thee, **that thou shalt say, Speak, LORD; for thy servant heareth.** So Samuel went and lay down in his place.

God may not speak personally to many in this manner; but he definitely speaks to us through his Word. Are we sensitive and listening to the whole Word of God to be zealous to learn it and to live by it?

Do we seek continually to fill ourselves with the nature of God; becoming fully like him by listening closely to his Word and keeping it, and by a continual prayerful consideration of all godliness?

3:10 And the LORD came, and stood, and called as at other times, Samuel, Samuel. Then Samuel answered, Speak; for thy servant heareth.

Jesus Christ then revealed directly to Samuel that the sons of Eli that had turned away from any zeal to keep the Word of God would be destroyed. This is an example for us so that we might learn to be zealously faithful to live by every Word of God.

Spiritual Israel has in this latter day forgotten this lesson and has turned aside from the Word of God to follow our own proud and selfish ways just like the sons of Eli did.

> **Deuteronomy 5:32** Ye shall observe to do therefore as the Lord your God hath commanded you: ye shall not turn aside to the right hand or to the left. **5:33** Ye shall walk in all the ways which the Lord your God hath commanded you, that ye may live, and that it may be well with you, and that ye may prolong your days in the land which ye shall possess.

1 Samuel 3:11 And the LORD said to Samuel, Behold, I will do a thing in Israel, at which both the ears of every one that heareth it shall tingle. **3:12** In that day I will perform against Eli all things which I have spoken concerning his house: when I begin, I will also make an end.

This is an example for us that the Eternal will also judge those of Spiritual Israel who turn away from zeal for the Word of God, and that Jesus Christ will judge those leaders, teachers and elders who fail to rebuke and remove sin out of the assemblies of the Eternal!

3:13 For I have told him that I will judge his house for ever for the iniquity which he knoweth; because **his sons made themselves vile, and he restrained them not.**

Will we learn from this terrible curse for Eli because he did not exercise his authority to rebuke sin and cast out the unrepentant wicked? Or will we continue in the same sin today?

The leaders, teachers and elders of today's Spiritual Israel are under the same curse, for they do not teach any zeal for keeping the whole Word of God; and instead they teach the brethren to follow them as their idols in place of any zeal for the Word of God.

They say: "Follow God" but then they say that to follow us is to follow God, and so they deceive the brethren away from any zeal for God and into a certain zeal for idols of men.

3:14 And therefore I have sworn unto the house of Eli, that the iniquity of Eli's house shall not be purged with sacrifice nor offering for ever.

Samuel was afraid to tell Eli his beloved teacher and father figure, what God had said.

3:15 And Samuel lay until the morning, and opened the doors of the house of the LORD. And Samuel feared to shew Eli the vision.

Eli asked the word of the Lord from Samuel.

3:16 Then Eli called Samuel, and said, Samuel, my son. And he answered, Here am I. **3:17** And he said, What is the thing that the LORD hath said unto thee? I pray thee hide it not from me: God do so to thee, and more also, if thou hide any thing from me of all the things that he said unto thee.

Eli then accepted the judgment of the Eternal.

Eli must have been vexed by the behavior of his sons himself, and might have expected that this was coming; so he did not weep and tear his garments in agony of spirit and repentance and entreat the mercy of the Eternal.

3:18 And Samuel told him every whit, and hid nothing from him. And he said, It is the LORD: let him do what seemeth him good.

As he grew up Samuel became known for his wisdom and had the fruits of a prophet to the level that no man could deny that Samuel had been called to be a prophet of the Eternal.

What man ordained Samuel? Did not God personally call him and ordain him to the office of prophet?

My friends and brethren, in this latter day Spiritual Israel, very many were ordained by men because of organizational loyalty or personal talent who WERE NOT called by GOD to the office that they were ordained to by men.

Remember the words of Christ in Matthew 7: We are to judge the words of all men by the Word of God; and we are to believe only those people who have the fruits of the office that God has called them to. Which fruits must be consistent and backed by a continual zeal to learn and to live by every Word of God like Samuel.

3:19 And Samuel grew, and the LORD was with him, and did let none of his words fall to the ground. **3:20** And all Israel from Dan even to Beersheba knew that Samuel was established to be a prophet of the LORD.

The Eternal began to have a very close relationship with Samuel, and was with the faithful Samuel.

3:21 And the LORD appeared again in Shiloh: for the LORD revealed himself to Samuel in Shiloh by the word of the LORD.

1 Samuel 4

Samuel became famous for his godly life, his godly wisdom and for his relationship with God; as God's called out prophet.

1 Samuel 4:1 And the word of Samuel came to all Israel.

Israel went forth to fight the Philistines and was defeated in battle.

. . . Now Israel went out against the Philistines to battle, and pitched beside Ebenezer: and the Philistines pitched in Aphek. **4:2** And the Philistines put themselves in array against Israel: and when they joined battle, Israel was smitten before the Philistines: and they slew of the army in the field about four thousand men.

Israel then reasoned among themselves and forgot their God, making an idol out of the Ark of the Covenant itself!

Dear brethren, I ask you if we have not done the same thing ourselves in this latter day spiritual Israel? Just as they idolized the Ark [the throne of God] instead of the God who sat on that throne: Today's Spiritual Ekklesia has made an idol out of our organizations, false traditions and human leaders!

4:3 And when the people were come into the camp, the elders of Israel said, Wherefore hath the LORD smitten us to day before the Philistines?

Let us fetch the ark of the covenant of the LORD out of Shiloh unto us, that, when it cometh among us, **it may save us** out of the hand of our enemies.

Then the two sons of Eli brought the Ark down to the battle without first inquiring of the Lord. Thus doing what they decided in order to gain fame among the people for themselves, instead of inquiring what God would have them do.

It is even so in today's Spiritual Israel today, we do as we please and we do not inquire of the Eternal as to what he would have us do.

4:4 So the people sent to Shiloh, that they might bring from thence the ark of the covenant of the LORD of hosts, which dwelleth between the cherubims: and the two sons of Eli, Hophni and Phinehas, were there with the ark of the covenant of God.

The Philistines also feared the Ark

4:5 And when the ark of the covenant of the LORD came into the camp, all Israel shouted with a great shout, so that the earth rang again. **4:6** And when the Philistines heard the noise of the shout, they said, What meaneth the noise of this great shout in the camp of the Hebrews? And they understood that the ark of the LORD was come into the camp.

The Philistines fear the Ark greatly seeing it as a mighty god [an idol] in itself.

Even so, today we love and exalt our organizations and leaders as idols above the Word of God, being filled with pride in our leaders, elders, false traditions and organizations and following them instead of living by every Word of God.

We even call God's Sabbath holy and then we pollute it because our idols of men have encouraged us to do so!

4:7 And the Philistines were afraid, for they said, God is come into the camp. And they said, Woe unto us! for there hath not been such a thing heretofore. **4:8** Woe unto us! who shall deliver us out of the hand of these mighty Gods? these are the Gods that smote the Egyptians with all the plagues in the wilderness.

The Philistine leaders then encouraged their men to fight the good fight.

4:9 Be strong and quit yourselves like men, O ye Philistines, that ye be not servants unto the Hebrews, as they have been to you: quit yourselves like men, and fight.

Hophni and Phinehas the sons of Eli, along with 30,000 were killed and the Ark was lost to the Philistines and the word of the Lord was fulfilled.

> **1 Samuel 3:11** And the LORD said to Samuel, Behold, I will do a thing in Israel, at which both the ears of every one that heareth it shall tingle. **3:12** In that day I will perform against Eli all things which I have spoken concerning his house: when I begin, I will also make an end.

1 Samuel 4:10 And the Philistines fought, and Israel was smitten, and they fled every man into his tent: and there was a very great slaughter; for there fell of Israel thirty thousand footmen. **4:11** And the ark of God was taken; and the two sons of Eli, Hophni and Phinehas, were slain.

A messenger comes to tell the people of the battle

4:12 And there ran a man of Benjamin out of the army, and came to Shiloh the same day with his clothes rent, and with earth upon his head.

Eli was sitting anxiously waiting for news

4:13 And when he came, lo, Eli sat upon a seat by the wayside watching: for his heart trembled for the ark of God. And when the man came into the city, and told it, all the city cried out. **4:14** And when Eli heard the noise of the crying, he said, What meaneth the noise of this tumult? And the man came in hastily, and told Eli.

Eli died hearing as his last words the fulfillment of the judgment of God.

4:15 Now **Eli was ninety and eight years old**; and his eyes were dim, that he could not see. **4:16** And the man said unto Eli, I am he that came out of the army, and I fled to day out of the army. And he said, What is there done, my son? **4:17** And the messenger answered and said, Israel is fled before the Philistines, and there hath been also a great slaughter among the people, and thy two sons also, Hophni and Phinehas, are dead, and the ark of God is taken.

4:18 And it came to pass, when he made mention of the ark of God, that he fell from off the seat backward by the side of the gate, and his neck brake, and he died: for he was an old man, and heavy. And he had judged Israel forty years.

On hearing of the death of her husband, Phinehas' wife delivered a son and died in childbirth.

4:19 And his daughter in law, Phinehas' wife, was with child, near to be delivered: and when she heard the tidings that the ark of God was taken, and that her father in law and her husband were dead, she bowed herself and travailed; for her pains came upon her. **4:20** And about the time of her death the women that stood by her said unto her, Fear not; for thou hast born a son. But she answered not, neither did she regard it.

4:21 And she named the child Ichabod, saying, The glory is departed from Israel: because the ark of God was taken, and because of her father in law and her husband.

The glory [presence of God] was removed from Israel and the ark was given by the hands of God to the Philistines; because of the transgressions of the priesthood of Eli and his sons which had led the people into sin. Where is the glory of the presence of God in the congregations of the greater church of God organizations today?

The glory of the Eternal is his righteousness; and the glory of the son's of God is their zeal to be like God their Father and to be righteous as HE is righteous; learning and living by every Word of God.

Today's Spiritual Ekklesia has left off from any zeal for learning and keeping the whole Word of God; we have rejected his glorious righteousness in order to do what is right in our own eyes; cleaving to our false traditions and idols of men!

How can we escape the judgment and correction of Almighty God?

4:22 And she said, The glory is departed from Israel: for the ark of God is taken.

1 Samuel 5

After the death and destruction of many worshipers of Dagon by Samson in the book of Judges, the Philistines rebuilt the temple of their fertility fish god Dagon; who was just another manifestation of Baal.

The pagan pantheon was mainly established at Babel and the various families of man took these gods with them under new names in their new languages. Outside of the true God, all the gods are but different names for the same Adversary and his demons.

The ark was placed beside Dagon, in the temple of Dagon; and God revealed by miracles that he would not share his preeminent God-hood with any false god: Even as today the Eternal will not tolerate the idolatry of men and organizations in the Spiritual Ekklesia.

The Eternal is God and beside him there is NO OTHER!

Just as Dagon fell down before the throne of the Eternal; the organizational idols of men and false traditions will be cast down before the Eternal God.

1 Samuel 5:1 And the Philistines took the ark of God, and brought it from Ebenezer unto Ashdod. **5:2** When the Philistines took the ark of God, they brought it into the house of Dagon, and set it by Dagon. **5:3** And when they of Ashdod arose early on the morrow, behold, Dagon was fallen upon his face to the earth before the ark of the LORD. And they took Dagon, and set him in his place again.

This was repeated the second day; only this time Dagon the fish god broke in pieces before the throne of the Eternal; just as today's church of God organizations who exalt men and organizations above the Word of Almighty God, are being broken into many pieces and corrected by the Eternal.

5:4 And when they arose early on the morrow morning, behold, Dagon was fallen upon his face to the ground before the ark of the LORD; and the head of Dagon and both the palms of his hands were cut off upon the threshold; only the stump of Dagon was left to him. **5:5** Therefore neither the priests of Dagon, nor any that come into Dagon's house, tread on the threshold of Dagon in Ashdod unto this day.

When severe this kind of affliction prevents normal activity and can be so severe as to prevent the hard physical work of cultivating the fields or any other physical work, causing hunger and severe distress to the nation.

5:6 But the hand of the LORD was heavy upon them of Ashdod, and he destroyed them, and smote them with emerods [hemorrhoids; piles; tumors; boils], even Ashdod and the coasts thereof.

The Philistines then acknowledged the superiority of the Eternal, but sought to hide from him rather than to repent and turn to him.

5:7 And when the men of Ashdod saw that it was so, they said, The ark of the God of Israel shall not abide with us: for his hand is sore upon us, and upon Dagon our god.

They took the Ark to Gath, and Gath was nearly destroyed.

5:8 They sent therefore and gathered all the lords of the Philistines unto them, and said, What shall we do with the ark of the God of Israel? And they answered, Let the ark of the God of Israel be carried about unto Gath. And they carried the ark of the God of Israel aboutthither. **5:9** And it was so, that, after they had carried it about, the hand of the LORD was against the city with a very great destruction: and he smote the men of the city, both small and great, and they had emerods in their secret parts.

They took the Ark to Ekron, and Ekron was nearly destroyed.

5:10 Therefore they sent the ark of God to Ekron. And it came to pass, as the ark of God came to Ekron, that the Ekronites cried out, saying, They have brought about the ark of the God of Israel to us, to slay us and our people.

And so the cities of the Philistines were taught that the God of Israel was the supreme God; and they counseled to send the Ark back to Israel..

5:11 So they sent and gathered together all the lords of the Philistines, and said, Send away the ark of the God of Israel, and let it go again to his own place, that it slay us not, and our people: for there was a deadly destruction throughout all the city; the hand of God was very heavy there.

Then the Philistines cried out in great agony because of the throne of God among them, which cast down any who would not repent and turn from their idols to bow before the Great and Mighty God to exalt him alone, and to learn and keep his Word without compromise or turning aside to the right or to the left.

5:12 And the men that died not were smitten with the emerods: and the cry of the city went up to heaven.

1 Samuel 6

At the end of seven months of severe affliction the Philistines called all their wise men and the priests of their gods together to decide what to do; and instead of repenting from Dagon to serve the Eternal; they rejected the Eternal and sent his throne out from among them.

1 Samuel 6:1 And the ark of the LORD was in the country of the Philistines seven months. **6:2** And the Philistines called for the priests and the diviners, saying, What shall we do to the ark of the LORD? tell us wherewith we shall send it to his place.

The Philistines determined to offer an offering without repentance and without turning to the Eternal; they decided to continue to worship their idols and to send the Ark [a throne which represented the authority of a ruler] of God back to Israel.

6:3 And they said, If ye send away the ark of the God of Israel, send it not empty; but in any wise return him a trespass offering: then ye shall be healed, and it shall be known to you why his hand is not removed from you.

From this it appears that a plague of small rodents also fell on the Philistines which consumed their granaries. So they were unable to work their fields and their food stocks seem to have been consumed by rodents.

6:4 Then said they, What shall be the trespass offering which we shall return to him? They answered, Five golden emerods, and five golden mice [small vermin; mice rats], according to the number of the lords of the Philistines: for one plague was on you all, and on your lords.

There was no thought of repentance at the correction and power of God; instead they thrust God out of their land.

The case is the same with most today who reject any zeal for the whole Word of God and cling to their own ways; yet they cry out to the Eternal in prayers and fasting's for deliverance from all their troubles.

6:5 Wherefore ye shall make images of your emerods, and images of your **mice that mar the land**; and ye shall give glory unto the God of Israel: **peradventure he will lighten his hand from off you, and from off your gods**, and from off your land.

They KNEW their history and they KNEW who the Eternal was; yet they would not repent to follow HIM!

6:6 Wherefore then do ye harden your hearts, as the Egyptians and Pharaoh hardened their hearts? when he had wrought wonderfully among them, did they not let the people go, and they departed?

This action of the Philistines later had a profound effect on David the king; for he followed their example [in ignorance, not knowing the scriptures on this point] in trying to transport the Ark contrary to the Word of God.

6:7 Now therefore make a new cart, and take two milch kine, on which there hath come no yoke, and tie the kine to the cart, and bring their calves home from them: **6:8** And take the ark of the LORD, and lay it upon the cart; and put the jewels of gold, which ye return him for a trespass offering, in a coffer by the side thereof; and send it away, that it may go.

The Philistines used the movement of the Ark as a test; to see if the Eternal had discomfited them, or if their trials were simply natural events.

6:9 And see, **if it goeth up by the way of his own coast to Bethshemesh, then he hath done us this great evil [has afflicted us]: but if not, then we shall know that it is not his hand that smote us: it was a chance that happened to us.**

6:10 And the men did so; and took two milch kine, and tied them to the cart, and shut up their calves at home: **6:11** And they laid the ark of the LORD upon the cart, and the coffer with the mice of gold and the images of their emerods.

The test of the Philistines made it clear to them that the Eternal God of Jacob and Moses had discomfited them to reveal that he was God indeed and beside him there is NO OTHER.

As the Ark [a type of God's throne] turned neither to the right nor to the left; we are to follow HIM and we are to live by every Word of God without any hint of turning aside.

6:12 And the **kine took the straight way to the way of Bethshemesh, and went along the highway, lowing as they went, and turned not aside to the right hand or to the left;** and the lords of the Philistines went after them unto the border of Bethshemesh.

Israel rejoiced at the recovery of the Ark representing the Eternal and his authority over his Covenant people.

Likewise today's brethren should rejoice that the authority of the Eternal and the righteousness of HIS Word are being proclaimed and restored in spiritual Israel today!

6:13 And they of Bethshemesh were reaping their wheat harvest in the valley: and they lifted up their eyes, and saw the ark, and rejoiced to see it.

When the Ark stood still among them, the men called for Levites to teach them what to do.

We should also seek to learn and to keep the whole Word of God today; we need to repent of doing what we think is right and we need to turn to live by every Word of God and do what the Eternal teaches and commands is right!

It is long past time that we turned to the Eternal in wholehearted repentance and service [which is the meaning of the burnt offering].

6:14 And the cart came into the field of Joshua, a Bethshemite, and stood there, where there was a great stone: and they clave the wood of the cart, and offered the kine a burnt offering unto the LORD.

6:15 And **the Levites took down the ark of the LORD, and the coffer that was with it, wherein the jewels of gold were, and put them on the great stone: and the men of Bethshemesh offered burnt offerings and sacrificed sacrifices the same day unto the LORD.**

The Philistines then returned home.

6:16 And when the five lords of the Philistines had seen it, they returned to Ekron the same day. **6:17** And these are the golden emerods which the

Philistines returned for a trespass offering unto the LORD; for Ashdod one, for Gaza one, for Askelon one, for Gath one, for Ekron one; **6:18** And the golden mice, according to the number of all the cities of the Philistines belonging to the five lords, both of fenced cities, and of country villages, even unto the great stone of Abel, whereon they set down the ark of the LORD: which stone remaineth unto this day [the day that this was written] in the field of Joshua, the Bethshemite.

In their joy at receiving the Ark the people broke the commandment of God; and Jesus Christ destroyed then without mercy taking 50,070 lives.

This is a mighty lesson that Jesus Christ is the Redeemer of the repentant who follow God's Word in all things. NO, we are not to worship our God in our own way: We are to worship the Eternal as he has commanded us to worship him.

Today's Spiritual Israel are also to worship God only as God has commanded us in the whole Word of God. We are not to take pagan things and re-label them "Christian" and claim that we do these evils in honor of the Eternal God.

We are to worship the Eternal Father and Jesus Christ the son, by doing what they require and by learning and living by every Word of God; We are NOT to worship our God by doing what we think is right and rejecting a wholehearted zeal to do what God has said is right.

NO, ABSOLUTELY NOT; God the Father and Jesus Christ will not tolerate sin against the Word of God!

6:19 And he smote the men of Bethshemesh, because they had looked into the ark of the LORD, even **he smote of the people fifty thousand and threescore and ten men**: and the people lamented, because the LORD had smitten many of the people with a great slaughter.

God is consistent in requiring that he be obeyed as he has commanded, and God will not be worshiped as men decide for themselves. Today's Spiritual Ekklesia should learn this lesson: we are to follow the Eternal and keep his Word with a sincere and whole heart; doing what God says, and NOT doing what we think is right.

6:20 And the men of Bethshemesh said, Who is able to stand before this holy LORD God? and to whom shall he go up from us? **6:21** And they sent messengers to the inhabitants of Kirjathjearim, saying, The Philistines have brought again the ark of the LORD; come ye down, and fetch it up to you.

1 Samuel 7

The Ark had been returned to Israel, yet God allowed the Philistines to continue to oppress the nation because Israel was still filled with idols.

Like the Philistines, Mosaic Israel feared God, but they would not obey him; it is the same with many today as they exalt their idols of men, organizations and the false teachings of the past; above any zeal to live by every Word of God.

1 Samuel 7:1 And the men of Kirjathjearim came, and fetched up the ark of the LORD, and brought it into the house of Abinadab in the hill, and sanctified Eleazar his son [a priest of Aaron] to keep the ark of the LORD. **7:2** And it came to pass, while the ark abode in Kirjathjearim, that the time was long; for it was **twenty years**: [then they lamented over the oppression of the Philistines] and all the house of Israel lamented after the LORD.

Samuel rose up to teach the people to put away the idols that had come between them and the Eternal; and told them to wholeheartedly follow the Eternal ONLY.

Samuel promised physical deliverance for wholeheartedly keeping the Mosaic Covenant; and if today's Spiritual Ekklesia would turn away from doing what we think is right, to wholeheartedly live by every Word of

God; Our Mighty One will raise us up on that day, giving us his salvation and the gift eternal life.

7:3 And Samuel spake unto all the house of Israel, saying, If ye do return unto the LORD with all your hearts, then put away the strange gods and Ashtaroth [idols, obelisks; including steeples and Christmas trees] from among you, and **prepare your hearts unto the LORD, and serve him only: and he will deliver you out of the hand of the Philistines.**

Finally Israel had had enough correction at the hands of the Philistines and destroyed their idols, turning to the Eternal to keep his Word.

It is time that we did the same thing in the spiritual sense and began to prove the teachings of men by the whole Word of God!

Let us also Return to God

> Brethren, we know that the violence of today and the coming wars will reset the conditions so that a genuine peace can be made. We know this because the Word of God tells us that "Peace and Safety" will be declared before the tribulation comes (1 Thess 5:3)! There will be an end to these wars which will bring a genuine peace deal; we have the Word of God telling us so!
>
> As you see these things being fulfilled; as you see these wars come and go and a genuine dialogue for peace take place; as you see a peace deal ratified; as you see the abomination, that man of sin, being set up in the Vatican and bringing a new Europe to life: You can know that the great tribulation WILL begin when he goes to the Holy Place!
>
> We are NOT to esteem any person who rejects and teaches others to reject any zeal to learn and to keep the whole Word of God. We are to reject all those who teach us to make idols of men and false traditions and who compromise with God's Word. They are the children of darkness, refusing the light of God for their own folly.
>
> Those faithful to God and his commandments should look about and mark out with respect all those who labor to turn the brethren to God, and who admonish all the brethren to turn with zeal to their God!
>
> **1 Thessalonians 5:12** And we beseech you, brethren, to know them which labour among you, and are over you in the Lord, and

admonish you; **5:13** And to esteem them very highly in love for their work's sake. And be at peace among yourselves.

2 Timothy 4:1 I charge thee therefore before God, and the Lord Jesus Christ, who shall judge the quick and the dead at his appearing and his kingdom; **4:2** Preach the word; be instant in season, out of season; reprove, rebuke, exhort with all long suffering and doctrine.

1 Thessalonians 5:14 Now we exhort you, brethren, warn them that are unruly [contentious against sound doctrine and conduct], comfort the feebleminded [the weak in understanding], support the [spiritually weak with sound doctrine] weak, be patient toward all men.

When we are abused or rejected, always follow godliness and do not give place to anger, but do good by teaching and living godliness.

5:15 See that none render evil for evil unto any man; but ever follow that which is good, both among yourselves, and to all men. **5:16** Rejoice evermore.

Rejoice in your calling and pray without ceasing for God's help through his Spirit, so that we may endure to the very end and overcome all things. Rejoice in your trials knowing that the Master Potter is molding us into a precious eternal vessel according to his will!

5:17 Pray without ceasing. **5:18** In every thing give thanks: for this is the will of God in Christ Jesus concerning you.

Be grateful to God for your calling and his many blessings and promises; which are sure and will be fulfilled for us if we faint not. Do not quench the Spirit by compromising with God's Word.

5:19 Quench not the Spirit.

5:20 Despise not prophesyings.

Do not have the attitude that we cannot know, so we should not even bother with prophecy. God reveals his will to those who are diligent to live by his Word when the time is at hand. Let us learn from past mistakes and embrace the truth discarding error and grow in knowledge, progressing in understanding. Watch diligently as these things unfold and remember the signs and warnings that God has given to those who love him and do that which is pleasing in his sight.

5:21 Prove all things; hold fast that which is good.

Prove all things by the Word of God! Utterly reject any compromise with God's Word and reject all toleration of sin. In the same manner that God our Father in heaven utterly rejects any spiritual uncleanness in his temple [his people]! Avoid even the mere appearance of evil so that the light of your example may shine brightly

5:22 Abstain from all appearance of evil.

5:23 And the very God of peace sanctify [set you apart from all worldliness and sin] you wholly; and I pray God **your whole spirit and soul and body be preserved blameless** [without any willful sin] unto the coming of our Lord Jesus Christ.

Become blameless as touching the Word of God, and fully internalize the mind and nature of God the Father and the Son, so that you will come into a complete unity of mind, spirit, attitude and deeds with Almighty God!

5:24 Faithful is he that calleth you, who also will do it.

God brought a great repentance by the word and teaching of Samuel. Oh, how today's spiritual Church of God needs such repentance!

1 Samuel 7:4 Then the children of Israel did put away Baalim and Ashtaroth, and served the LORD only.

The people gathered together with Samuel, fasting the true fast of sincere repentance and water was poured out; picturing the Word and Spirit of God being poured out like water.

This was done long before Ezra established the water pouring service at the Feast of Tabernacles.

7:5 And Samuel said, Gather all Israel to Mizpeh, and I will pray for you unto the LORD. **7:6** And they gathered together to Mizpeh, and **drew water, and poured it out before the LORD,** and fasted on that day, and said there, We have sinned against the LORD. And Samuel judged [taught] the children of Israel in Mizpeh.

The Philistines hearing of this massing of people went out against them.

7:7 And when the Philistines heard that the children of Israel were gathered together to Mizpeh, the lords of the Philistines went up against

Israel. And when the children of Israel heard it, they were afraid of the Philistines.

These now repentant people cried out to the Eternal for deliverance; just like those of Spiritual Israel today need to cry out in sincere repentance from sin for deliverance from the forces of evil.

7:8 And the children of Israel said to Samuel, Cease not to cry unto the LORD our God for us, that he will save us out of the hand of the Philistines. **7:9** And Samuel took a sucking lamb, and offered it for a burnt offering wholly unto the LORD: and Samuel cried unto the LORD for Israel; and the LORD heard him.

Then Jesus Christ stood up to deliver his sincerely repentant people.

7:10 And as Samuel was offering up the burnt offering, the Philistines drew near to battle against Israel: but the LORD thundered with a great thunder on that day upon the Philistines, and discomfited them; and they were smitten before Israel.

When the Philistines fled at the thundering of the Eternal; Israel pursued them and a great victory was won.

Brethren, if we sincerely take a stand to learn and live by every Word of God continually; then we may have problems in this physical life in order that we may learn and be molded into what God has in mind for us: but God will go forth to deliver his faithful and chosen on that day.

7:11 And the men of Israel went out of Mizpeh, and pursued the Philistines, and smote them, until they came under Bethcar.

Samuel then set up a memorial stone which stone represents the ROCK of our Salvation, the God Being who later gave up his God-hood to be made flesh as Jesus Christ the Messiah.

7:12 Then Samuel took a stone, and set it between Mizpeh and Shen, and called the name of it Ebenezer, saying, Hitherto hath the LORD helped us.

The Philistines were subdued all the days of Samuel.

7:13 So the Philistines were subdued, and they came no more into the coast of Israel: and the hand of the LORD was against the Philistines all the days of Samuel. **7:14** And the cities which the Philistines had taken from Israel were restored to Israel, from Ekron even unto Gath; and the coasts thereof did Israel deliver out of the hands of the Philistines. And there was peace between Israel and the Amorites.

Samuel became a kind of circuit judge and continually taught the people to be faithful to the whole Word of God; and during this time, beginning after the famine in Israel and the defeat of the Philistines there was peace; and near the beginning of that time of peace when Samuel was just beginning as an accepted Judge over Israel, Ruth came to Judah and married Boaz.

7:15 And Samuel judged Israel all the days of his life. **7:16 And he went from year to year in circuit to Bethel, and Gilgal, and Mizpeh, and judged Israel in all those places. 7:17 And his return was to Ramah;** for there was his house; and there he judged Israel; and there he built an altar unto the LORD.

1 Samuel 8

1 Samuel 8:1 And it came to pass, when Samuel was old, that he made his sons judges over Israel.

The sons of Samuel also turned aside from God like the sons of Eli

8:2 Now the name of his firstborn was Joel; and the name of his second, Abiah: they were judges in Beersheba. **8:3** And his sons walked not in his ways, but turned aside after lucre, and took bribes, and perverted judgment.

The people then sought stability for the nation through a dynastic kingdom. This is a lesson for us in governance, that it does not matter what form of governance is in an organization; it is faithfulness to God and zeal for the whole Word of God that is the important thing in any ruler.

Any organization regardless of its governance structure; is only God's government if it is zealous and faithful to the HEAD which is God the Father, Jesus Christ and their Word.

It is a fact that an authoritative government is powerful as an entity, but it is the easiest to subvert and turn aside from God, because only a handful of men need be perverted to lead the others astray.

In God's true government each person to obey and follow their HEAD [God the Father and Jesus Christ] by proving all the words of men by every Word of God and following men ONLY as they follow God the Father and Jesus Christ.

8:4 Then all the elders of Israel gathered themselves together, and came to Samuel unto Ramah, **8:5** And said unto him, Behold, thou art old, and thy sons walk not in thy ways: **now make us a king to judge us like all the nations.**

Samuel was offended because he thought they were rejecting him.

8:6 But the thing displeased Samuel, when they said, Give us a king to judge us. And Samuel prayed unto the LORD.

This very thing was prophesied by Moses.

God prophecies of a coming king by Moses

> **Deuteronomy 17:14** When thou art come unto the land which the LORD thy God giveth thee, and shalt possess it, and shalt dwell therein, and shalt say, **I will set a king over me**, like as all the nations that are about me;
>
> **17:15** Thou shalt in any wise **set him king over thee, whom the LORD thy God shall choose**: one from among thy brethren shalt thou set king over thee: thou mayest not set a stranger over thee, which is not thy brother.
>
> In the New Covenant, the faithfully obedient to God brethren must ONLY choose to follow the man who demonstrates by his fruits that God has chosen him! That leader MUST be a person who is a brother in the faith and has proven by his fruits to be the choice of God (Mat 7).
>
> We have been led far astray because we have not questioned and proved the men that we follow by their fruits from the scriptures!
>
> We have broken this commandment of Deuteronomy as well as the many commandments on the subject in the New Testament. A great many of the leaders in the various church groups have proven by their fruits of a lack of zeal for God and his law, and their compromising with God's Word that they are NOT godly men.
>
> We have been led astray because we have been willing to blindly and without question follow anyone who makes some grand claim and gives lip service to the faith, while doing whatever they please instead of doing as God has commanded.

Neither Physical nor Spiritual leaders are to use their positions to feed themselves and not the flock. They are NOT to take the best things for themselves nor seek the exaltation of the people.

They are to be faithful to the Eternal in all things; to exalt the Eternal and to obey him in all things; to faithfully serve the Eternal by feeding the flock sound doctrine and a good knowledge of TRUTH; and to speak the Word of God without fear or compromise before all peoples.

17:16 But he shall not multiply horses [make himself rich] to himself, nor cause the people to return to Egypt [shall not lead the people into sin and bondage to enrich himself], to the end that he should multiply horses: forasmuch as the LORD hath said unto you, Ye shall henceforth return no more that way.

The ruler or leader must not exercise his office for personal gain.

17:17 Neither shall he multiply wives to himself, that his heart turn not away: neither shall he greatly multiply to himself silver and gold.

The leader of the people both secular and spiritual and the elders; must have a personal copy of the Word of God and must study in it every day of their lives, to learn it and to keep it.

Every one of is called to become a priest and or king [ruler], and we are all to have personal copies of God's Word and we must study it to learn it and to keep it, all the days of our lives.

17:18 And it shall be, when he sitteth upon the throne of his kingdom, **that he shall write him a copy of this law in a book out of that which is before the priests the Levites:**

17:19 And **it shall be with him, and he shall read therein all the days of his life: that he may learn to fear the LORD his God, to keep all the words of this law and these statutes, to do them:**

17:20 That his heart be not lifted up [in pride] **above his brethren, and that he turn not aside from the commandment, to the right hand, or to the left:** to the end that he may prolong his days in his kingdom, he, and his children, in the midst of Israel.

Brethren, those who set themselves up as leaders and elders [kings, rulers] of the spiritual Church of God, must also follow these instructions!

1 Samuel 8:7 And the LORD said unto Samuel, Hearken unto the voice of the people in all that they say unto thee: for they have not rejected thee, but they have rejected me, that I should not reign over them.

YHVH then goes on to say that the people have turned away from God.

8:8 According to all the works which they have done since the day that I brought them up out of Egypt even unto this day, wherewith **they have forsaken me, and served other gods, so do they also unto thee.**

God tells Samuel to inform the people what kings do to their subjects, and then tells him to follow the wishes of the people.

8:9 Now therefore hearken unto their voice: howbeit yet **protest solemnly unto them, and shew them the manner of the king that shall reign over them.**

8:10 And Samuel told all the words of the LORD unto the people that asked of him a king.

This is the manner of all physical rulers including business and corporate leaders. The ruler will make himself officials and administrators and accrue power and wealth to himself.

8:11 And he said, This will be the manner of the king that shall reign over you: **He will take your sons, and appoint them for himself, for his chariots, and to be his horsemen; and some shall run before his chariots. 8:12** And he will appoint him captains over thousands, and captains over fifties; and will set them to ear his ground, and to reap his harvest, and to make his instruments of war, and instruments of his chariots. **8:13** And he will take your daughters to be confectionaries, and to be cooks, and to be bakers.

The ruler will take as he chooses; today we call that taxes.

8:14 And he will take your fields, and your vineyards, and your oliveyards, even the best of them, and give them to his servants. **8:15** And he will take the tenth of your seed, and of your vineyards, and give to his officers, and to his servants. **8:16** And he will take your menservants, and your maidservants, and your goodliest young men, and your asses, and put them to his work. **8:17** He will take the tenth of your sheep: and ye shall be his servants.

And when we cry out because of the oppression, God will neither hear nor answer, because we have only received what we asked for by desiring to serve men.

8:18 And ye shall cry out in that day because of your king which ye shall have chosen you; and the LORD will not hear you in that day.

The people insisted and Samuel prayed to the Eternal.

8:19 Nevertheless the people refused to obey the voice of Samuel; and they said, Nay; but we will have a king over us; **8:20** That we also may be like all the nations; and that our king may judge us, and go out before us, and fight our battles. **8:21** And Samuel heard all the words of the people, and he rehearsed them in the ears of the LORD.

So God said: go and make them a king as they desire.

8:22 And the LORD said to Samuel, Hearken unto their voice, and make them a king. And Samuel said unto the men of Israel, Go ye every man unto his city.

These people wanted a king to take responsibility for them and to rule over them: instead of being loyal to the whole Word of God, they would rather by loyal to some man.

It is the same in the called out of Spiritual Israel today!

We look to men to rule over us and to lead us; and we reject following the whole Word of God in order to follow these men away from any zeal for living by every Word of God. We have a zeal for keeping the words of the men that we can see, and we have no zeal to learn and to live by every Word of God.

1 Samuel 9

Kish of Benjamin was a powerful man in Israel and his son Saul was a big and impressive man.

1 Samuel 9:1 Now there was a man of Benjamin, whose name was Kish, the son of Abiel, the son of Zeror, the son of Bechorath, the son of Aphiah, a Benjamite, a mighty man of power. **9:2** And he had a son, whose name was Saul, a choice young man, and a goodly: and there was not among the children of Israel a goodlier [impressive and handsome] person than he: from his shoulders and upward he was higher than any of the people.

Saul goes to seek the lost animals of his father

9:3 And the asses of Kish Saul's father were lost. And Kish said to Saul his son, Take now one of the servants with thee, and arise, go seek the asses. **9:4** And he passed through mount Ephraim, and passed through the land of Shalisha, but they found them not: then they passed through the land of Shalim, and there they were not: and he passed through the land of the Benjamites, but they found them not. **9:5** And when they were come to the land of Zuph, Saul said to his servant that was with him, Come, and let us return; lest my father leave caring for the asses, and take thought for us.

Saul decides to return home empty, but his servant advises Saul to inquire of God.

9:6 And he said unto him, Behold now, there is in this city a man of God, and he is an honourable man; all that he saith cometh surely to pass: now let us go thither; peradventure he can shew us our way that we should go.

They are willing to pay Samuel for his advice

9:7 Then said Saul to his servant, But, behold, if we go, what shall we bring the man? for the bread is spent in our vessels, and there is not a present to bring to the man of God: what have we? **9:8** And the servant answered Saul again, and said, Behold, I have here at hand the fourth part of a shekel of silver: that will I give to the man of God, to tell us our way.

Saul then goes to seek out Samuel

9:9 (Beforetime in Israel, when a man went to enquire of God, thus he spake, Come, and let us go to the seer: for he that is now called a Prophet was beforetime called a Seer.) **9:10** Then said Saul to his servant, Well said; come, let us go. So they went unto the city where the man of God was. **9:11** And as they went up the hill to the city, they found young maidens going out to draw water, and said unto them, Is the seer here?

The maids tell Saul to make haste and find Samuel, before Samuel becomes occupied with the sacrifice.

9:12 And they answered them, and said, He is; behold, he is before you: make haste now, for he came to day to the city; for there is a sacrifice of the people to day in the high place: **9:13** As soon as ye be come into the city, ye shall straightway find him, before he go up to the high place to eat: for the people will not eat until he come, because he doth bless the sacrifice; and afterwards they eat that be bidden. Now therefore get you up; for about this time ye shall find him.

Rushing into the city they catch up to Samuel as he is going to the sacrifice.

9:14 And they went up into the city: and when they were come into the city, behold, Samuel came out against them, for to go up to the high place.

The God Being who later became flesh as Jesus Christ, told Samuel to anoint Saul king in a clear small voice in his ear.

9:15 Now the LORD had told Samuel in his ear a day before Saul came, saying, **9:16** To morrow about this time I will send thee a man out of the land of Benjamin, and thou shalt anoint him to be captain over my people Israel, that he may save my people out of the hand of the Philistines: for I have looked upon my people, because their cry is come unto me.

God opened the eyes of Samuel to recognize the man that he should anoint king.

The sceptre had already been promised by the prophetic blessings to rest with Judah. Yet if Saul had only been faithful to God, his line would have been joined to David of Judah and David would have had a son by Saul's daughter who would have been king.

9:17 And when Samuel saw Saul, the LORD said unto him, Behold the man whom I spake to thee of! this same shall reign over my people.

Saul not recognizing Samuel asked him the way to the house of the prophet.

9:18 Then Saul drew near to Samuel in the gate, and said, Tell me, I pray thee, where the seer's house is.

Samuel identified himself and bids Saul go up to the tabernacle for the sacrifice.

9:19 And Samuel answered Saul, and said, I am the seer: go up before me unto the high place; for ye shall eat with me to day, and to morrow I will let thee go, and will tell thee all that is in thine heart.

Samuel tells Saul that the lost animals are found and then tells Saul that the desire and heart of Israel is on him and his father's house. Saul was the people's choice.

9:20 And as for thine asses that were lost three days ago, set not thy mind on them; for they are found. And on whom is all the desire of Israel? Is it not on thee, and on all thy father's house?

Saul was humble and bewildered before the man of God.

9:21 And Saul answered and said, Am not I a Benjamite, of the smallest of the tribes of Israel? and my family the least of all the families of the tribe of Benjamin? wherefore then speakest thou so to me?

Samuel sets Saul in the chief seat at the sacrificial meal.

9:22 And Samuel took Saul and his servant, and brought them into the parlour, and made them sit in the chiefest place among them that were bidden, which were about thirty persons.

The choicest portion was then given to Saul as a mark of great honor.

9:23 And Samuel said unto the cook, Bring the portion which I gave thee, of which I said unto thee, Set it by thee. **9:24** And the cook took up the shoulder, and that which was upon it, and set it before Saul. And Samuel said, Behold that which is left! set it before thee, and eat: for unto this time hath it been kept for thee since I said, I have invited the people. So Saul did eat with Samuel that day.

Afterwards Samuel spoke with Saul for some time.

9:25 And when they were come down from the high place into the city, Samuel communed with Saul upon the top of the house.

Then in the early morning Saul is sent on his way and Samuel walks with him to the city gate conversing as they went.

9:26 And they arose early: and it came to pass about the spring of the day, that Samuel called Saul to the top of the house, saying, Up, that I may send thee away. And Saul arose, and they went out both of them, he and Samuel, abroad.

Then Samuel tells Saul to send his servant on ahead while Samuel tells Saul the Word of the Eternal.

9:27 And as they were going down to the end of the city, Samuel said to Saul, Bid the servant pass on before us, (and he passed on), but stand thou still a while, that I may shew thee the word of God.

1 Samuel 10

Samuel anoints Saul king and then gives him a string of prophecies to help him gain faith and confidence.

1 Samuel 10:1 Then Samuel took a vial of oil, and poured it upon his head, and kissed him, and said, Is it not because the LORD hath anointed thee to be captain over his inheritance?

10:2 When thou art departed from me to day, then thou shalt find two men by Rachel's sepulchre in the border of Benjamin at Zelzah; and they will say unto thee, The asses which thou wentest to seek are found: and, lo, thy father hath left the care of the asses, and sorroweth for you, saying, What shall I do for my son? **10:3** Then shalt thou go on forward from thence, and thou shalt come to the plain of Tabor, and there shall meet thee three men going up to God to Bethel, one carrying three kids, and another carrying three loaves of bread, and another carrying a bottle of wine: **10:4** And they will salute thee, and give thee two loaves of bread; which thou shalt receive of their hands.

Saul was given the Spirit of God

The life of Saul should be a graphic example for us, that not every called out person or ordained man who starts out with God's Spirit; continues in the path of his calling.

Saul was an example for the people [and especially to David] of how NOT to lead; so that we could learn that absolute loyalty to God and the Word of God is required for godly leadership.

10:5 After that thou shalt come to the hill of God, where is the garrison of the Philistines: and it shall come to pass, when thou art

come thither to the city, that thou shalt meet a company of prophets coming down from the high place with a psaltery, and a tabret, and a pipe, and a harp, before them; and they shall prophesy: **10:6 And the Spirit of the LORD will come upon thee, and thou shalt prophesy with them, and shalt be turned into another man.**

This series of signs was to demonstrate to Saul that God would be with him as long as he did not depart from God.

10:7 And let it be, when these signs are come unto thee, that thou do as occasion serve thee; for God is with thee.

Saul was told to wait at Gilgal seven days for Samuel to come and give him instructions from God.

10:8 And thou shalt go down before me to Gilgal; and, behold, I will come down unto thee, to offer burnt offerings, and to sacrifice sacrifices of peace offerings: seven days shalt thou tarry, till I come to thee, and shew thee what thou shalt do.

All these signs came in one day and Saul was given God's Spirit

10:9 And it was so, that when he had turned his back to go from Samuel, **God gave him another heart: and all those signs came to pass that day.** **10:10** And when they came thither to the hill, behold, a company of prophets met him; and the Spirit of God came upon him, and he prophesied among them.

Saul is recognized by the people as the man chosen of God to be king

10:11 And it came to pass, when all that knew him beforetime saw that, behold, he prophesied among the prophets, then the people said one to another, What is this that is come unto the son of Kish? Is Saul also among the prophets? **10:12** And one of the same place answered and said, But who is their father? Therefore it became a proverb, Is Saul also among the prophets? **10:13** And when he had made an end of prophesying, he came to the high place.

Saul's uncle inquires of Saul about all that he has done.

10:14 And Saul's uncle said unto him and to his servant, Whither went ye? And he said, To seek the asses: and when we saw that they were no where, we came to Samuel. **10:15** And Saul's uncle said, Tell me, I pray thee, what Samuel said unto you.

10:16 And Saul said unto his uncle, He told us plainly that the asses were found. But of the matter of the kingdom, whereof Samuel spake, he told him not.

Saul told no one of the anointing of Samuel to make him king.

Samuel called the people to Mizpeh to present Saul to them as the king that God had chosen to rule over them. First Samuel rebuked the people for desiring a hereditary king instead of the Eternal; he rebuked them for desiring to follow a man instead of directly following the God and Husband of their Covenant.

In today's Spiritual Ekklesia very many have done this exact thing; turning away from any zeal to learn and live by every Word of God and a direct personally responsible relationship with God to follow idols of men. They are no longer proving the words of men by the whole Word of God and have turned towards zealously following men and corporate entities and exalting them above the Word of God.

Our King is God the Father and our Head is Jesus Christ; to follow any other is spiritual treason, and to turn away from their Word is insurrection against the God of our calling.

> **1 Corinthians 11:3** But I would have you know, that the head of every man is Christ; and the head of the woman is the man; and the head of Christ is God.

1 Samuel 10:17 And Samuel called the people together unto the LORD to Mizpeh; **10:18** And said unto the children of Israel, Thus saith the LORD God of Israel, I brought up Israel out of Egypt, and delivered you out of the hand of the Egyptians, and out of the hand of all kingdoms, and of them that oppressed you: **10:19** And ye have this day rejected your God, who himself saved you out of all your adversities and your tribulations; and ye have said unto him, Nay, but set a king over us. Now therefore present yourselves before the LORD by your tribes, and by your thousands.

The tribe of Benjamin was placed near Samuel, and they sought for Saul

10:20 And when Samuel had caused all the tribes of Israel to come near, the tribe of Benjamin was taken. **10:21** When he had caused the tribe of

Benjamin to come near by their families, the family of Matri was taken, and Saul the son of Kish was taken: and when they sought him, he could not be found.

Samuel then asked YHVH where Saul was and was told that Saul had hidden himself.

This indicated very early on that Saul feared the people more than he feared to obey God; for Saul knew that he had been chosen by God and anointed king, yet he shrank back for fear of men.

There are two separate issues: Fear of men and humility before God. In the beginning Saul was somewhat humble before God but was more afraid of the people; shrinking back from what God had called him to do for fear of the people. Saul was too afraid of the people to fulfill his God given responsibilities.

Then as time passed Saul became more and more proud against God while continuing to fear the people, which is what Samuel later rebuked him for.

10:22 Therefore they enquired of the LORD further, if the man should yet come thither. And the LORD answered, Behold he hath hid himself among the stuff.

Then Saul was presented to the people who looked at his physical stature and not at his spiritual stature.

Even in today's Spiritual Ekklesia, many are greatly impressed by the outward appearance of skilled and talented elders and leaders, without considering their spiritual character and whether they are zealous to live by every Word of God.

The Eternal sometimes chooses spiritually weak leaders like Saul, to TEST our loyalty to God. Moses warned us of this very thing in Deuteronomy 13.

> **Deuteronomy 13:1** If there arise among you a prophet, or a dreamer of dreams, and giveth thee a sign or a wonder, **13:2** And the sign or the wonder come to pass, whereof he spake unto thee, saying, Let us go after other gods, which thou hast not known, and let us serve them;
>
> **13:3 Thou shalt not hearken unto the words of that prophet, or that dreamer of dreams: for the Lord your God proveth [TESTS us] you, to know whether ye love the Lord your God with all your heart and with all your soul. 13:4 Ye shall walk after the**

Lord your God, and fear him, and keep his commandments, and obey his voice, and ye shall serve him, and cleave unto him.

13:5 And that prophet, or that dreamer of dreams, shall be put to death; because he hath spoken to turn you away from the Lord your God, which brought you out of the land of Egypt, and redeemed you out of the house of bondage, to thrust thee out of the way which the Lord thy God commanded thee to walk in. So shalt thou put the evil away from the midst of thee.

Equating loyalty to men with loyalty to God is idolatry and is an abomination to Almighty God.

1 Samuel 10:23 And they ran and fetched him thence: and when he stood among the people, he was higher than any of the people from his shoulders and upward. **10:24** And Samuel said to all the people, **See ye him whom the LORD hath chosen, that there is none like him among all the people? And all the people shouted, and said, God save the king.**

Samuel then informed the new king and the people about what God had commanded for the kingdom.

10:25 Then Samuel told the people the manner of the kingdom, and wrote it in a book, and laid it up before the LORD. And Samuel sent all the people away, every man to his house.

A band of men was inspired by God to gather around and support Saul, while others were contrary to him.

10:26 And Saul also went home to Gibeah; and there went with him **a band of men, whose hearts God had touched. 10:27** But the children of Belial [Beliel; a name of Satan meaning sons of perdition] said, How shall this man save us? And they despised him, and brought no presents. But he held his peace.

1 Samuel 11

Saul was given a challenge so that God could begin to establish his name as king over Israel.

Spiritually those who would be godly have always faced problems to build up the character and reputation of godly leaders.

An Ammonite takes a city of Israel and the people not yet trusting Saul agreed to serve him in tribute, but a very heavy tribute is laid upon them forcing them to appeal to Saul.

1 Samuel 11:1 Then Nahash the Ammonite came up, and encamped against Jabeshgilead: and all the men of Jabesh said unto Nahash, Make a covenant with us, and we will serve thee. **11:2** And Nahash the Ammonite answered them, On this condition will I make a covenant with you, that I may thrust out all your right eyes, and lay it for a reproach upon all Israel.

The elders sought help from Saul before accepting such terrible terms. This is clearly allowed by God to establish Saul as king, since the demands were totally irrational.

11:3 And the elders of Jabesh said unto him, Give us seven days' respite, that we may send messengers unto all the coasts of Israel: and then, if there be no man to save us, we will come out to thee.

The messengers arrived in Gibeah, and Saul arriving from work in the fields hears their story.

11:4 Then came the messengers to Gibeah of Saul, and told the tidings in the ears of the people: and all the people lifted up their voices, and wept. **11:5** And, behold, Saul came after the herd out of the field; and Saul said, What aileth the people that they weep? And they told him the tidings of the men of Jabesh.

Saul became furious at this terrible outrage being planned against the people and God's Spirit fell upon him to inspire him as to what to do.

11:6 And the Spirit of God came upon Saul when he heard those tidings, and his anger was kindled greatly.

Saul then summoned the men of war and threatened them with the pieces of oxen to arouse them to action.

11:7 And he took a yoke of oxen, and hewed them in pieces, and sent them throughout all the coasts of Israel by the hands of messengers, saying, **Whosoever cometh not forth after Saul and after Samuel, so shall it be done unto his oxen. And the fear of the LORD fell on the people, and they came out with one consent.**

Then 330,000 men gathered to Saul to help against this evil.

11:8 And when he numbered them in Bezek, the children of Israel were three hundred thousand, and the men of Judah thirty thousand.

Then messengers were sent to the threatened city to inform them that help was on the way.

11:9 And they said unto the messengers that came, Thus shall ye say unto the men of Jabeshgilead, To morrow, by that time the sun be hot, ye shall have help. And the messengers came and shewed it to the men of Jabesh; and they were glad.

The people of Jabesh then told the Ammonites that they would come out to them the next day; and eased them into thinking that there was no danger of battle.

11:10 Therefore the men of Jabesh said, To morrow we will come out unto you, and ye shall do with us all that seemeth good unto you.

In the cool of the early morning Saul sets upon the Ammonites in three companies of men; totally destroying them and saving Jabesh from a cruel fate.

11:11 And it was so on the morrow, that Saul put the people in three companies; and they came into the midst of the host in the morning watch, and slew the Ammonites until the heat of the day: and it came to pass, that they which remained were scattered, so that two of them were not left together.

The people then rejoiced in Saul and he was established as king; the people even wanting to kill all who opposed Saul as king.

11:12 And the people said unto Samuel, Who is he that said, Shall Saul reign over us? bring the men, that we may put them to death.

Saul starts off well, issuing a general amnesty and giving the glory of victory to the Eternal.

11:13 And Saul said, There shall not a man be put to death this day: **for to day the LORD hath wrought salvation in Israel.**

Then Saul who was ordained by God and anointed by Samuel was made king by all the people.

11:14 Then said Samuel to the people, Come, and let us go to Gilgal, and renew the kingdom there. **11:15** And all the people went to Gilgal; and there they made Saul king before the LORD in Gilgal; and there they sacrificed sacrifices of peace offerings before the LORD; and there Saul and all the men of Israel rejoiced greatly.

In the beginning Saul did not exalt himself but remained working in his father's fields until God opened up the way for him to be established as king over Israel; and then Saul forgave his foes in Israel and gave God the glory.

Saul started off well, but he would later fall astray from the way of God by his fear of the people, and his desire for the adulation of the people.

Many have done this exact same thing; being filled with zeal for God in the beginning and later turning aside; no longer rebuking sin, leaving off from any zeal to live by every Word of God and watering down the outreach into a business model instead of the early messages of solid doctrine and warning.

1 Samuel 12

Samuel reasons with the people

1 Samuel 12:1 And Samuel said unto all Israel, Behold, I have hearkened unto your voice in all that ye said unto me, and have made a king over you. **12:2** And now, behold, the king walketh before you: and I am old and grayheaded; and, behold, my sons are with you: and I have walked before you from my childhood unto this day.

Samuel asks the people why they have rejected him and demanded a king.

12:3 Behold, here I am: witness against me before the LORD, and before his anointed: whose ox have I taken? or whose ass have I taken? or whom have I defrauded? whom have I oppressed? or of whose hand have I received any bribe to blind mine eyes therewith? and I will restore it you.

12:4 And they said, Thou hast not defrauded us, nor oppressed us, neither hast thou taken ought of any man's hand. **12:5** And he said unto them, The LORD is witness against you, and his anointed is witness this day, that ye have not found ought in my hand. And they answered, He is witness.

Samuel then rehearses that it is the Eternal who delivers his people; and that we are to follow ONLY those men who are faithful servants of the Eternal God.

12:6 And Samuel said unto the people, It is the LORD that advanced Moses and Aaron, and that brought your fathers up out of the land of Egypt.

12:7 Now therefore stand still, that I may reason with you before the LORD of all the righteous acts of the LORD, which he did to you and to your fathers.

12:8 When Jacob was come into Egypt, and your fathers cried unto the LORD, then **the LORD sent Moses and Aaron,** which brought forth your fathers out of Egypt, and made them dwell in this place. **12:9** And **when they forgat the LORD their God, he sold them into the hand of Sisera, captain of the host of Hazor, and into the hand of the Philistines, and into the hand of the king of Moab,** and they fought against them.

12:10 And they cried unto the LORD, and said, We have sinned, because we have forsaken the LORD, and have served Baalim and Ashtaroth: but now deliver us out of the hand of our enemies, and we will serve thee.

12:11 And **the LORD sent** Jerubbaal [Gideon], and Bedan, and Jephthah, and Samuel, and delivered you out of the hand of your enemies on every side, and ye dwelled safe.

Then the people demanded a king; choosing to follow a man instead of following the Eternal God.

Most in today's Spiritual Ekklesia also want men to come between us and God, wanting to follow and obey men instead of looking directly to God. The desire of most in today's Spiritual Ekklesia is to shirk personal responsibility for our actions: not understanding that following men contrary to God is idolatry and brings destruction upon us.

12:12 And when ye saw that Nahash the king of the children of Ammon came against you, ye said unto me, Nay; but a king shall reign over us: when the LORD your God was your king.

They desired a king and the Eternal gave them the kind of king that they wanted, a man who was physically impressive. This was done to teach us that the important thing is the godliness of a man, not his physical characteristics.

12:13 Now therefore behold the king whom ye have chosen, and whom ye have desired! and, behold, the LORD hath set a king over you.

Most in today's Spiritual Ekklesia want to have corporate organizations and men to rule over them, instead of living by every Word of God; just like physical Israel wanted a king. This is because they fear to take responsibility for their actions and therefore desire to follow others so that they can excuse themselves by saying "we were following the elders" when they are convicted of sin.

God warned physical Israel that if they remained faithful to his Word, he would remain faithful to them, but if they turned away from a wholehearted zeal to live by every Word of God to follow apostate rulers, he would turn against them (Deu 28-30).

The very same warning holds true for today's called out Spiritual Israel! Each individual must be absolutely zealously wholeheartedly faithful to the Eternal and every Word of God; no matter what any other human being says.

When a person stands before God and answers for his sins by saying that he was faithful to the king or to a certain leader or elder; what do you think God will answer? Will God not ask why we followed a man and were not faithful to HIM?

Now hear the Word of the Eternal Almighty God of Jacob:

12:14 If ye will fear the LORD, and serve him, and obey his voice, and not rebel against the commandment of the LORD, then shall both ye and also the king that reigneth over you continue following the LORD your God:

Brethren, we are to test every word of men, and compare them with the Word of God; and we must keep only what is absolutely consistent with the whole Word of God.

If we follow men contrary to the Word of God, regardless of whatever title such men claim: Almighty God will surely be against us!

12:15 But if ye will not obey the voice of the LORD, but rebel against the commandment of the LORD, then shall the hand of the LORD be against you, as it was against your fathers.

Samuel then gives a sign that out of season in the dry summer months, God would demonstrate his power by thunder and rain.

12:16 Now therefore stand and see this great thing, which the LORD will do before your eyes. **12:17** Is it not wheat harvest [summer] to day? I will call unto the LORD, and he shall send thunder and rain; that ye may perceive and see that your wickedness is great, which ye have done in the sight of the LORD, in asking you a king.

I expect that this was no ordinary thunder storm but one of great and awesome intensity; and great thunder is accompanied by great lightening.

12:18 So Samuel called unto the LORD; and the LORD sent thunder and rain that day: and all the people greatly feared the LORD and Samuel.

Then the people asked for forgiveness for seeking a king to come between them and God and resolved to obey God first and the man second.

We of the spiritually called out, need to repent of this very same sin; we need to repent of following men and exalting those men as equal to or above Almighty God in our lives.

12:19 And all the people said unto Samuel, Pray for thy servants unto the LORD thy God, that we die not: for we have added unto all our sins this evil, to ask us a king.

Samuel then adjures the people to follow God above all else and to respect authorities according to their faithful godliness.

Never follow any leader, king or elder away from a zealous keeping of the whole Word of God! This is idolatry and it is the mark of the beast!

Nevertheless, always follow all legitimate authorities over you; when they are not in conflict with the Word of God!

12:20 And Samuel said unto the people, Fear not: ye have done all this wickedness: **yet turn not aside from following the LORD, but serve the LORD with all your heart; 12:21 And turn ye not aside: for then should ye go after vain things, which cannot profit nor deliver; for they are vain.**

Do not forsake the Word of God for the words of men; for God has called us to godliness.

12:22 For the LORD will not forsake his people for his great name's sake: because it hath pleased the LORD to make you his people.

12:23 Moreover as for me, God forbid that I should sin against the LORD in ceasing to pray for you: but **I will teach you the good and the right way: 12:24 Only fear the LORD, and serve him in truth with all your heart: for consider how great things he hath done for you.**

Those who lack uncompromising zeal for learning and living by every Word of God will be destroyed.

12:25 But **if ye shall still do wickedly, ye shall be consumed, both ye and your king.**

1 Samuel 13

Saul established a core standing army of three thousand

1 Samuel 13:1 Saul reigned one year; and when he had reigned two years over Israel, **13:2** Saul chose him three thousand men of Israel; whereof two thousand were with Saul in Michmash and in mount Bethel, and a thousand were with Jonathan in Gibeah of Benjamin: and the rest of the people he sent every man to his tent.

Saul's son Jonathan a valiant godly man, attacks and destroys a garrison of the Philistines, provoking war. After which Saul called all Israel to gather for the impending war.

13:3 And Jonathan smote the garrison of the Philistines that was in Geba, and the Philistines heard of it. And Saul blew the trumpet throughout all the land, saying, Let the Hebrews hear. **13:4** And all Israel heard say that Saul had smitten a garrison of the Philistines, and that Israel also was had in abomination with the Philistines. And the people were called together after Saul to Gilgal.

The Philistines massed a huge army against Israel in response to the attack by Jonathan.

13:5 And the Philistines gathered themselves together to fight with Israel, thirty thousand chariots, and six thousand horsemen, and people as the sand which is on the sea shore in multitude: and they came up, and pitched in Michmash, eastward from Bethaven.

Israel feared and fled from the army of the Philistines.

13:6 When the men of Israel saw that they were in a strait, (for the people were distressed,) then the people did hide themselves in caves, and in thickets, and in rocks, and in high places, and in pits. **13:7** And some of the Hebrews went over Jordan to the land of Gad and Gilead. As for Saul, he was yet in Gilgal, and all the people followed him trembling.

It had been appointed that Samuel would join Saul in seven days as the representative of God, to go with the army because the battle was the Lord's; but Samuel was delayed and many people left Saul, God desiring to TEST Saul.

13:8 And he tarried seven days, according to the set time that Samuel had appointed: but Samuel came not to Gilgal; and **the people were scattered from him.**

Then Saul fearing that the people would leave him and that he would be overwhelmed by the Philistines offered sacrifices contrary to the Word of God. Saul sought to worship God by his own way instead of doing what God had said and waiting on God.

13:9 And Saul said, Bring hither a burnt offering to me, and peace offerings. And he offered the burnt offering.

Then Samuel arrived and corrected Saul

13:10 And it came to pass, that as soon as he had made an end of offering the burnt offering, behold, Samuel came; and Saul went out to meet him, that he might salute him.

13:11 And Samuel said, What hast thou done? And Saul said, Because I saw that the people were scattered from me, and that thou camest not within the days appointed, and that the Philistines gathered themselves together at Michmash; **13:12** Therefore said I, The Philistines will come down now upon me to Gilgal, and I have not made supplication unto the LORD: I forced myself therefore, and offered a burnt offering.

13:13 And Samuel said to Saul, **Thou hast done foolishly: thou hast not kept the commandment of the LORD thy God, which he commanded thee:** for now would the LORD have established thy kingdom upon Israel for ever.

Saul failed the test of zeal to keep the Word of God; and his kingdom was given to another.

If they also depart from the Word of God to do as they think is right, instead of doing what the Eternal says is right: The same thing will happen to today's Spiritual Ekklesia who have been promised kingdoms for their faithful uncompromising obedience to God.

13:14 But now thy kingdom shall not continue: the LORD hath sought him a man after his own heart, and the LORD hath commanded him to be captain over his people, because thou hast not kept that which the LORD commanded thee.

Saul was left with only 600 out of all his thousands

Spiritually many are called but very few will remain steadfast in uncompromising faithful loyalty and zeal to the Eternal King and his Word.

>**Matthew 22:14** For many are called, but few are chosen.

Many are called but only a few will overcome and be chosen for a part in the resurrection to spirit as kings and priests in the Kingdom of God the Father and the Priesthood of Jesus Christ.

1 Samuel 13:15 And Samuel arose, and gat him up from Gilgal unto Gibeah of Benjamin. And Saul numbered the people that were present with him, about six hundred men.

13:16 And Saul, and Jonathan his son, and the people that were present with them, abode in Gibeah of Benjamin: but the Philistines encamped in Michmash.

Then the Philistines came to the attack in three parts.

13:17 And the spoilers came out of the camp of the Philistines in three companies: one company turned unto the way that leadeth to Ophrah, unto the land of Shual: **13:18** And another company turned the way to Bethhoron: and another company turned to the way of the border that looketh to the valley of Zeboim toward the wilderness.

God was about to deliver Israel by the hand of Saul.

13:19 Now there was no smith found throughout all the land of Israel: for the Philistines said, Lest the Hebrews make them swords or spears: **13:20** But all the Israelites went down to the Philistines, to sharpen every man his share, and his coulter, and his axe, and his mattock. **13:21** Yet they had a file for the mattocks, and for the coulters, and for the forks, and for the axes, and to sharpen the goads.

Israel went out to fight with only 600 lightly armed men against a huge army of men and chariots with weapons of war. Yet Israel would be invincible as long as they followed the Eternal!

God may allow trials and sufferings in this physical life to build our character and make us into what he wants us to become; but we will be spiritually invincible, as long as we are zealously faithful to live by every Word of God and to follow our espoused Husband wherever he goes.

13:22 So it came to pass in the day of battle, that there was neither sword nor spear found in the hand of any of the people that were with Saul and Jonathan: but with Saul and with Jonathan his son was there found.

13:23 And the garrison of the Philistines went out to the passage of Michmash.

1 Samuel 14

Jonathan launches an independent raid on the Philistines

1 Samuel 14:1 Now it came to pass upon a day, that Jonathan the son of Saul said unto the young man that bare his armour, Come, and let us go over to the Philistines' garrison, that is on the other side. But he told not his father.

14:2 And Saul tarried in the uttermost part of Gibeah under a pomegranate tree which is in Migron: and the people that were with him were about six hundred men; **14:3** And Ahiah, the son of Ahitub, Ichabod's brother, the son of Phinehas, the son of Eli, the LORD's priest in Shiloh, wearing an ephod. And the people knew not that Jonathan was gone.

14:4 And between the passages, by which Jonathan sought to go over unto the Philistines' garrison, there was a sharp rock on the one side, and a sharp rock on the other side: and the name of the one was Bozez, and the name of the other Seneh.

14:5 The forefront of the one was situate northward over against Michmash, and the other southward over against Gibeah.

Jonathan is very bold and full of faith in God; and it is a true thing that God saves by either many or by few. Very often God accomplishes his purpose by the weak and small, so that all will know that the deliverance was from God and not from any man, so that no flesh may glory. Today many wrongly look to men and not to God.

14:6 And Jonathan said to the young man that bare his armour, Come, and let us go over unto the garrison of these uncircumcised: **it may be that the LORD will work for us: for there is no restraint to the LORD to save by many or by few. 14:7** And his armourbearer said unto him, Do all that is in thine heart: turn thee; behold, I am with thee according to thy heart.

Jonathan decides to reveal their presence to a group of Philistines. Jonathan then seeks a sign from God through the words of the Philistines.

14:8 Then said Jonathan, Behold, we will pass over unto these men, and we will discover ourselves unto them. **14:9** If they say thus unto us, Tarry until we come to you; then we will stand still in our place, and will not go up unto them. **14:10** But if they say thus, **Come up unto us;** then we will go up: for the LORD hath delivered them into our hand: and this shall be a sign unto us.

God inspires the Philistines to challenge Jonathan and his bearer to come up to fight, fulfilling the sign that Jonathan sought, revealing that God had given him the victory.

14:11 And both of them discovered themselves unto the garrison of the Philistines: and the Philistines said, Behold, the Hebrews come forth out of the holes where they had hid themselves. **14:12** And the men of the garrison answered Jonathan and his armourbearer, and said, **Come up to us, and we will shew you a thing** [in modern parlance: "we will teach you a lesson"]. **And Jonathan said unto his armourbearer, Come up after me: for the LORD hath delivered them into the hand of Israel.**

Jonathan and his bearer went up in absolute faith in God and slew many Philistines, filling the men of Israel with fear concerning a Philistine response. When we trust in God there is no reason to fear any man.

> **Daniel 3:16** Shadrach, Meshach, and Abednego, answered and said to the king, O Nebuchadnezzar, we are not careful [not afraid to answer or to stand up to kings and rulers of men] to answer thee in this matter.

> Our mighty God is able to deliver his faithful even in this physical life, but if he chooses not to do so in order to prove our loyalty to

him to the death; then the truly faithful will still assuredly serve the God of Jacob and Moses and not any other.

3:17 If it be so, **our God whom we serve is able to deliver us from the burning fiery furnace, and he will deliver us out of thine hand, O king.**

Oh, how far today's Spiritual Ekklesia has fallen away from the Word of God and the example of his faithful; exalting and serving men and their corporate entities above the Word of God!

3:18 But if not, be it known unto thee, O king, that we will not serve thy gods, nor worship the golden image [Representing all idolatry, including following ANY man, contrary to the whole word of God.] which thou hast set up.

1 Samuel 14:13 And Jonathan climbed up upon his hands and upon his feet, and his armourbearer after him: and they fell before Jonathan; and his armourbearer slew after him. **14:14** And that first slaughter, which Jonathan and his armourbearer made, **was about twenty men**, within as it were an half acre of land, which a yoke of oxen might plow.

The remaining army of Saul melted away for fear, not having the faith of Jonathan who went to battle with his armourbearer and faith in God.

14:15 And there was trembling in the host, in the field, and among all the people: the garrison, and the spoilers, they also trembled, and the earth [seemed to quake for their fears] quaked: so it was a very great trembling. **14:16** And the watchmen of Saul in Gibeah of Benjamin looked; and, behold, the multitude melted away, and they went on beating down one another.

Saul numbers the people to see how many have fled and who remains, but Jonathan was missing, being out fighting the Philistines.

14:17 Then said Saul unto the people that were with him, Number now, and see who is gone from us. And when they had numbered, behold, Jonathan and his armourbearer were not there.

Saul asked for the Ark of God and the high priest, to consult with God.

14:18 And Saul said unto Ahiah [the high priest], Bring hither the ark of God. For the ark of God was at that time with the children of Israel.

Then the Philistines attacked in response to the slaughter by Jonathan; and Saul tells the priest to remove the Ark for safe keeping.

14:19 And it came to pass, while Saul talked unto the priest, that the noise that was in the host of the Philistines went on and increased: and Saul said unto the priest, Withdraw thine hand.

Saul then assembled what was left of his army and a great victory was won over the Philistines; even the collaborators with the Philistines changed sides and fought for Israel.

14:20 And Saul and all the people that were with him assembled themselves, and they came to the battle: and, behold, every man's sword was against his fellow, and there was a very great discomfiture. **14:21** Moreover the Hebrews that were with the Philistines before that time, which went up with them into the camp from the country round about, even they also turned to be with the Israelites that were with Saul and Jonathan.

When those of the army of Israel who had fled heard of the victory, they turned back and joined Saul to finish off the Philistine army.

14:22 Likewise all the men of Israel which had hid themselves in mount Ephraim, when they heard that the Philistines fled, even they also followed hard after them in the battle.

14:23 So the LORD saved Israel that day: and the battle passed over unto Bethaven.

Saul had made a foolish vow to God that distressed Israel greatly, for Saul had vowed to kill any person that did not fast that day and Israel had to fight fasting.

14:24 And the men of Israel were distressed that day: for Saul had adjured the people, saying, Cursed be the man that eateth any food until evening, that I may be avenged on mine enemies. So none of the people tasted any food.

Thus was Saul, great in war and very weak and foolish spiritually.

14:25 And all they of the land came to a wood; and there was honey upon the ground. **14:26** And when the people were come into the wood, behold, the honey dropped; but no man put his hand to his mouth: for the people feared the oath.

Jonathan mistakenly breaks his father's vow, out of ignorance

14:27 But Jonathan heard not when his father charged the people with the oath: wherefore he put forth the end of the rod that was in his hand, and dipped it in an honeycomb, and put his hand to his mouth; and his eyes were enlightened [he was strengthened].

Then the people warned Jonathan, but the deed was done

14:28 Then answered one of the people, and said, Thy father straitly charged the people with an oath, saying, Cursed be the man that eateth any food this day. And the people were faint.

Jonathan then rebuked his father's vow, pointing out how much greater a victory they might have had had every man been strong.

God's Word is sweeter than honey to those that truly love the Eternal; let us never leave off from true zeal for the whole Word of God to learn and to internalize the Word of God and to keep it; for therein is our spiritual strength!

> **Psalm 119:103** How sweet are thy words unto my taste! yea, sweeter than honey to my mouth!

It is through following and living by every Word of God that spiritual victory will be won and sin can be overcome; resulting in entry into the Promised Land of eternal life!

> **Psalm 19:7** The law of the Lord is perfect, converting the soul: the testimony of the Lord is sure, making wise the simple. **19:8** The statutes of the Lord are right, rejoicing the heart: the commandment of the Lord is pure, enlightening the eyes.
>
> **19:9** The fear of the Lord is clean, enduring for ever: the judgments of the Lord are true and righteous altogether. **19:10** More to be desired are they than gold, yea, than much fine gold: sweeter also than honey and the honeycomb.
>
> **19:11** Moreover by them is thy servant warned [to depart from evil]: and in keeping of them there is great reward. **19:12** Who can understand his errors? cleanse thou me from secret faults.
>
> **19:13** Keep back thy servant also from presumptuous sins; let them not have dominion over me: then shall I be upright, and I shall be innocent from the great transgression. **19:14** Let the words of my mouth, and the meditation of my heart, be acceptable in thy sight, O Lord, my strength, and my redeemer.

1 Samuel 14:29 Then said Jonathan, My father hath troubled the land: see, I pray you, how mine eyes have been enlightened, because I tasted a little of this honey. **14:30** How much more, if haply the people had eaten freely to day of the spoil of their enemies which they found? for had there not been now a much greater slaughter among the Philistines? **14:31** And they smote the Philistines that day from Michmash to Aijalon: and the people were very faint.

At the setting sun, the people made haste to eat without properly bleeding and preparing the flesh for consumption.

Physically blood is the life of all higher creatures, and the shedding of blood carries with it the thought of death which is the wages of sin.

Spiritually, blood is to be shed for sin; [The wages of sin being death, Romans 6:23] and therefore eating blood carries with it the thought of partaking of sin and death.

14:32 And the people flew upon the spoil, and took sheep, and oxen, and calves, and slew them on the ground: and the people did eat them with the blood.

Saul sought to correct the people for this sin, and made a place for them to properly kill for food. This is one of the few times that Saul stood up for godliness against the people.

14:33 Then they told Saul, saying, Behold, the people sin against the LORD, in that they eat with the blood. And he said, Ye have transgressed: roll a great stone unto me this day. **14:34** And Saul said, Disperse yourselves among the people, and say unto them, Bring me hither every man his ox, and every man his sheep, and slay them here, and eat; and sin not against the LORD in eating with the blood. And all the people brought every man his ox with him that night, and slew them there.

Saul quickly built an altar and corrected the people, lest they be struck down for their sins.

14:35 And Saul built an altar unto the LORD: the same was the first altar that he built unto the LORD.

Then Saul asked God if he should go to fight the Philistines and God would not answer him that day.

14:36 And Saul said, Let us go down after the Philistines by night, and spoil them until the morning light, and let us not leave a man of them. And they said, Do whatsoever seemeth good unto thee. Then said the priest, Let us draw near hither unto God. **14:37** And Saul asked counsel of God, Shall I go down after the Philistines? wilt thou deliver them into the hand of Israel? But he answered him not that day.

Then Saul thought that God did not answer because someone had broken his vow.

14:38 And Saul said, Draw ye near hither, all the chief of the people: and know and see wherein this sin hath been this day. **14:39** For, as the LORD liveth, which saveth Israel, though it be in Jonathan my son, he shall surely die. But there was not a man among all the people that answered him.

Saul then cast lots by the high priest between himself and the people to find the guilty persons.

14:40 Then said he unto all Israel, Be ye on one side, and I and Jonathan my son will be on the other side. And the people said unto Saul, Do what seemeth good unto thee.

The lot fell on the guilty one, Jonathan the son of Saul.

14:41 Therefore Saul said unto the LORD God of Israel, Give a perfect lot. And Saul and Jonathan were taken: but the people escaped. **14:42** And Saul said, Cast lots between me and Jonathan my son. And Jonathan was taken. **14:43** Then Saul said to Jonathan, Tell me what thou hast done. And Jonathan told him, and said, I did but taste a little honey with the end of the rod that was in mine hand, and, lo, I must die. **14:44** And Saul answered, God do so and more also: for thou shalt surely die, Jonathan.

The people rose up and saved Jonathan, and the army of Israel was stopped from pursuing the Philistines.

14:45 And the people said unto Saul, Shall Jonathan die, who hath wrought this great salvation in Israel? God forbid: as the LORD liveth, there shall not one hair of his head fall to the ground; for he hath wrought with God this day. So the people rescued Jonathan, that he died not. **14:46** Then Saul went up from following the Philistines: and the Philistines went to their own place.

Saul was then fully established as king of Israel and he became a great warrior king; destroying many enemies of Israel, which helped to prepare the kingdom for his successor David.

14:47 So Saul took the kingdom over Israel, and fought against all his enemies on every side, against Moab, and against the children of Ammon, and against Edom, and against the kings of Zobah, and against the Philistines: and whithersoever he turned himself, he vexed them. **14:48** And he gathered an host, and smote the Amalekites, and delivered Israel out of the hands of them that spoiled them.

Saul's family and his army captain Abner.

After the death of Saul, Abner later joined David.

14:49 Now the sons of Saul were Jonathan, and Ishui, and Melchishua: and the names of his two daughters were these; the name of the firstborn Merab, and the name of the younger Michal [Me-Khal **pronunciation link**]: **14:50** And the name of Saul's wife was Ahinoam, the daughter of Ahimaaz: and the name of **the captain of his host was Abner**, the son of Ner, Saul's uncle.

> **Abner** (Hebrew אבנר "Avner" meaning "father of [or is a] light"), was first cousin to Saul and commander-in-chief of his army (1 Samuel 14:50, 20:25). He is often referred to as the son of Ner.

14:51 And Kish was the father of Saul; and **Ner the father of Abner** was the son of Abiel.

Saul fought continually throughout the days of his kingship to destroy the enemies of Israel and to establish his dynasty.

14:52 And there was sore war against the Philistines all the days of Saul: and when Saul saw any strong man, or any valiant man, he took him unto him.

1 Samuel 15

Then the God Being who later gave up his God-hood to become flesh as Jesus Christ instructed Saul to attack the Amalekites, who were a vicious and cruel people.

1 Samuel 15:1 Samuel also said unto Saul, The LORD sent me to anoint thee to be king over his people, over Israel: now therefore hearken thou unto the voice of the words of the LORD.

Jesus Christ commands Saul to destroy Amalek and leave not so much as a lamb alive. This is the Real Jesus, not the false tolerant of sin Jesus of the permissive set.

These Amalekites were a type of sin like the Canaanites, and their destruction was to be an example of the total destruction in the lake of fire that will befall all those who compromise with the Word of God.

Do you cook or buy food and drink or anything else on Sabbath because some man told you to when God's Word condemns all who do so? If we remain unrepentant of our idolatry of men and the sin that they lead us into, we will face strong correction and if still unrepentant we will be totally destroyed.

15:2 Thus saith the LORD of hosts, I remember that which Amalek did to Israel, how he laid wait for him in the way, when he came up from Egypt.

15:3 Now go and smite Amalek, and utterly destroy all that they have, and spare them not; but slay both man and woman, infant and suckling, ox and sheep, camel and ass.

Saul then gathered 210,000 men for the fight. Up to this point he had obeyed God and Samuel but he soon sins in this matter.

This is a lesson that all of the spiritually called out are to continually live by every Word of God regardless of any pressure or temptation to do otherwise.

15:4 And Saul gathered the people together, and numbered them in Telaim, two hundred thousand footmen, and ten thousand men of Judah.

Saul sent the Bedouin away and then attacked the Amalekites, destroying them as commanded by God, except that he disobeyed in regard to the animals. This was a TEST from God as to whether they would obey God even when it did not make sense to them and was to their apparent hurt.

How many of us fail the same kind of test today, failing to obey because some point does not make sense to us at the time?

Saul then warned the Kenites a nomadic tribe which came out of Midian and the in law family of Moses, who are today called Bedouins; to flee from among the Amalekites.

15:5 And Saul came to a city of Amalek, and laid wait in the valley. **15:6** And Saul said unto the Kenites, Go, depart, get you down from among the Amalekites, lest I destroy you with them: for ye shewed kindness to all the children of Israel, when they came up out of Egypt. So the Kenites departed from among the Amalekites.

15:7 And Saul smote the Amalekites from Havilah until thou comest to Shur, that is over against Egypt. **15:8** And he took Agag the king of the Amalekites alive, and utterly destroyed all the people with the edge of the sword.

Always the politician who sought to please the people above obeying God, Saul allowed Israel to keep the good things of the spoil contrary to the Word of God.

The physical sin here was direct rebellion and disobedience to a clear command of God. Even so many in today's Spiritual Ekklesia seek to please the worldly in their outreach programs instead of pleasing God by preaching the true gospel of warning and zeal to learn and to live by every Word of God.

15:9 But Saul and the people spared Agag, and the best of the sheep, and of the oxen, and of the fatlings, and the lambs, and all that was good, and would not utterly destroy them: but every thing that was vile and refuse, that they destroyed utterly.

Then Jesus Christ regretted making Saul king because of his repeated disobedience; just like large numbers of today's leaders, elders and brethren also apostatize from living by every Word of God, into trying to please men.

15:10 Then came the word of the LORD unto Samuel, saying, **15:11** It repenteth me that I have set up Saul to be king: for he is turned back from following me, and hath not performed my commandments. And it grieved Samuel; and he cried unto the LORD all night.

Samuel prayed for Saul and agonized over Saul's sins, before going up to meet him.

15:12 And when Samuel rose early to meet Saul in the morning, it was told Samuel, saying, Saul came to Carmel, and, behold, he set him up a place, and is gone about, and passed on, and gone down to Gilgal. **15:13** And Samuel came to Saul: and Saul said unto him, Blessed be thou of the LORD: I have performed the commandment of the LORD.

Saul blamed the people and did not take responsibility for his actions: Just like many today think that they can stand before God and shirk any responsibility for their own actions by blaming their sins on others and saying: "I was just obeying church leaders."

The Nazi's made the same excuse saying "I had to obey my boss." NO you didn't! You could have resigned or even died rather than sin!

Saul and thousands of others proved that they would willingly commit sin if they thought it was to their personal advantage; and Almighty God will reject our own similar excuses just like he rejected the same excuse from king Saul!

15:14 And Samuel said, What meaneth then this bleating of the sheep in mine ears, and the lowing of the oxen which I hear? **15:15** And Saul said, They have brought them from the Amalekites: for the people spared the best of the sheep and of the oxen, to sacrifice unto the LORD thy God; and the rest we have utterly destroyed.

Samuel then told Saul the judgment of God.

15:16 Then Samuel said unto Saul, Stay, and I will tell thee what the LORD hath said to me this night. And he said unto him, Say on.

This very thing could be said to many of us in today's Spiritually Ekklesia.

Were we not called and anointed to be kings and priests of the Great King and eternal High Priest of humanity?

Were we not anointed and commissioned to drive all sin and disobedience to God and all compromise with the word of God out of ourselves; and to prepare ourselves to do the same thing in future for all of humanity?

Were we not called and anointed to fully internalize the very nature of Jesus Christ the King and God the Mighty Father; by uncompromisingly overcoming and destroying all sin from within us?

Today most of our leaders and very many of the brethren followed their idols of men and corporations away from any zeal for learning and keeping of the whole Word of God in passionate zeal; and have fallen away into a zeal for idols of men and false traditions, to follow them contrary to the Word of God.

15:17 And Samuel said, When thou wast little in thine own sight, wast thou not made the head of the tribes of Israel, and the LORD anointed thee king over Israel? **15:18** And the LORD sent thee on a journey, and said, Go and utterly **destroy the sinners** the Amalekites, and fight against them until they be consumed.

We are called to be kings and priests of our Mighty Father and the Great King and High Priest Jesus Christ! How is it then that we dare to turn aside from any zeal for them, to follow our idols of men, contrary to the Word of God?

15:19 Wherefore then didst thou not obey the voice of the LORD, but didst fly upon the spoil, and didst evil in the sight of the LORD? **15:20** And Saul said unto Samuel, Yea, I have obeyed the voice of the LORD, and have gone the way which the LORD sent me, and have brought Agag the king of Amalek, and have utterly destroyed the Amalekites.

Saul then interjects his defense, blaming the people and saying that the animals were taken to sacrifice to God.

God desires obedience much more than sacrifice and he forbids us to worship him by our own methods, instead of worshiping him according to HIS instructions.

In this affair Jesus was teaching us that all unrepentant sinners will ultimately be destroyed along with all their possessions.

15:21 But the people took of the spoil, sheep and oxen, the chief of the things which should have been utterly destroyed, to sacrifice unto the LORD thy God in Gilgal.

Then Samuel continued with a lesson that was meant for us as well as Saul.

We are called to OBEY the voice of our God, so that we may learn to be LIKE HIM!

15:22 And Samuel said, **Hath the LORD as great delight in burnt offerings and sacrifices, as in obeying the voice of the LORD? Behold, to obey is better than sacrifice, and to hearken than the fat of rams.**

Calling the Sabbath holy and then polluting it by transgressing God's Word on how to keep the Sabbath holy; because some mere mortal man said polluting the Sabbath is acceptable, is REBELLION against God and is no different than open witchcraft!

Brethren, we reject God when we reject any zeal to learn and to keep his Word, in favor of a zeal to follow and obey men: That is the sin of Idolatry!

Make no mistake; this is about eternal life and eternal death.

If we are not zealous to faithfully learn and to uncompromisingly keep the whole Word of God, no matter what any man says [regardless of the title he claims for himself]; we will be rejected from the resurrection to eternal life.

15:23 For rebellion is as the sin of witchcraft, and stubbornness is as iniquity and idolatry. Because thou hast rejected the word of the LORD, he hath also rejected thee from being king.

Saul remorsefully admits the sin of disobedience and the sin of exalting people above the Word of God.

Do you fear men more than you fear God so that you exalt the words of men above the Word of God to maintain membership in some social club church? Or will you keep God's Word above the words of men?

15:24 And Saul said unto Samuel, I have sinned: for **I have transgressed the commandment of the LORD, and thy words: because I feared the people, and obeyed their voice.**

Saul then asked Samuel to accompany him to worship God. This was a political act because Samuel going up to the tabernacle with Saul would imply Samuel's approval of Saul before the people.

15:25 Now therefore, I pray thee, pardon my sin, and turn again [go with me] with me, that I may worship the LORD.

Samuel rejects this loaded invitation and Saul begins to beg, for he knows what the people will think if Samuel turns his back on him.

15:26 And Samuel said unto Saul, I will not return with thee: for thou hast rejected the word of the LORD, and the LORD hath rejected thee from being king over Israel. **15:27** And as Samuel turned about to go away, he laid hold upon the skirt of his mantle, and it rent.

Samuel informs Saul that the judgment of God is final.

When we [yes, even the spiritually called out] repeatedly turn aside from the faithful keeping of the Word of God to do what we or other men think is right; the time will come when the patience of Jesus Christ will run out and he will reject us, because we have repeatedly rejected any love for him by refusing to do those things that please him (Rev 3:16).

15:28 And Samuel said unto him, The LORD hath rent the kingdom of Israel from thee this day, and hath given it to a neighbour of thine, that is better than thou.

Jesus Christ will not change his mind.

Many who have been called to become pillars in the kingdom will not be among the chosen, they will not be there!

Many others who have been called to be pillars and then went astray for a time will be in the resurrection IF they learn their lesson and repent, yet they will NOT be the pillars they were called to be, but will be at a lower level for all eternity.

15:29 And also the Strength of Israel will not lie nor repent: for he is not a man, that he should repent.

Saul begs Samuel again to worship God with him and this time Samuel assents.

15:30 Then he said, I have sinned: yet honour me now, I pray thee, before the elders of my people, and before Israel, and turn again with me, that I may worship the LORD thy God. **15:31** So Samuel turned again after Saul; and Saul worshipped the LORD.

Then Samuel does what God commanded Saul to do and kills Agag.

15:32 Then said Samuel, Bring ye hither to me Agag the king of the Amalekites. And Agag came unto him delicately. And Agag said, Surely the bitterness of death is past. **15:33** And Samuel said, As the sword hath made women childless, so shall thy mother be childless among women. And Samuel hewed Agag in pieces before the LORD in Gilgal.

Samuel continually mourned for Saul the mighty warrior king, but did not visit him again.

15:34 Then Samuel went to Ramah; and Saul went up to his house to Gibeah of Saul. **15:35** And Samuel came no more to see Saul until the day of his death: nevertheless Samuel mourned for Saul: and the LORD repented that he had made Saul king over Israel.

1 Samuel 16

God sent Samuel to anoint a new king.

1 Samuel 16:1 And the LORD said unto Samuel, How long wilt thou mourn for Saul, seeing I have rejected him from reigning over Israel? fill thine horn with oil, and go, I will send thee to Jesse the Bethlehemite: for I have provided me a king among his sons.

God reveals to Samuel what he should do.

16:2 And Samuel said, How can I go? if Saul hear it, he will kill me. And the LORD said, Take an heifer [a virgin female cow, usually under a year or two old] with thee, and say, I am come to sacrifice to the LORD. **16:3** And call Jesse to the sacrifice, and I will shew thee what thou shalt do: and thou shalt anoint unto me him whom I name unto thee.

Samuel came to Bethlehem and called Jesse and his sons to the sacrifice. Jesse being the son of Obed the son of Boaz and Ruth and a man of great wealth and reputation for godliness.

16:4 And Samuel did that which the LORD spake, and came to Bethlehem. And the elders of the town trembled at his coming, and said, Comest thou peaceably?

The elders of Bethlehem feared lest Samuel had come to rebuke them in some matter.

16:5 And he said, Peaceably: I am come to sacrifice unto the LORD: sanctify yourselves, and come with me to the sacrifice. And he sanctified Jesse and his sons, and called them to the sacrifice.

Jesus Christ teaches us not to look on outward appearances and impressive goodly features, or talents and skills; but on the fruits of a wholehearted dedication to love and live by every Word of God.

16:6 And it came to pass, when they were come, that he looked on Eliab, and said, Surely the LORD's anointed is before him. **16:7** But the LORD said unto Samuel, **Look not on his countenance, or on the height of his stature**; because I have refused him: for the

LORD seeth not as man seeth; for **man looketh on the outward appearance, but the LORD looketh on the heart.**

All seven sons of Jesse were seen by Samuel and God rejected them all, even though they were all impressive in appearance.

Why did Christ not just chose David first?

Because Jesus was teaching a lesson to us that very many impressive men with excellent speaking ability are not godly in their character.

We must learn to judge (Mat 7, Mat 24) who we choose to follow, by their wholehearted zeal for the whole Word of God and not by their persuasive tongues or impressive appearance or leadership skills.

16:8 Then Jesse called Abinadab, and made him pass before Samuel. And he said, Neither hath the LORD chosen this. **16:9** Then Jesse made Shammah to pass by. And he said, Neither hath the LORD chosen this. **16:10** Again, Jesse made seven of his sons to pass before Samuel. And Samuel said unto Jesse, The LORD hath not chosen these.

Then David was called from keeping the sheep

Jesse was a rich man with fields and flocks and it is quite reasonable that David as the owners son, had charge over several if not many shepherds. David doubtless had experience in leadership as well as in caring for sheep. This is also an example for us that we can draw and learn spiritual lessons from any situation if our minds are continually carefully considering the Word and Will of God.

Samuel tells Jesse to fetch David in haste

16:11 And Samuel said unto Jesse, Are here all thy children? And he said, There remaineth yet the youngest, and, behold, he keepeth the sheep. And Samuel said unto Jesse, Send and fetch him: for we will not sit down till he come hither.

Here we see that Samuel did not choose David; David was chosen by Jesus Christ. In the Ekklesia today we can know who Jesus Christ has sent, by their zeal to learn, to keep and to teach the whole Word of God!

16:12 And he sent, and brought him in. Now he was ruddy, and withal of a beautiful countenance, and goodly to look to. And the LORD said, Arise, anoint him: for this is he.

We are to ordain those whom God has called who will be known by their long term fruits of godliness and passionate enthusiasm to live by every Word of God. We are NOT to ordain men because they are loyal to some man or organization.

16:13 Then Samuel took the horn of oil, and anointed him in the midst of his brethren: and the Spirit of the LORD came upon David from that day forward. So Samuel rose up, and went to Ramah.

At that moment God's Spirit departed from Saul, yet he remained king until God had fully trained his replacement.

Just as physical Israel could have bad kings, and there were many bad kings; so Spiritual Israel can have bad leaders and elders in their assemblies. Remember the many New Testament warnings that many evil men would infiltrate the assemblies and persecute the faithful.

16:14 But the Spirit of the LORD departed from Saul, and an evil spirit from the LORD troubled him.

Saul's servants soon noticed the change and recognized the presence of evil. How is it that so many of us are so blind to the present reality?

16:15 And Saul's servants said unto him, Behold now, an evil spirit from God troubleth thee.

Saul must have been greatly troubled over the end of his dynasty before it really began; and also would have feared insurrection against himself.

His personal fears would have driven him to distraction, finding terrors in every shadow and imagining enemies out to destroy him. Like Herod during his rule, no person, no matter how loyal was safe from suspicion and possible insane enraged personal attacks.

This kind of mental affliction has plagued many leaders throughout history.

Saul's servants sought out a man of music to calm the king.

16:16 Let our lord now command thy servants, which are before thee, to seek out a man, who is a cunning player on an harp: and it shall come to pass, when the evil spirit from God is upon thee, that he shall play with his hand, and thou shalt be well. **16:17** And Saul said unto his servants, Provide me now a man that can play well, and bring him to me.

David is appointed as Saul's musician and he learns much in the household of Saul. Saul sees David as a valiant courageous man and also enjoys his music, and makes David his armourbearer.

David, always an avid student would have watched and learned from everything he saw.

16:18 Then answered one of the servants, and said, Behold, I have seen a son of Jesse the Bethlehemite, that is cunning in playing, and a mighty valiant man, and a man of war, and prudent in matters, and a comely person, and the LORD is with him. **16:19** Wherefore Saul sent messengers unto Jesse, and said, Send me David thy son, which is with the sheep.

16:20 And Jesse took an ass laden with bread, and a bottle of wine, and a kid, and sent them by David his son unto Saul. **16:21** And **David came to Saul, and stood before him: and he loved him greatly; and he became his armourbearer. 16:22** And Saul sent to Jesse, saying, Let David, I pray thee, stand before me; for he hath found favour in my sight.

When Saul was troubled David's playing calmed him and brought Saul peace of mind and rest.

16:23 And it came to pass, when the evil spirit from God was upon Saul, that David took an harp, and played with his hand: so Saul was refreshed, and was well, and the evil spirit departed from him.

1 Samuel 17

The story of David and Goliath is often portrayed as a classic story of an underdog winning out over his far more powerful rival. There is much more to the story than that!

Goliath was an example of unrepentant sinners and of the sin of enmity against God and the Word of God; while David was a type of all God's faithful who are filled with courage through their trust and faith in the Eternal and his deliverance for all those who are zealous to follow him and to live by every Word of God.

Brethren, we can ALL be David's, approaching and fighting sin with an expectation of total victory; through living by every Word of God and an absolute unshakable faith in our Mighty God!

David was full of courage to face the mightiest of enemies, because he KNEW that he had been zealous for and faithful to Almighty God; and that God would go before him and give him the victory!

We too can confront sin victoriously if we are full of zeal to learn and to live by every Word of God; we can be full of faith KNOWING that our Lord dwells within us and will fight for us against all sin, giving us total victory over sin and its wages of death.

If we try to confront sin by our own strength, we have failed before we begin! If we are passionately zealous to learn and to keep the whole Word of God, and to follow the Word of God wherever God leads; the victory is assured!

The Philistines and Israel were each camped on the opposite heights of a valley.

1 Samuel 17:1 Now the Philistines gathered together their armies to battle, and were gathered together at Shochoh, which belongeth to Judah, and pitched between Shochoh and Azekah, in Ephesdammim. **17:2** And Saul and the men of Israel were gathered together, and pitched by the valley of Elah, and set the battle in array against the Philistines. **17:3** And the Philistines stood on a mountain on the one side, and Israel stood on a mountain on the other side: and there was a valley between them.

When our trials, persecutions and the temptations to turn aside from uncompromising zeal for the whole Word of God seem like insurmountable Goliath's in our eyes; let us turn to our Mighty Deliverer and put our complete trust in he who alone is Mighty to Save!

17:4 And there went out a champion out of the camp of the Philistines, named Goliath, of Gath, whose height was six cubits and a span [about ten feet tall]. **17:5** And he had an helmet of brass upon his head, and he was armed with a coat of mail; and the weight of the coat was five thousand shekels of brass. **17:6** And he had greaves of brass upon his legs, and a target of brass between his shoulders. **17:7** And the staff of his spear was like a weaver's beam; and his spear's head weighed six hundred shekels of iron: and one bearing a shield went before him.

Satan challenges us with the persecutions he inspires against us and with all manner of temptations that indeed appear desirable but are snares to bring our downfall.

He is like a great roaring lion against whom there is no defense; and the evils that beset us often seem like insurmountable Goliath's or Red Sea's that we simply cannot resist.

Brethren, this is all an illusion to frighten and intimidate us! Satan is but a wisp of vapor before the Might of our God! Be faithful and strong to live by every Word of God, and God will give us the victory; just like the Eternal delivered Moses, Joshua, Daniel and David!

James 4:7 **Submit yourselves therefore to God. Resist the devil, and he will flee from you.**

4:8 Draw nigh to God, and he will draw nigh to you. Cleanse your hands, ye sinners; and purify your hearts, ye double minded.

4:9 Be afflicted [fast], and mourn [repent from sin] , and weep: let your laughter [delight in sin] be turned to mourning, and your joy [in wantonness] to heaviness.

4:10 Humble yourselves in the sight of the Lord, and he shall lift you up.

Satan challenges us like Goliath challenged Israel, trying to deceive us into thinking that we are alone in the fight and terrifying us into giving up the struggle.

Brethren we are not alone! No not at all! Our Champion is greater than ten thousand thousand million Satan's; before the Eternal, Satan the roaring lion cringes and the very mountains melt away!

1 Samuel 17:8 And he stood and cried unto the armies of Israel, and said unto them, Why are ye come out to set your battle in array? am not I a Philistine, and ye servants to Saul? choose you a man for you, and let him come down to me. **17:9** If he be able to fight with me, and to kill me, then will we be your servants: but if I prevail against him, and kill him, then shall ye be our servants, and serve us. **17:10** And the Philistine said, I defy the armies of Israel [God's Covenant people Mosaic Israel and today's New Covenant Spiritual Israel] this day; give me a man, that we may fight together.

17:11 When Saul and all Israel heard those words of the Philistine, they were dismayed, and greatly afraid.

Do not be discouraged or dismayed by the struggle to resist sin, rather turn to an even greater zeal for God; run to the arms of our Mighty Deliverer, the High Tower of our Salvation and put our trust in HIM resisting all sin and compromise with God's Word!

So what, if we suffer in this world for zeal for our God and his Word: Did not Joseph also suffer, before being exalted to the ruler-ship of Egypt [Which is to say that he was exalted over the allegorical type of bondage to sin!]?

This happened as an example for us so that we might also be formed and tempered through affliction, to learn to be just and godly kings [rulers] and priests! Read Hebrews 11.

17:12 Now David was the son of that Ephrathite of Bethlehemjudah, whose name was Jesse; and he had eight sons: and the man went among men for an old man [Jesse was old in Saul's time] in the days of Saul.

David and three other sons of Jesse followed Saul to the war, but David returned home to care for the sheep when the battle was delayed.

17:13 And the three eldest sons of Jesse went and followed Saul to the battle: and the names of his three sons that went to the battle were Eliab the firstborn, and next unto him Abinadab, and the third

Shammah. **17:14** And David was the youngest: and the three eldest followed Saul. **17:15** But David went and returned from Saul to feed his father's sheep at Bethlehem.

The standoff lasted for 40 days and then Jesse sent David to his brothers with a gift of some food.

17:16 And the Philistine drew near morning and evening, and presented himself forty days.

17:17 And Jesse said unto David his son, Take now for thy brethren an ephah of this parched corn, and these ten loaves, and run to the camp of thy brethren; **17:18** And carry these ten cheeses unto the captain of their thousand, and look how thy brethren fare, and take their pledge.

David went to his brothers as his father had asked.

17:19 Now Saul, and they, and all the men of Israel, were in the valley of Elah, fighting with the Philistines. **17:20** And David rose up early in the morning, and left the sheep with a keeper, and took, and went, as Jesse had commanded him; and he came to the trench, as the host was going forth to the fight, and shouted for the battle. **17:21** For Israel and the Philistines had put the battle in array, army against army.

Then David saw how Israel reacted to Goliath, running in fear; just as today so many of us are filled with fear over any real or imagined difficulty in living by the Word of God.

17:22 And David left his carriage in the hand of the keeper of the carriage, and ran into the army, and came and saluted his brethren. **17:23** And as he talked with them, behold, there came up the champion, the Philistine of

Gath, Goliath by name, out of the armies of the Philistines, and spake according to the same words: and David heard them.

Then someone told David about king Saul's offer

Do we not have an even better offer from a much greater King? Will we not be given in marriage as a faithful bride to the King of kings under God the Father, and granted freedom from sin and from death itself; if we are zealous for our Mighty King and willing to do battle with the spiritual enemy?

The Deliverer of the Faithful will go forward before his beloved who have the courage to stand up and FIGHT sin with the sword of TRUTH and are full of absolute Faith in our Deliverer!

The Mighty God of Jacob will go before the courageous faithful servants of God, to give them eternal victory over Satan and sin, and the final enemy, DEATH itself!

17:24 And all the men of Israel, when they saw the man, fled from him, and were sore afraid. **17:25** And the men of Israel said, Have ye seen this man that is come up? surely to defy Israel is he come up: and it shall be, that the man who killeth him, the king will enrich him with great riches, and will give him his daughter, and make his father's house free in Israel.

17:26 And David spake to the men that stood by him, saying, What shall be done to the man that killeth this Philistine, and taketh away the reproach from Israel? for who is this uncircumcised Philistine, that he should defy the armies of the living God? **17:27** And the people answered him after this manner, saying, So shall it be done to the man that killeth him.

David's brother rebukes him for his courageous zeal for God.

It is so even today in Spiritual Israel, that the spiritually insipid, lukewarm, morally permissive often rebuke the zealous who keep the whole Word of God with passionate courage and enthusiasm.

17:28 And Eliab his eldest brother heard when he spake unto the men; and Eliab's anger was kindled against David, and he said, Why camest thou down hither? and with whom hast thou left those few sheep in the wilderness? I know thy pride, and the naughtiness of thine heart; for thou art come down that thou mightest see the battle. **17:29** And David said, What have I now done? Is there not a cause? **17:30** And he turned from him toward another, and spake after the same manner: and the people answered him again after the former manner.

David's words came to Saul, and David was called before Saul.

Remember that our words and deeds of courage and trust and faithfulness in the Eternal will come up before God the Father in heaven and he takes note of them.

> **Malachi 3:16** Then **they that feared the Lord spake often one to another: and the Lord hearkened, and heard it, and a book of remembrance was written before him for them that feared the Lord, and that thought upon his name. 3:17** And they shall be mine, saith the Lord of hosts, in that day when I make up my jewels; and I will spare them, as a man spareth his own son that serveth him.

1 Samuel 17:31 And when the words were heard which David spake, they rehearsed them before Saul: and he sent for him.

Then David told Saul that he would go forth to fight against the enemies of God.

We all should be David's; willing to fight sin and all compromise with the Word of God with all the heart and courage of a Mighty Man of God!

If we do, the Great King will go before us and give us the victory and the reward of eternal life with him for our faithfulness, our zeal for God and for our courage to take a stand for the Word of God!

17:32 And David said to Saul, Let no man's heart fail [be afraid] because of him; thy servant will go and fight with this Philistine.

Saul questioned David about his ability to fight Goliath not knowing that it is God who will fight for his beloved faithful.

Consider that David had been anointed king by Samuel and that David had faith that God would make him king as God had promised. It was not David that fought Goliath, it was Almighty God that went before David to give him victory over the enemy of God.

David was faithful believing in the promise of God's anointing, and full of the courage and works of faith; and God delivered him!

Consider that the New Covenant first fruits Spiritual Ekklesia have also been anointed to become kings (Rev 5:10)! Not yet having received a kingdom! Our anointing and our kingdom being conditional on our zeal for our God and his Word, and on our courage and faith to take a stand to live by every Word of God against all sin!

17:33 And Saul said to David, Thou art not able to go against this Philistine to fight with him: for thou art but a youth, and he a man of war from his youth.

David then declared his deeds to Saul.

17:34 And David said unto Saul, Thy servant kept his father's sheep, and there came a lion, and a bear, and took a lamb out of the flock: **17:35** And I went out after him, and smote him, and delivered it out of his mouth: and when he arose against me, I caught him by his beard, and smote him, and slew him.

David then said that just as he was courageous to protect his flock, he will be courageous to take a stand on the Word of God to stand up to sin and wickedness.

David KNEW where his deliverance came from and he passionately loved the Word of God! We would do well to follow David's example!

17:36 Thy servant slew both the lion and the bear: and this uncircumcised Philistine shall be as one of them, seeing he hath defied the armies of the living God. **17:37** David said moreover, **The LORD that delivered me out of the paw of the lion, and out of the paw of the bear, he will deliver me out of the hand of this Philistine.** And Saul said unto David, Go, and the LORD be with thee.

David refuses Saul's armour saying that he had not practiced with it.

This rejection of the armour of Saul to rely on the protection of the Eternal is also an interesting example for us that we are not to put our salvation and spiritual trust in men, or in physical assets; we are to put our trust fully in the Eternal.

17:38 And Saul armed David with his armour, and he put an helmet of brass upon his head; also he armed him with a coat of mail. **17:39** And David girded his sword upon his armour, and he assayed to go; for he had not proved it. And David said unto Saul, I cannot go with these; for I have not proved them. And David put them off him.

David then went out to meet the Philistine, Goliath.

17:40 And he took his staff in his hand, and chose him five smooth stones out of the brook, and put them in a shepherd's bag which he had, even in a scrip; and his sling was in his hand: and he drew near to the Philistine. **17:41** And the Philistine came on and drew near unto David; and the man that bare the shield went before him.

Goliath is insulted that Israel has sent out such a young man to fight him. Yet God has set this situation up to demonstrate that God can and will defend even the smallest and weakest person who is uncompromisingly faithful to HIM; against all the power of Satan and sin!

It is not in or by our own strength that victory is won over sin, but by our faithfulness to believe and to follow the Mighty God; for he alone can and will deliver all those who are willing to faithfully live by every Word of God!

17:42 And when the Philistine looked about, and saw David, he disdained him: for he was but a youth, and ruddy, and of a fair countenance. **17:43** And the Philistine said unto David, Am I a dog, that thou comest to me with staves? And the Philistine cursed David by his gods. **17:44** And the Philistine said to David, Come to me, and I will give thy flesh unto the fowls of the air, and to the beasts of the field.

David then declares his faith in God for everyone in both armies to hear; openly declaring that he is standing up for the Eternal, and that the Eternal will destroy the enemy [which enemy was an allegory of Satan and sin]!

17:45 Then said David to the Philistine, Thou comest to me with a sword, and with a spear, and with a shield: but **I come to thee in the name of the LORD of hosts, the God of the armies of Israel, whom thou hast defied. 17:46 This day will the LORD deliver thee into mine hand;** and I will smite thee, and take thine head from thee; and I will give the carcases of the host of the Philistines this day unto the fowls of the air, and to the wild beasts of the earth; **that all the earth may know that there is a God in Israel.**

The battle against sin is the Lord's; and we need only be zealous to learn and to live by every Word of God, and to follow the Eternal wherever he goes calling on him to fight for us and to deliver us!

17:47 And all this assembly shall know that the LORD saveth not with sword and spear [by the strength of man]: for **the battle is the LORD's,** and he will give you into our hands.

David fearlessly and full of faith, rushed forward to oppose the enemy who reproached God.

17:48 And it came to pass, when the Philistine arose, and came, and drew nigh to meet David, that David hastened, and ran toward the army to meet the Philistine. **17:49** And David put his hand in his bag, and took thence a stone, and slang it, and smote the Philistine in his forehead, that the stone sunk into his forehead; and he fell upon his face to the earth. **17:50** So David prevailed over the Philistine with a sling and with a stone, and smote the Philistine, and slew him; but there was no sword in the hand of David.

When we trust in God to deliver us, and we are faithful to serve him fully; he will give us ultimate victory over Satan, sin and death itself!

17:51 Therefore David ran, and stood upon the Philistine, and took his sword, and drew it out of the sheath thereof, and slew him, and cut off his head therewith. And when the Philistines saw their champion was dead, they fled.

17:52 And the men of Israel and of Judah arose, and shouted, and pursued the Philistines, until thou come to the valley, and to the gates of Ekron. And the wounded of the Philistines fell down by the way to Shaaraim, even unto Gath, and unto Ekron. **17:53** And the children of Israel returned from chasing after the Philistines, and they spoiled their tents. **17:54** And David took the head of the Philistine, and brought it to Jerusalem; but he put his armour in his tent.

On this day, God began to exalt David in fame above Saul, causing Saul to inquire about David. Before this David had merely been a musician in the background of Saul's court; now Saul begins to take real notice of him.

17:55 And when Saul saw David go forth against the Philistine, he said unto Abner, the captain of the host, Abner, whose son is this youth? And Abner said, As thy soul liveth, O king, I cannot tell. **17:56** And the king said, Enquire thou whose son the stripling is.

General Abner brings David and introduces him to king Saul.

17:57 And as David returned from the slaughter of the Philistine, Abner took him, and brought him before Saul with the head of the Philistine in his hand. **17:58** And Saul said to him, Whose son art thou, thou young man? And David answered, I am the son of thy servant Jesse the Bethlehemite.

1 Samuel 18

Jonathan who had proved his zeal and courage by taking on the Philistines in the name of YHVH meets David the champion of Israel who defeated Goliath in the name of YHVH. Obviously they were both men of faith and of courageous action based on their faith, and they become the closest of fast friends.

The lesson here concerns the unity that springs from a mutual zeal and faith to follow the Eternal. Simply getting along while disagreeing on the things that matter is not spiritual unity!

It is true and passionate unity with Jesus Christ, God the Father and the whole Word of God to learn it and to keep it; that brings true spiritual unity with all others who are also united with God!

1 Samuel 18:1 And it came to pass, when he had made an end of speaking unto Saul, that the soul [heart, spirit] of Jonathan was knit with the soul of David, and Jonathan loved him as his own soul.

Saul kept David where he could see him and control him, suspecting that the fame of David surpassed even his own.

18:2 And Saul took him that day, and would let him go no more home to his father's house. **18:3** Then Jonathan and David made a covenant, because he loved him as his own soul.

David and Jonathan made a covenant of friendship.

18:4 And Jonathan stripped himself of the robe that was upon him, and gave it to David, and his garments, even to his sword, and to his bow, and to his girdle.

Saul made David the Chief of Staff of his army, and David began to learn the art of war and practiced it under Saul, helping Saul to defeat the enemies of Israel round about them. So the fame of David grew while Saul diminished in the love and respect of the people because of his bouts of madness.

David was not given the kingdom when he was called by God through Samuel but was first trained in how to lead. He also gained a reputation for godliness by his righteous faithful conduct; even being loyal as far as he could be to a bad king.

David obeyed the king in the LORD, but David never obeyed the king to commit sin!

Just like David, the called out and anointed of the New Covenant must be trained up and gain experience and establish a reputation of godliness before God and man. We must prepare ourselves to rule and teach the earth through the struggles in our own physical lives.

Did you think that "Preaching the Gospel" was only about warning humanity today? No, there is far more to it than that: in doing so we are learning to lead the whole of humanity in his kingdom!

Therefore if we water down the gospel into a business model outreach, finding out what the people think they need or want and pandering to that instead of diligently teaching the whole Word of God, we disqualify ourselves from taking part in the resurrection to spirit.

If we set an example of compromise and situation ethics to do whatever we want, with no zeal to live by every Word of God: We are unfit to be a part of the Bride of Christ!

18:5 And David went out whithersoever Saul sent him, and behaved himself wisely: and **Saul set him over the men of war**, and **he was accepted in the sight of all the people, and also in the sight of Saul's servants.**

Saul kept David under close scrutiny because of the rejoicing among the people at the victory over Goliath and the Philistines.

Even so Satan keeps a watchful eye on those who are zealous for the whole Word of God, with the courage to follow the Lamb wherever he goes. Satan KNOWS that we are qualifying to replace him and his government [like David was qualifying to replace Saul] and he is doing his best to obstruct, discourage and tempt us to turn aside and fail.

18:6 And it came to pass as they came, when David was returned from the slaughter of the Philistine, that the women came out of all cities of Israel, singing and dancing, to meet king Saul, with tabrets, with joy, and with instruments of musick.

When we stand solidly on the foundation of the whole Word of God we are mocked and attacked by others; yet some are establishing a reputation of faithfulness and godliness that cannot be denied, and we are being prepared to gain eternal life and a kingdom under the Lord that we faithfully follow.

18:7 And the women answered one another as they played, and said, **Saul hath slain his thousands, and David his ten thousands. 18:8** And Saul was very wroth, and the saying displeased him; and he said, They have ascribed unto David ten thousands, and to me they have ascribed but thousands: and what can he have more but the

kingdom? **18:9 And Saul eyed David from that day and forward.**

The day after they returned from victory over the Philistines; Saul is taken by a sudden impulse to slay the man he had just appointed his military leader, David; who Saul now sees as his competitor for the throne.

18:10 And it came to pass **on the morrow**, that the evil spirit from God came upon Saul, and he prophesied in the midst of the house: and David played with his hand, as at other times: and there was a javelin in Saul's hand. **18:11** And **Saul cast the javelin; for he said, I will smite David even to the wall with it. And David avoided out of his presence twice.**

Brethren, Satan alternately attacks and tempts us because he is AFRAID of us and our potential to replace him!

Make no mistake, Satan KNOWS that his time is close to an end and he knows that God is not with him but is with his faithful: and Satan is AFRAID of those who are passionately zealous to follow the God the Father and the Lamb of God and keep his Word!

Why should we fear and try to alleviate our physical situations by compromising with the Word of our Mighty Deliverer, when that will only bring us to our own destruction? Why should we fear the being who is terrified of US and trying to turn us aside from our calling to replace him?

Why should we fear the evil one, when we have been called to God the Father and the Mighty Deliverer and Great ROCK of our Salvation, Jesus Christ, the Being who has conquered Satan, sin and DEATH itself?

18:12 And Saul was afraid of David, because the LORD was with him, and was departed from Saul.

After a short time Saul sent David away and demoted him to be a captain over a garrison of a thousand.

18:13 Therefore Saul removed him from him, and made him his captain over a thousand; and he went out and came in before the people.

Yet David remained faithful to the whole Word of God and to Saul as far as God's Word would allow.

18:14 And David behaved himself wisely in all his ways; and the LORD was with him.

Saul was hoping that David would make a mistake and rebel or somehow displease God as he himself had done; and when David proved faithful the fear of Saul increased.

The more we grow in true zeal and faithfulness for the whole Word of God; the more the fear and anger of Satan also increases; until he is beside himself with terror and rage at his imminent downfall.

18:15 Wherefore when Saul saw that he behaved himself very wisely, he was afraid of him.

In all this the brethren began to love David because of his righteous example before them and for all his mighty deeds of faith.

18:16 But all Israel and Judah loved David, because he went out and came in before them.

Then Saul devises a stratagem to have David killed by the Philistines.

18:17 And Saul said to David, Behold my elder daughter Merab, her will I give thee to wife: only be thou valiant for me, and fight the LORD's battles. For Saul said, Let not mine hand be upon him, but let the hand of the Philistines be upon him.

David expresses humility at the offer of the king and Merab was given to another.

18:18 And David said unto Saul, Who am I? and what is my life, or my father's family in Israel, that I should be son in law to the king? **18:19** But it came to pass at the time when Merab Saul's daughter should have been given to David, that she was given unto Adriel the Meholathite to wife.

Then Saul used his younger daughter Michal]Me-khal] as a snare to try and kill David.

18:20 And Michal Saul's daughter loved David: and they told Saul, and the thing pleased him. **18:21** And Saul said, I will give him her, that she may be a snare to him, and that the hand of the Philistines may be against him. Wherefore Saul said to David, Thou shalt this day be my son in law in the one of the twain.

Saul asks his servants to entice David to take Michal as his wife.

18:22 And Saul commanded his servants, saying, Commune with David secretly, and say, Behold, the king hath delight in thee, and all his servants love thee: now therefore be the king's son in law. **18:23** And Saul's servants spake those words in the ears of David. And David said, Seemeth it to you a light thing to be a king's son in law, seeing that I am a poor man, and lightly esteemed? **18:24** And the servants of Saul told him, saying, On this manner spake David.

Then Saul asks for a dowry not of money but of Philistines.

18:25 And Saul said, Thus shall ye say to David, The king desireth not any dowry, but **an hundred foreskins of the Philistines, to be avenged of the king's enemies. But Saul thought to make David fall by the hand of the Philistines.**

18:26 And when his servants told David these words, it pleased David well to be the king's son in law: and [David rose up to attack the Philistines] the days were not expired. **18:27** Wherefore David arose and went, he and his men, and **slew of the Philistines two hundred men**; and David brought their foreskins, and they gave them in full tale to the king, that he might be the king's son in law. And Saul gave him Michal his daughter to wife.

David then brought Saul double what he had requested for his daughter; and Saul was even more jealous of David's fame and the approval of the people for David was increased.

18:28 And Saul saw and knew that the LORD was with David, and that Michal Saul's daughter loved him. **18:29** And **Saul was yet the more afraid of David; and Saul became David's enemy continually.**

18:30 Then the princes of the Philistines went forth: and it came to pass, after they went forth, that **David behaved himself more wisely than all the servants of Saul; so that his name was much set by.**

1 Samuel 19

Saul became enraged and commanded that David should be killed.

1 Samuel 19:1 And Saul spake to Jonathan his son, and to all his servants, that they should kill David.

But Saul's son Jonathan who had made a covenant of friendship with David reported the matter to David.

19:2 But Jonathan Saul's son delighted much in David: and Jonathan told David, saying, Saul my father seeketh to kill thee: now therefore, I pray thee, take heed to thyself until the morning, and abide in a secret place, and hide thyself: **19:3** And I will go out and stand beside my father in the field where thou art, and I will commune with my father of thee; and what I see, that I will tell thee.

Jonathan intercedes with his father for David and Saul relents.

19:4 And Jonathan spake good of David unto Saul his father, and said unto him, Let not the king sin against his servant, against David; because he hath not sinned against thee, and because his works have been to thee-ward very good: **19:5** For he did put his life in his hand, and slew the Philistine, and the LORD wrought a great salvation for all Israel: thou sawest it, and didst rejoice: wherefore then wilt thou sin against innocent blood, to slay David without a cause? **19:6** And Saul hearkened unto the voice of Jonathan: and Saul sware, As the LORD liveth, he shall not be slain.

Jonathan sought to bring peace between Saul and his friend David.

19:7 And Jonathan called David, and Jonathan shewed him all those things. And Jonathan brought David to Saul, and he was in his presence, as in times past.

Then another occasion arose to inflame the jealousy of Saul. By now we should be able to see that Satan was inflaming Saul to destroy David.

Satan uses men and inspires them to fulfill his agenda, but Almighty God is fully able to work all things out for his glory and the good of all those who love him enough to do his will.

The closer we are to God the more Satan will fear us and the more he will attack or try to tempt us to turn aside.

19:8 And there was war again: and David went out, and fought with the Philistines, and slew them with a great slaughter; and they fled from him. **19:9** And the evil spirit from the LORD was upon Saul, as he sat in his house with his javelin in his hand: and David played [music] with his hand.

Saul thrust his javelin against David and David eluded the thrust which penetrated the wall, and David hid himself and later escaped in the night.

19:10 And Saul sought to smite David even to the wall with the javelin: but he slipped away out of Saul's presence, and he smote the javelin into the wall: and David fled, and escaped that night.

David runs home where Michal his wife bids him flee for she knows her father.

19:11 Saul also sent messengers unto David's house, to watch him, and to slay him in the morning: and Michal David's wife told him, saying, If thou save not thy life to night, to morrow thou shalt be slain. **19:12** So Michal let David down through a window: and he went, and fled, and escaped.

Michal then delays the assassins

19:13 And Michal took an image, and laid it in the bed, and put a pillow of goats' hair for his bolster, and covered it with a cloth. **19:14** And when Saul sent messengers to take David, she said, He is sick. **19:15** And Saul sent the messengers again to see David, saying, Bring him up to me in the bed, that I may slay him. **19:16** And when the messengers were come in, behold, there was an image in the bed, with a pillow of goats' hair for his bolster.

David flees to Samuel at Naioth; while Michal justifies herself to Saul.

19:17 And Saul said unto Michal, Why hast thou deceived me so, and sent away mine enemy, that he is escaped? And Michal answered Saul, He said unto me, Let me go; why should I kill thee? **19:18** So David fled, and escaped, and came to Samuel to Ramah, and told him all that Saul had done to him. And he and Samuel went and dwelt in Naioth. **19:19** And it was told Saul, saying, Behold, David is at Naioth in Ramah.

Saul then sent assassins to Naioth and God defended David, overcoming Saul's agents by the Holy Spirit. God Spirit does not dwell within the unrepentant, but God's Spirit can certainly inspire an action in an unconverted person so that God's will is done; we see this with Cyrus who God inspired.

19:20 And Saul sent messengers to take David: and when they saw the company of the prophets prophesying, and Samuel standing as appointed over them, the **Spirit of God was upon the messengers of Saul, and they also prophesied.**

The same thing happened a second and a third time

19:21 And when it was told Saul, he sent other messengers, and they prophesied likewise. And Saul sent messengers again the third time, and they prophesied also.

Then Saul went himself and was also taken by the Spirit of God. This reveals that God's Spirit can WORK with and inspire a person without being IN that person.

God can use anyone for his purposes; however his Spirit is only given to dwell within the sincerely repentant who commit to zealously live by every Word of God and to go and sin no more! (Acts 5:32)

19:22 Then went he [Saul] also to Ramah, and came to a great well that is in Sechu: and he asked and said, Where are Samuel and David? And one said, Behold, they be at Naioth in Ramah. **19:23** And he went thither to Naioth in Ramah: and the Spirit of God was upon him also, and he went on, and prophesied, until he came to Naioth in Ramah.

19:24 And he stripped off his clothes [he removed his royal robes to his undergarments] also, and prophesied before Samuel in like manner, and lay down naked all that day and all that night. Wherefore they say, Is Saul also among the prophets?

1 Samuel 20

Jonathan meets with David to warn him. Consider the depth of the love of Jonathan for God and for David. Jonathan quite probably knew that David would replace him as king because of the sins of his father Saul, yet Jonathan still loved David and in no way sought to destroy or supplant him like Saul did.

1 Samuel 20:1 And David fled from Naioth in Ramah, and came and said before Jonathan, What have I done? what is mine iniquity? and what is my sin before thy father, that he seeketh my life? **20:2** And he said unto him, God forbid; thou shalt not die: behold, my father will do nothing either great or small, but that he will shew it me: and why should my father hide this thing from me? it is not so.

David replied that Saul knows of the friendship between himself and Jonathan and will surely keep these matters secret from Jonathan.

20:3 And David sware moreover, and said, Thy father certainly knoweth that I have found grace in thine eyes; and he saith, Let not Jonathan know this, lest he be grieved: but truly as the LORD liveth, and as thy soul liveth, there is but a step between me and death. **20:4** Then said Jonathan unto David, Whatsoever thy soul desireth, I will even do it for thee.

David then said that tomorrow is the new moon which is a Feast of the Lord [for feasting on the special new moon sacrifices]; and that he will hide away from Saul today, tomorrow the new moon day; and then on the third day Jonathan should bring him news.

Before Hezekiah the moon cycle was exactly 12 thirty day months making a 360 day year, then the solar/lunar cycle changed and after Hezekiah the Sanhedrin [the 70] set the new moons at Jerusalem and also set the new year from Jerusalem. They did not go searching across the nation but set the new year by the barley in the immediate vicinity of Jerusalem where it would be cut when the nation was to be gathered at Jerusalem for the Feast. See the Calendar articles at theshiniglight.info for more.

There is no mystery in how Saul, David and Israel knew it would be the New Moon the next day since before about the eighth century B.C. the moon rode the sky in the precise 30 day cycles of original creation; the new moon would have begun at the end of the 30th day every month.

The change in the moon's cycle to an average of twenty-nine and one half days did not take place until about the eighth century B. C.

Originally there were 12 thirty day months in a solar year, this changed later and they had to be much more careful about establishing the new moon and began to intercalate to keep the months in line with the solar year.

Early civilizations around the world used calendars with months of 30 days and years of 360 days. These calendars functioned well until sometime in the 8th century B.C. when suddenly it became necessary to change them. Then most civilizations around the world began to modify their calendars to allow for 5 extra days for the year and 6 fewer days for a lunar year of 12 full months; a modern lunar year is 354 days (12 months x 29.5 days).

The number of days in a year change was marked by the second King of Rome, Numa Pompilius, and by his Jewish contemporary, King Hezekiah. Later other civilizations adopted the new 365 day solar year as well. These events are linked by some with the shadow on the sundial going back 10 degrees in the days of Hezekiah.

There was a change in the number of days in a solar year and in the lunar month in about the 8th century B.C. which made setting the new moon more difficult and necessitated the intercalation of a 13th month every so often to keep the lunar year in line with seasons and the solar year about the time of Hezekiah.

This Biblical Calendar continued after that through the days of Jesus Christ until the apostate modern Rabbinic Calendar was finalized; changing from the scriptural first light of the new moon to begin months, to start the Rabbinic months with the darkness of conjunctions in 1178 A.D.

20:5 And David said unto Jonathan, Behold, to morrow is the new moon, and I should not fail to sit with the king at meat: but let me go, that I may hide myself in the field unto the third day at even. **20:6** If thy father at all miss me, then say, David earnestly asked leave of me that he might run to Bethlehem his city: for there is a yearly sacrifice there for all the family.

David believed that Saul was set to kill him when he came to the new moon feast; and therefore Saul would be very angry to find David not present.

20:7 If he say thus, It is well; thy servant shall have peace: but **if he be very wroth, then be sure that evil is determined by him.**

The two men then remember their covenant and pledged their friendship anew.

20:8 Therefore thou shalt deal kindly with thy servant; for thou hast brought thy servant into a covenant of the LORD with thee: notwithstanding, if there be in me iniquity, slay me thyself; for why shouldest thou bring me to thy father? **20:9** And Jonathan said, Far be it from thee: for if I knew certainly that evil were determined by my father to come upon thee, then would not I tell it thee?

Then David asked how he will be told, what if Saul is angry with Jonathan as well?

20:10 Then said David to Jonathan, Who shall tell me? or what if thy father answer thee roughly? **20:11** And Jonathan said unto David, Come, and let us go out into the field. And they went out both of them into the field.

Jonathan and David again pledge their loyalty and friendship.

Consider that Jonathan is being disloyal to his father and to the king, in order to be loyal to David and to what is right before God. Jonathan lives by the Word of God and not by the word of the king.

In this story Saul as king of physical Israel, pictures the bad leaders in today's Spiritual Ekklesia who are leading the brethren away from any zeal for the Word of God to follow after themselves; teaching that they are God's shepherds and that the people must follow them, thus leading them astray.

Saul is a type of apostasy from God the Father and Jesus Christ, while David and Jonathan are a type of the deep, deep, passionate love and faithfulness between God the Father and Jesus Christ and their faithful friends.

Remember that anyone who says that he loves Jesus and then refuses to DO what the Word of God teaches and commands; is NO FRIEND of Jesus Christ!

The called out to God the Father and Jesus Christ must always put God the Father and Jesus Christ and every Word of God FIRST; before and above the words of any men.

20:12 And Jonathan said unto David, O LORD God of Israel, when I have sounded my father about to morrow any time, or the third day, and, behold, if there be good toward David, and I then send not unto thee, and shew it thee; **20:13** The LORD do so and much more to Jonathan: but if it please my father to do thee evil, then I will shew it thee, and send thee away, that thou mayest go in peace: and the LORD be with thee, as he hath been with my father.

Jonathan, understanding that David will be king in his place someday asks David to show him kindness when he is exalted; because Jonathan loved him and spared his life.

Jonathan knows that God will destroy all the enemies of David and that David will be king.

Friends, in this story David is an allegory of Jesus Christ enduring much persecution to be given the kingdom by God the Father; and Jonathan is an allegory of the faithful love of Christ's friends.

> **John 15:14** Ye are my friends, **if ye do whatsoever I command you.** [Jesus Christ inspired the whole Word of God] **15:15** Henceforth I call you not servants; for the servant knoweth not what his lord doeth: but I have called you friends; for all things that I have heard of my Father I have made known unto you.

Oh, that we are as faithful to our friend Jesus Christ, as Jonathan was to David: To be absolutely true blue dependable friends to follow Christ, to please him and to keep the Word and ways of God in Christ-like zeal without any hint of compromise, to love him in deeds as well as in words!

If we are as faithful to the whole Word of God and to the New Covenant of our baptismal commitment as Jonathan was to David; we shall surely dwell with the mercy and loving kindness of the LORD of our covenant forever!

1 Samuel 20:14 And thou shalt not only while yet I live shew me the kindness of the LORD, that I die not: **20:15 But also thou shalt not cut off thy kindness from my house for ever**: no, not when the LORD hath cut off the enemies of David every one from the face of the earth.

Jonathan made a covenant with David; accepting that David would be king and pledging that Jonathan would follow and serve David forever.

This is the same covenant that we make with Jesus Christ at our baptism; that he is our King and that we will serve him fully, faithfully; and with the passion of the deepest strongest love forever.

Oh, the foolishness and ignorance of those selfish souls who say they love Jesus and then reject any zeal to live by every Word of God, to please him and to love him in words and deeds.

20:16 So Jonathan made a covenant with the house of David, saying, Let the LORD even require it at the hand of David's enemies. **20:17** And Jonathan caused David to swear again, because he loved him: for he loved him as he loved his own soul.

Jonathan then instructs David in how he should be contacted

20:18 Then Jonathan said to David, To morrow is the new moon: and thou shalt be missed, because thy seat will be empty. **20:19** And when thou hast stayed three days, then thou shalt go down quickly, and come to the place where thou didst hide thyself when the business was in hand, and shalt remain by the stone Ezel.

20:20 And I will shoot three arrows on the side thereof, as though I shot at a mark. **20:21** And, behold, I will send a lad, saying, Go, find out the arrows. If I expressly say unto the lad, Behold, the arrows are on this side of thee, take them; then come thou: for there is peace to thee, and no hurt; as the LORD liveth. **20:22** But if I say thus unto the young man, Behold, the arrows are beyond thee; go thy way: for the LORD hath sent thee away.

Jonathan again says that his covenant with David is a vow before God forever. Even so our baptismal covenant commitment is an eternal vow of love and commitment to serve the coming King of the world.

20:23 And as touching the matter which thou and I have spoken of, behold, the LORD be between thee and me for ever.

David waited but I expect that David knew the answer, and that this was for the sake of Jonathan so that he might know full well the depth of his father's hatred. In this situation Saul was a type of Satan who is full of fear, frustration and anger that he will lose his kingdom to one better than himself.

20:24 So David hid himself in the field: and when the new moon was come, the king sat him down to eat meat.

The new moon sacrificial feast begins and Saul thinks that perhaps David is not present because of uncleanness. Yes, God did command us to observe the new moons and to be physically and spiritually clean.

20:25 And the king sat upon his seat, as at other times, even upon a seat by the wall: and Jonathan arose, and Abner sat by Saul's side, and David's place was empty. **20:26** Nevertheless Saul spake not any thing that day: for he thought, Something hath befallen him, he is not clean; surely he is not clean.

On the second day of the month Saul asks Jonathan why David is not present. For if David was unclean for the feast he should have showed up the day after the new moon feast.

20:27 And it came to pass on the morrow, which was the second day of the month, that David's place was empty: and Saul said unto Jonathan his son, Wherefore cometh not the son of Jesse to meat, neither yesterday, nor to day?

Jonathan then gives an answer.

20:28 And Jonathan answered Saul, David earnestly asked leave of me to go to Bethlehem: **20:29** And he said, Let me go, I pray thee; for our family hath a sacrifice in the city; and my brother, he hath commanded me to be there: and now, if I have found favour in thine eyes, let me get away, I pray thee, and see my brethren. Therefore he cometh not unto the king's table.

Saul erupts in fury against Jonathan; informing him that he is giving away the kingdom to David. Here we see clearly that Saul understood that David would be given the kingdom and that his hatred of David was political.

20:30 Then Saul's anger was kindled against Jonathan, and he said unto him, Thou son of the perverse rebellious woman, do not I know that thou hast chosen the son of Jesse to thine own confusion, and unto the confusion of thy mother's nakedness? **20:31** For **as long as the son of Jesse liveth upon the ground, thou shalt not be established, nor thy kingdom.** Wherefore now send and fetch him unto me, for he shall surely die.

Jonathan then demands to know what David has done to deserve to die; and Saul makes his intentions very clear.

20:32 And Jonathan answered Saul his father, and said unto him, Wherefore shall he be slain? what hath he done? **20:33** And Saul cast a javelin at him to smite him: whereby Jonathan knew that it was determined of his father to slay David.

Jonathan left the table because he, the supposed crown prince, had been humiliated before the nobles by the king; Jonathan grieving also for his father's apostasy and Saul's commitment to destroy David.

20:34 So Jonathan arose from the table in fierce anger, and did eat no meat the second day of the month: for he was grieved for David, because his father had done him shame.

Jonathan then goes to the appointed place and warns David of Saul's determination to kill him.

20:35 And it came to pass in the morning, that Jonathan went out into the field at the time appointed with David, and a little lad with him. **20:36** And he said unto his lad, Run, find out now the arrows which I shoot. And as the lad ran, he shot an arrow beyond him. **20:37** And when the lad was come to the place of the arrow which Jonathan had shot, Jonathan cried after the lad, and said, Is not the arrow beyond thee? **20:38** And Jonathan cried after the lad, Make speed, haste, stay not. And Jonathan's lad gathered up the arrows, and came to his master. **20:39** But the lad knew not any thing: only Jonathan and David knew the matter.

Jonathan sent his servant away and stayed to speak with David.

20:40 And Jonathan gave his artillery unto his lad, and said unto him, Go, carry them to the city.

Jonathan knew that God had given his, Jonathan's, kingdom to David, because of the sins of his father Saul!

Oh, how Jonathan loved God and was willing to give up 'his' kingdom to love and obey God's judgment, and for the love of his friend David!

20:41 And as soon as the lad was gone, David arose out of a place toward the south, and fell on his face to the ground, and bowed himself three times: and they kissed one another, and wept one with another, until David exceeded.

20:42 And Jonathan said to David, Go in peace, **forasmuch as we have sworn both of us in the name of the LORD, saying, The LORD be between me and thee, and between my seed and thy seed for ever.** And he arose and departed: and Jonathan went into the city.

1 Samuel 21

David fled to the High Priest at Nob and starving he asked for bread.

1 Samuel 21:1 Then came David to Nob to Ahimelech the priest: and Ahimelech was afraid at the meeting of David, and said unto him, Why art thou alone, and no man with thee? **21:2** And David said unto Ahimelech the priest, The king hath commanded me a business, and hath said unto me, Let no man know any thing of the business whereabout I send thee, and what I have commanded thee: and I have appointed my servants to such and such a place.

Clearly David was accompanied by soldiers who were loyal to God and to David, who was God's anointed but not yet crowned, king of Israel.

21:3 Now therefore what is under thine hand? give me five loaves of bread in mine hand, or what there is present. **21:4** And the priest answered David, and said, There is no common bread under mine hand, but there is hallowed bread; **if the young men have kept themselves at least from women.**

David points out that the bread, now removed from the tables of the Lord was in a manner common, no longer being on the table before God.

We must understand that David had been fleeing from Saul for three days without food and they were weak and about to be overtaken and murdered because of their hunger.

21:5 And David answered the priest, and said unto him, Of a truth women have been kept from us about these three days, since I came out, and the vessels of the young men are holy, and the bread is in a manner common, yea, though it were sanctified this day in the vessel. **21:6** So the priest gave him hallowed bread: **for there was no bread there but the shewbread, that was taken from before the LORD,** to put hot bread in the day when it was taken away.

Doeg was there to worship God; but he was a servant of Saul who valued the immediate physical reward promised by Saul more than he valued obedience to God.

21:7 Now a certain man of the servants of Saul was there that day, detained before the LORD; and his name was Doeg, an Edomite, the chiefest of the herdmen that belonged to Saul.

David asked the high priest for a weapon, and is given the sword of Goliath.

21:8 And David said unto Ahimelech, And is there not here under thine hand spear or sword? for I have neither brought my sword nor my weapons with me, because the king's business required haste. **21:9** And the priest said, The sword of Goliath the Philistine, whom thou slewest in the valley of Elah, behold, it is here wrapped in a cloth behind the ephod: if thou wilt take that, take it: for there is no other save that here. And David said, There is none like that; give it me.

David fled to the Philistines but becomes greatly afraid when his identity is made known. Here David has a crisis of faith and we need to learn from this episode to trust in our Mighty One and not to fail in our faith no matter what our fears. David made many mistakes in his life, but when he became aware of them he repented quickly and deeply.

The degree of a person's conversion can be judged by how quickly and how sincerely they repent:

    1. How zealous we are to learn and to keep the whole Word of God.

    2. How quickly we repent when a sin becomes known to us.

    3. How sincerely and thoroughly we repent, so that the sin is not repeated; or whether we take the satanic position of justifying and excusing our sin.

21:10 And David arose and fled that day for fear of Saul, and went to Achish the king of Gath. **21:11** And the servants of Achish said unto him,

Is not this **David the king** [by this time everyone in the region knew that David was the anointed king of Israel] of the land? did they not sing one to another of him in dances, saying, Saul hath slain his thousands, and David his ten thousands? **21:12** And David laid up these words in his heart, and was sore afraid of Achish the king of Gath.

David plays the mad man to save himself from the superstitious Philistines; in this fearing these wicked men more than he trusted in the deliverance of God. Surely David learned a hard lesson that day when he, the anointed king, slinked away in disgrace.

Brethren, the issue in our lives is not whether we have problems or breakdowns of faith: All people have problems and trials of faith!

The issue is how we deal with our missteps!

Do we destroy our spiritual house by justifying ourselves to protect our pride in ourselves and our own ways? Or do we build up our spiritual character house, by sincerely and carefully considering our sins and then deeply sincerely repenting, grinding our personal pride to powder before our God and resolving with all our hearts to go and sin no more with God's help?

21:13 And he changed his behaviour before them, and feigned himself mad in their hands, and scrabbled on the doors of the gate, and let his spittle fall down upon his beard. **21:14** Then said Achish unto his servants, Lo, ye see the man is mad: wherefore then have ye brought him to me? **21:15** Have I need of mad men, that ye have brought this fellow to play the mad man in my presence? shall this fellow come into my house?

1 Samuel 22

1 Samuel 22:1 David therefore departed thence, and escaped to **the cave Adullam: and when his brethren and all his father's house heard it, they went down thither to him.**

22:2 And every one that was in distress, and every one that was in debt, and every one that was discontented, gathered themselves unto him; and he became a captain over them: and there were with him about four hundred men.

David's parents were given a safe haven in Moab, and the downtrodden gathered around David. Indeed even today it is mostly the downtrodden that are called to gather themselves to God the Father and Jesus Christ, see the parable of the wedding in Matthew 22.

22:3 And David went thence to Mizpeh of Moab: and he said unto the king of Moab, Let my father and my mother, I pray thee, come forth, and be with you, **till I know what God will do for me. 22:4** And he brought them before the king of Moab: and they dwelt with him all the while that David was in the hold.

God warned David by his prophet Gad to leave his redoubt. When we wait upon God to do as he wills; all things work together for God's glory and for our good.

22:5 And the prophet Gad said unto David, Abide not in the hold; depart, and get thee into the land of Judah. Then David departed, and came into the forest of Hareth.

Saul then offers great rewards to his tribe of Benjamin if they would kill David. When we are zealously faithful to God, Satan does all that he can to destroy our faith and zeal and to turn us aside from qualifying to replace himself.

22:6 When Saul heard that David was discovered, and the men that were with him, (now Saul abode in Gibeah under a tree in Ramah, having his spear in his hand, and all his servants were standing about him;) **22:7** Then Saul said unto his servants that stood about him, Hear now, ye Benjamites; will the son of Jesse give every one of you fields and vineyards, and make you all captains of thousands, and captains of hundreds;

Doeg then betrays David and the high priest to Saul.

22:8 That all of you have conspired against me, and there is none that sheweth me that my son hath made a league with the son of Jesse, and there is none of you that is sorry for me, or sheweth unto me that my son hath stirred up my servant against me, to lie in wait, as at this day? **22:9** Then answered Doeg the Edomite, which was set over the servants of Saul, and said, I saw the son of Jesse coming to Nob, to Ahimelech the son of Ahitub. **22:10** And he enquired of the LORD for him, and gave him victuals, and gave him the sword of Goliath the Philistine.

Then Saul called the priests and the high priest and his family to come to him.

22:11 Then the king sent to call Ahimelech the priest, the son of Ahitub, and all his father's house, the priests that were in Nob: and they came all of them to the king. **22:12** And Saul said, Hear now, thou son of Ahitub. And he answered, Here I am, my lord.

Saul accused the high priest of conspiring against the king.

22:13 And Saul said unto him, Why have ye conspired against me, thou and the son of Jesse, in that thou hast given him bread, and a sword, and hast enquired of God for him, that he should rise against me, to lie in wait, as at this day?

The high priest pleads ignorance of the dispute between Saul and David.

22:14 Then Ahimelech answered the king, and said, And who is so faithful among all thy servants as David, which is the king's son in law, and goeth at thy bidding, and is honourable in thine house? **22:15** Did I then begin to enquire of God for him? be it far from me: let not the king impute any thing unto his servant, nor to all the house of my father: for thy servant knew nothing of all this, less or more.

Saul then commanded that the high priest and his family be put to death.

22:16 And the king said, Thou shalt surely die, Ahimelech, thou, and all thy father's house.

No man of Israel dared to commit this terrible sin of destroying the godly, no not even at the fear of his own life from the king.

Satan tries his very best to destroy the spiritually faithful; and he may destroy the flesh, but he cannot destroy the spirit unless we allow him to turn us aside into rebellion against any part of the whole Word of God. We are to be zealously faithful to God the Father and Jesus Christ unto our physical death, and if we are, Jesus Christ will raise us up to spirit on that day.

22:17 And the king said unto the footmen that stood about him, Turn, and slay the priests of the LORD: because their hand also is with David, and because they knew when he fled, and did not shew it to me. But the servants of the king would not put forth their hand to fall upon the priests of the LORD.

The Edomite then obeyed the king

Remember that Edom [Esau] despised the birthright of his calling to sell it for a bowl of stew. Will we also despise the birthright of our calling to be priests and kings for eternity in order to exalt men as our idols in place of the Word of God?

22:18 And the king said to Doeg, Turn thou, and fall upon the priests. And Doeg the Edomite turned, and he fell upon the priests, and slew on that day fourscore and five persons [85 priests] that did wear a linen ephod.

Then the Edomite utterly destroyed all the priests, and all that lived in Nob the city of the priests.

If we turn aside from passionately faithfully following every Word of God to obey wicked and deceitful rulers of men, exalting them above the Word of God, we shall be destroyed spiritually. If we are faithful unto godliness to the very death like these priests who were destroyed physically, we shall be raised from the grave of death into life eternal.

22:19 And Nob, the city of the priests, smote he with the edge of the sword, both men and women, children and sucklings, and oxen, and asses, and sheep, with the edge of the sword.

Only one escaped to become the next High Priest and a fellow with David and because of this outrageous act of the king, the priests in the other cities of Israel and the people turned to prefer David above Saul.

22:20 And one of the sons of Ahimelech the son of Ahitub, named Abiathar, escaped, and fled after David. **22:21** And Abiathar shewed David that Saul had slain the LORD's priests.

David pledges to protect Abiathar

22:22 And David said unto Abiathar, I knew it that day, when Doeg the Edomite was there, that he would surely tell Saul: I have occasioned the death of all the persons of thy father's house. **22:23** Abide thou with me, fear not: for he that seeketh my life seeketh thy life: but with me thou shalt be in safeguard.

1 Samuel 23

David continues to fulfill the duty of his calling and anointing, to God and his people and thereby continues to rise in the respect of the people.

Many false teachers have crept into the assemblies today; where they try to destroy the faithful by teaching a false permissive Christ to lead the brethren astray from the Word of God.

Each of us was anointed to become a king and priest of the High Priesthood of Jesus Christ forever (Rev 1:6, 5:10). If we betray our anointing to exalt and obey apostate leaders above the Word of God, by obeying any man contrary to the Word of God we are making such men our idols; and we disqualify ourselves from our calling.

We are to remain faithful to the anointing of our calling and we are not to exalt the words of any man or organization above the Word of God; not even if he is a king, physical high priest, or leader in the Spiritual Ekklesia.

Let us make our calling sure through living by every Word of God; and NOT obeying any man contrary to the Word of God, no not even if he has the power of physical life and death.

1 Samuel 23:1 Then they told David, saying, Behold, the Philistines fight against Keilah, and they rob the threshingfloors. **23:2** Therefore **David enquired of the LORD**, saying, Shall I go and smite these Philistines?

And the LORD said unto David, Go, and smite the Philistines, and save Keilah.

David seeks out the Word of God before taking action!

We should also seek out the Word of God to study it and to pray and seek out God's will, always.

23:3 And David's men said unto him, Behold, we be afraid here in Judah: how much more then if we come to Keilah against the armies of the Philistines? **23:4** Then David enquired of the LORD yet again. And the LORD answered him and said, Arise, go down to Keilah; for I will deliver the Philistines into thine hand. **23:5** So David and his men went to Keilah, and fought with the Philistines, and brought away their cattle, and smote them with a great slaughter. So David saved the inhabitants of Keilah.

The ephod was a cloak of royal blue worn over the ankle length white shirt of a priest

23:6 And it came to pass, when Abiathar the son of Ahimelech fled to David to Keilah, that he came down with an ephod in his hand.

Saul now thinks that he has David trapped and Saul's madness causes him to loose all dignity and pursue a civil war. Only David's restraint keeps a bloody civil war from Israel.

23:7 And it was told Saul that David was come to Keilah. And Saul said, God hath delivered him into mine hand; for he is shut in, by entering into a town that hath gates and bars. **23:8** And Saul called all the people together to war, to go down to Keilah, to besiege David and his men.

David inquires of God by the new high priest, who wore the ephod of his office. The day will come when the chosen will also wear the white linen shirt and the royal blue cloak of the eternal priesthood of their calling.

23:9 And David knew that Saul secretly practised mischief against him; and he said to Abiathar the priest, **Bring hither the ephod. 23:10** Then said David, O LORD God of Israel, thy servant hath certainly heard that Saul seeketh to come to Keilah, to destroy the city for my sake. **23:11** Will the men of Keilah deliver me up into his hand? will Saul come down, as thy servant hath heard? O LORD God of Israel, I beseech thee, tell thy servant. And the LORD said, He will come down.

23:12 Then said David, Will the men of Keilah deliver me and my men into the hand of Saul? And the LORD said, They will deliver thee up.

At the Word of God, David departed Keilah and was saved yet again by obeying and following the Word of God. During this time David was being tested and trained up by God to become a truly godly king.

In the same manner we are called out of this society to be tested, trained and molded into what God wants us to be, in order to prepare us to be rulers and priests of the High Priesthood of Jesus Christ and the kingdom of God for all eternity.

Some of today's called out, like David, will pass the test of total loyalty to God; and others like Doeg will fail that test and instead exalt and obey men above the Word of God, only to be rejected by Jesus Christ from having any part in his faithful collective bride!

23:13 Then David and his men, which were about six hundred, arose and departed out of Keilah, and went whithersoever they could go. And it was told Saul that David was escaped from Keilah; and he forbare to go forth. **23:14** And David abode in the wilderness in strong holds, and remained in a mountain in the wilderness of Ziph. And Saul sought him every day, but God delivered him not into his hand. **23:15** And David saw that Saul was come out to seek his life: and David was in the wilderness of Ziph in a wood.

Jonathan reminds David that he will be king and encourages David in the promises of God.

Let us all be filled with a Jonathan like love of God's Word and decisions, even if it appears to be to our personal disadvantage; and let us be full of love for other like-minded faithful!

23:16 And Jonathan Saul's son arose, and went to David into the wood, **and strengthened his hand in God. 23:17** And he said unto him, Fear not: for the hand of Saul my father shall not find thee; and **thou shalt be king over Israel, and I shall be next unto thee; and that also Saul my father knoweth.**

These two men renewed their covenant before God to the effect that David would be king and Jonathan would stand at his side.

23:18 And **they two made a covenant before the LORD**: and David abode in the wood, and Jonathan went to his house.

Then certain men betrayed David for a reward from Saul; trusting in that rebel against God rather than trusting in the Word of God.

Again the story is a contrast between David's loving faithfulness to God; or an idolatrous faithfulness to the words of men above the Word of God.

Saul and Jonathan and all the people KNEW that David had been anointed and ordained as Saul's successor, yet some were willing to conspire against the Lord's anointed David in order to obey men instead of obeying God.

23:19 Then came up the Ziphites to Saul to Gibeah, saying, Doth not David hide himself with us in strong holds in the wood, in the hill of Hachilah, which is on the south of Jeshimon? **23:20** Now therefore, O king, come down according to all the desire of thy soul to come down; and our part shall be to deliver him into the king's hand.

Saul gives the betrayers his instruction to spy out all the secret places of David.

23:21 And Saul said, Blessed be ye of the LORD; for ye have compassion on me. **23:22** Go, I pray you, prepare yet, and know and see his place where his haunt is, and who hath seen him there: for it is told me that he dealeth very subtilly. **23:23** See therefore, and take knowledge of all the lurking places where he hideth himself, and come ye again to me with the certainty, and I will go with you: and it shall come to pass, if he be in the land, that I will search him out throughout all the thousands of Judah.

David hears that Saul was coming against him and he leaves his abode to go and remain at Maon.

23:24 And they arose, and went to Ziph before Saul: but David and his men were in the wilderness of Maon, in the plain on the south of Jeshimon. **23:25** Saul also and his men went to seek him. And [some warned David] they told David; wherefore he came down into a rock, and abode in the wilderness of Maon. And when Saul heard that, he pursued after David in the wilderness of Maon.

David then escaped to avoid battle with Saul.

23:26 And Saul went on this side of the mountain, and David and his men on that side of the mountain: and David made haste to get away for fear of Saul; for Saul and his men compassed David and his men round about to take them.

Saul was distracted by a Philistine incursion and had to turn aside from pursuing David. Did God send these Philistines to divert Saul? God can use the unconverted to perform his will.

23:27 But there came a messenger unto Saul, saying, Haste thee, and come; for the Philistines have invaded the land. **23:28** Wherefore Saul returned from pursuing after David, and went against the Philistines: therefore they called that place Selahammahlekoth.

The diversion of Saul allowed David to flee to an oasis by the Dead Sea.

23:29 And David went up from thence, and dwelt in strong holds at Engedi.

1 Samuel 24

Saul is told that David is in Engedi and goes there to kill him.

1 Samuel 24:1 And it came to pass, when Saul was returned from following the Philistines, that it was told him, saying, Behold, David is in the wilderness of Engedi. **24:2** Then Saul took three thousand chosen men out of all Israel, and went to seek David and his men upon the rocks of the wild goats.

When one squats down the long ankle length shirt worn in those days covered the feet, hence the expression

24:3 And he came to the sheepcotes by the way, where was a cave; and Saul went in to cover his feet: and David and his men remained in the sides of the cave.

David's men advise him to kill Saul while he is there, but David sneaks up and cuts off a corner of Saul's shirt as it lies on the ground.

24:4 And the men of David said unto him, Behold the day of which the LORD said unto thee, Behold, I will deliver thine enemy into thine hand, that thou mayest do to him as it shall seem good unto thee. Then David arose, and cut off the skirt of Saul's robe privily.

David then repented of his disrespectful action against the king.

24:5 And it came to pass afterward, that David's heart smote him, because he had cut off Saul's skirt. **24:6** And he said unto his men, The LORD forbid that I should do this thing unto my master, the LORD's anointed, to stretch forth mine hand against him, seeing he is the anointed of the LORD.

24:7 So David stayed his servants with these words, and suffered them not to rise against Saul. But Saul rose up out of the cave, and went on his way. **24:8** David also arose afterward, and went out of the cave, and cried after Saul, saying, My lord the king. And when Saul looked behind him, **David stooped with his face to the earth, and bowed himself.**

David then presents his defense against the rumors that he sought to kill Saul.

24:9 And David said to Saul, Wherefore hearest thou men's words, saying, Behold, David seeketh thy hurt? **24:10** Behold, this day thine eyes have seen how that the LORD had delivered thee to day into mine hand in the cave: and some bade me kill thee: but mine eye spared thee; and I said, I will not put forth mine hand against my lord; for he is the LORD's anointed.

David goes so far as to call Saul his father [Saul was David's father in law and the head of the nation], before the armies gathered there.

24:11 Moreover, my father, see, yea, see the skirt of thy robe in my hand: for in that I cut off the skirt of thy robe, and killed thee not, know thou and see that there is neither evil nor transgression in mine hand, and I have not sinned against thee; yet thou huntest my soul to take it. **24:12** The LORD judge between me and thee, and the LORD avenge me of thee: but mine hand shall not be upon thee.

Wickedness proceeds from evil thoughts; evil thoughts are what Paul calls evil concupiscence. We are not to dwell on evil thoughts and plans, but on the goodness of the whole Word of God.

24:13 As saith the proverb of the ancients, **Wickedness proceedeth from the wicked:** but mine hand shall not be upon thee.

David humbles himself before Saul, saying that he [David] is nothing.

24:14 After whom is the king of Israel come out? after whom dost thou pursue? after a dead dog, after a flea. **24:15** The LORD therefore be judge, and judge between me and thee, and see, and plead my cause, and deliver me out of thine hand.

Out of shame Saul then repented of his desire to kill David

24:16 And it came to pass, when David had made an end of speaking these words unto Saul, that Saul said, Is this thy voice, my son David? And Saul lifted up his voice, and wept. **24:17** And he said to David, Thou art more righteous than I: for thou hast rewarded me good, whereas I have rewarded thee evil. **24:18** And thou hast shewed this day how that thou hast dealt well with me: forasmuch as when the LORD had delivered me into thine hand, thou killedst me not. **24:19** For if a man find his enemy, will he let him go well away? wherefore the LORD reward thee good for that thou hast done unto me this day.

Saul acknowledges before the two armies that he knows that David will be king and asks for peace between their houses.

24:20 And now, behold, I know well that thou shalt surely be king, and that the kingdom of Israel shall be established in thine hand. **24:21** Swear now therefore unto me by the LORD, that thou wilt not cut off my seed after me, and that thou wilt not destroy my name out of my father's house.

David swore to Saul, but was distrustful of Saul and remained in hiding.

24:22 And David sware unto Saul. And Saul went home; but David and his men gat them up unto the hold.

1 Samuel 25

1 Samuel 25:1 And Samuel [Hebrew; Shemuel, God has heard] died; and all the Israelites were gathered together, and lamented him, and buried him in his house at Ramah. And David arose, and went down to the wilderness of Paran.

Nabal of Carmel [by Haifa]

This is a classic story of pride and the deceitfulness of riches.

Here we have a very rich man who has been made proud by his wealth and looks down on the poor and weak whom he regards as beneath him; yet Jesus Christ looks on the heart of a person.

In numerous places Christ teaches us not to judge by the seeing of the eyes or by the wealth or poverty of a person; but to judge by the spiritual things of faithfulness to the Word of God. We are told not to depend on physical riches which can vanish in a day; but to seek out and lay up spiritual riches that will last for eternity.

This is also about the pride that brings the downfall of a person; a pride that is so obviously evident in today's Spiritual Ekklesia where they will do anything to cleave to their false traditions against the Word of God.

It is important to realize that the story of Abigail is a lesson for us today.

Abigail was the wife of Nabal and we all know that a wife is to be subject to her husband in the Lord. Here we have a foolish man with a virtuous wife, which can be a problem in some marriages. This is an allegory that we are to be faithful to GOD and his Word first, before any human authority.

When Abigail knew that her husband and family were in jeopardy, she went out to save them, contrary to her husband's wishes.

Brethren, this is an allegory and lesson for US; that we must put the Word of God FIRST, above the words of any man or corporation, no matter what title they call themselves. Abigail did what was right in God's eyes, by serving God and doing what was right and wise by God's Word.

Knowing that God had chosen and anointed David to be king she discretely and wisely did the right thing by the Word of God even though it was contrary to the wishes of her husband; giving us a lesson that we must also wisely obey God above the men who claim authority over us.

Our FIRST obligation is to learn and to live by every Word of God. We are to obey men in authority only so long as they do not require us to sin against the Word of God!

Will we be steadfast to the whole Word of God to do what is wise and right in God's eyes like Abigail? Or will we follow idols of men and the false traditions of men?

25:2 And there was a man in Maon, whose possessions were in Carmel; and the man was very great, and he had three thousand sheep, and a thousand goats: and he was shearing his sheep in Carmel.

Nabal was selfish and nasty, but he had a wise and beautiful wife.

25:3 Now the name of the man was Nabal; and the name of his wife Abigail: and she was a woman of good understanding, and of a beautiful countenance: but the man was churlish and evil in his doings; and **he was of the house of Caleb**.

David hears that Nabal has brought his sheep together for shearing and sends ten men to him to request food from him.

25:4 And David heard in the wilderness that Nabal did shear his sheep. **25:5** And David sent out ten young men, and David said unto the young men, Get you up to Carmel, and go to Nabal, and greet him in my name: **25:6** And thus shall ye say to him that liveth in prosperity, Peace be both to thee, and peace be to thine house, and peace be unto all that thou hast.

When they requested food from him these men told Nabal how they had had peace with his shepherds and had helped them.

25:7 And now I have heard that thou hast shearers: now thy shepherds which were with us, we hurt them not, neither was there ought missing unto them, all the while they were in Carmel.

David's men presented their petition with the greatest respect.

25:8 Ask thy young men, and they will shew thee. Wherefore let the young men find favour in thine eyes: for we come in a good day: give, I pray thee, whatsoever cometh to thine hand unto thy servants, and to thy son David. **25:9** And when David's young men came, they spake to Nabal according to all those words in the name of David, and ceased.

Nabal then ignores the fact that even Saul says that David will be king and prefers to think of David's band as a band of outcasts and runaway servants. He sees and judges with the sight of his eyes and cannot see the heart and spirit of men to judge them as God judges men.

> **Isaiah 11:1** And there shall come forth a rod out of the stem of Jesse, and a Branch shall grow out of his roots: [Jesus Christ; [Hebrew: Yeshua HaMashiach].
>
> **11:2** And the spirit of the Lord shall rest upon him, the spirit of wisdom and understanding, the spirit of counsel and might, the spirit of knowledge and of the fear of the Lord; **11:3** And shall make him of quick understanding in the fear of the Lord: and **he shall not judge after the sight of his eyes, neither reprove after the hearing of his ears:**
>
> **11:4** But with righteousness shall he judge the poor, and reprove with equity for the meek of the earth: and he shall smite the earth: with the rod of his mouth, and with the breath of his lips shall he slay the wicked.

Nabal the rich and lordly despised David as the leader of a band of poor downtrodden outcasts; and Nabal the proud rejected the poor in spirit that God finds acceptable.

1 Samuel 25:10 And Nabal answered David's servants, and said, Who is David? and who is the son of Jesse? there be many servants now a days that break away every man from his master. **25:11** Shall I then take my bread, and my water, and my flesh that I have killed for my shearers, and give it unto men, whom I know not whence they be? **25:12** So David's young men turned their way, and went again, and came and told him all those sayings.

David then took 400 men to punish against Nabal, because after all David is the anointed king.

25:13 And David said unto his men, Gird ye on every man his sword. And they girded on every man his sword; and David also girded on his sword: and there went up after David about four hundred men; and two hundred abode by the stuff.

A servant of Nabal tells has wife Abigail and she rushes to placate the anger of David.

25:14 But one of the young men told Abigail, Nabal's wife, saying, Behold, David sent messengers out of the wilderness to salute our master; and he railed on them. **25:15** But the men were very good unto us, and we were not hurt, neither missed we any thing, as long as we were conversant with them, when we were in the fields: **25:16** They were a wall unto us both by night and day, all the while we were with them keeping the sheep. **25:17** Now therefore know and consider what thou wilt do; for evil is determined against our master, and against all his household: for he is such a son of Belial, that a man cannot [reason with him] speak to him.

Abigail rushes to make peace with David.

25:18 Then Abigail made haste, and took two hundred loaves, and two bottles of wine, and five sheep ready dressed, and five measures of parched corn, and an hundred clusters of raisins, and two hundred cakes of figs, and laid them on asses.

Abigail meets David

25:19 And she said unto her servants, Go on before me; behold, I come after you. But she told not her husband Nabal. **25:20** And it was so, as she rode on the ass, that she came down by the covert on the hill, and, behold, David and his men came down against her; and she met them.

25:21 Now David had said, Surely in vain have I kept all that this fellow hath in the wilderness, so that nothing was missed of all that pertained unto him: and he hath requited me evil for good. **25:22** So and more also do God unto the enemies of David, if I leave of all that pertain to him by the morning light any that pisseth against the wall [no man would be left alive].

Abigail petitions David for the lives of her family and the servants of Nabal.

25:23 And when Abigail saw David, she hasted, and lighted off the ass, and fell before David on her face, and bowed herself to the

ground, **25:24** And fell at his feet, and said, Upon me, my lord, upon me let this iniquity be: and let thine handmaid, I pray thee, speak in thine audience, and hear the words of thine handmaid. **25:25** Let not my lord, I pray thee, regard this man of Belial, even Nabal: for as his name is, so is he; Nabal [fool] is his name, and folly is with him: but I thine handmaid saw not the young men of my lord, whom thou didst send.

25:26 Now therefore, my lord, as the LORD liveth, and as thy soul liveth, seeing the LORD hath withholden thee from coming to shed blood, and from avenging thyself with thine own hand, now let thine enemies, and they that seek evil to my lord, be as Nabal.

25:27 And now this blessing which thine handmaid hath brought unto my lord, let it even be given unto the young men that follow my lord.

Abigail knows that David is a man of God and anointed to be king, a fact which her husband disdained. She adds a little diplomacy by saying that David has not sinned in all his days.

25:28 I pray thee, forgive the trespass of thine handmaid: **for the LORD will certainly make my lord a sure house; because my lord fighteth the battles of the LORD, and evil hath not been found in thee all thy days.**

Abigail speaks of Saul and makes a prophecy of David. This prophecy is for all the people that God has called out, if they will only be faithful to follow God teh Father and Jesus Christ to live by every Word of God.

Brethren, ALL of the called out early harvest have been anointed to become kings and priests of Jesus Christ [Melchizedek], anointed with the Holy Spirit to learn to fulfill those offices in a godly manner.

If we persevere and if we are faithful to learn and to live by every Word of God to follow the Lamb wherever he goes; like David we will overcome the enemy [Satan and sin] by the power of God and enter the Promised Land of eternal life.

25:29 Yet a man [Saul, and for us Satan] is risen to pursue thee, and to seek thy soul: but the soul of my lord [David and the spiritually called out] shall be bound in the bundle of [eternal] life with the LORD thy God; and the souls of thine enemies, [spiritually the enemy is Satan, his demons and sin] them shall he sling out, as out of the middle of a sling. **25:30** And it shall come to pass, when the LORD shall have done to my lord according to all the good that he hath spoken concerning thee, and shall have appointed [and will also exalt God's faithful to the eternal kingship and priesthood of Jesus Christ] thee ruler over Israel;

The phrase: "Obedience is better than sacrifice" means that if we faithfully obey God and do not sin, we would not need to repent and would not need a sacrifice.

25:31 That this shall be no grief unto thee, nor offence of heart unto my lord, either that thou hast shed blood causeless, or that my lord hath avenged himself: but when the LORD shall have dealt well with my lord, then remember thine handmaid.

God used this woman to save David from committing a great sin of murdering many for the sin of one. Always consider very carefully the advice of your wives and others who have proven themselves faithful to God, whatever their physical condition or poverty.

25:32 And David said to Abigail, Blessed be the LORD God of Israel, which sent thee this day to meet me: **25:33** And blessed be thy advice, and blessed be thou, which hast kept me this day from coming to shed blood, and from avenging myself with mine own hand. **25:34** For in very deed, as the LORD God of Israel liveth, which hath kept me back from hurting thee, except thou hadst hasted and come to meet me, surely there had not been left unto Nabal by the morning light any that pisseth against the wall [male].

David accepts the words and food from Abigail and is turned back from his purpose.

25:35 So David received of her hand that which she had brought him, and said unto her, Go up in peace to thine house; see, I have hearkened to thy voice, and have accepted thy person.

Abigail returns home to find her husband having a feast for himself; just like very many of today's church leaders and elders Nabal took all the very best for himself.

25:36 And Abigail came to Nabal; and, behold, he held a feast in his house, like the feast of a king; and Nabal's heart was merry within him, for he was very drunken: wherefore she told him nothing, less or more, until the morning light.

In the morning when Abigail told Nabal all that had happened [she was honest and was no sneak] Nabal fell down dead, for God had judged him.

25:37 But it came to pass in the morning, when the wine was gone out of Nabal, and his wife had told him these things, that his heart died within him, and he became as a stone. **25:38** And it came to pass about ten days after, that **the LORD smote Nabal, that he died.**

The lesson is that the proud who exalt their own ways and seek to be chief among the people in place of God, will be judged.

Then David took Abigail to wife just as Jesus Christ will take his faithful followers who diligently live by every Word of God, to be his collective bride at the marriage of the Lamb before the Father's throne in heaven (Rev 15).

25:39 And when David heard that Nabal was dead, he said, Blessed be the LORD, that hath pleaded the cause of my reproach from the hand of Nabal, and hath kept his servant from evil: for the LORD hath returned the wickedness of Nabal upon his own head. And David sent and communed with Abigail, to take her to him to wife. **25:40** And when the servants of David were come to Abigail to Carmel, they spake unto her, saying, David sent us unto thee, to take thee to him to wife.

Abigail, a type of the virtuous bride of Christ, then agreed to the marriage in godly humility.

So it is that the virtuous who are full of the wisdom of God through internalizing the Word of God and who are passionately zealous to do all that our Lord requires; loving to please him and to internalize his very nature: Will be resurrected to spirit to become a part of the collective bride of Christ at the resurrection to spirit.

Abigail pledged in submissive humility to wash the very feet of David's servants, and our baptismal pledge is to serve God the Father and Jesus Christ in submissive humility for all eternity.

25:41 And she arose, and bowed herself on her face to the earth, and said, Behold, **let thine handmaid be a servant to wash the feet of the servants of my lord. 25:42** And Abigail hasted, and arose and rode upon an ass, with five damsels of hers that went after her; and she went after the messengers of David, and became his wife.

David then had two wives Abigail and Ahinoam; for Saul in his rage had given Michal to another.

25:43 David also took Ahinoam of Jezreel; and they were also both of them his wives. **25:44** But Saul had given Michal his daughter, David's wife, to Phalti the son of Laish, which was of Gallim.

1 Samuel 26

The life of David as the anointed but yet not crowned king of physical Israel is an analogy of the life of the spiritually anointed and not yet crowned New Covenant called out to be kings and priests of the kingdom of God (Rev 1:6, 5:10).

David wrongfully suffered at the hands of king Saul; and those anointed to replace Satan the god-king of this world, also wrongfully suffer at the hands of the spiritual Adversary.

David was tested by God and through his trials he was trained by God to be a good king; and the New Covenant Spiritual Ekklesia are being tested, purged, polished, and trained up to be good kings in the kingdom of God.

David is betrayed again: No wonder David wrote:

> **Psalm 146:3** Put not your trust in princes, nor in the son of man, in whom there is no help.

1 Samuel 26:1 And the Ziphites came unto Saul to Gibeah, saying, Doth not David hide himself in the hill of Hachilah, which is before Jeshimon?

Saul forgot his remorse at the cave and again goes out to kill David.

26:2 Then Saul arose, and went down to the wilderness of Ziph, having three thousand chosen men of Israel with him, to seek David in the wilderness of Ziph. **26:3** And Saul pitched in the hill of Hachilah, which is before Jeshimon, by the way. But David abode in the wilderness, and he saw that Saul came after him into the wilderness.

David learned where the very bed of Saul was and asked for volunteers to enter Saul's camp with him.

26:4 David therefore sent out spies, and understood that Saul was come in very deed. **26:5** And David arose, and came to the place where Saul had pitched: and David beheld the place where Saul lay, and Abner the son of Ner, the captain of his host: and Saul lay in the trench, and the people pitched round about him. **26:6** Then answered David and said to Ahimelech the Hittite, and to Abishai the son of Zeruiah, brother to Joab, saying, Who will go down with me to Saul to the camp? And Abishai said, I will go down with thee.

David's men were willing to destroy Saul, but David rejected their desire that Saul should die so that David might be king. David did not lust for Saul's office and was willing to wait on God to perform God's will.

26:7 So David and Abishai came to the people by night: and, behold, Saul lay sleeping within the trench, and his spear stuck in the ground at his bolster: but Abner and the people lay round about him. **26:8** Then said Abishai to David, God hath delivered thine enemy into thine hand this day: now therefore let me smite him, I pray thee, with the spear even to the earth at once, and I will not [will not need to] smite him the second time.

David continually sets an example of godly humility and forbearance, longsuffering and patience to wait on God rather than exalting himself. Yet David did not follow Saul in Saul's wickedness but lived by every Word of God.

Today we should follow David's example of patient faithfulness to live by every Word of God.

26:9 And David said to Abishai, Destroy him not: for who can stretch forth his hand against the LORD's anointed, and be guiltless? **26:10** David said furthermore, As the LORD liveth, **the LORD shall smite him; or his day shall come to die; or he shall descend into battle, and perish. 26:11** The LORD forbid that I should stretch forth mine hand against the LORD's anointed: but, I pray thee, take thou now the spear that is at his bolster, and the cruse of water, and let us go. **26:12** So David took the spear and the cruse of water from Saul's bolster; and they gat them away, and no man saw it, nor knew it, neither awaked: for they were all asleep; because a deep sleep from the LORD was fallen upon them.

David informs Saul publicly in front of his army, of his mercy to Saul, which only increased the reputation of David among the army and people. Those who exalt and call themselves by great titles fighting for political pre-eminence in the Ekklesia should consider the example of David, and remember the words of Jesus Christ.

> **Matthew 20:25** But Jesus called them unto him, and said, Ye know that **the princes of the Gentiles exercise dominion over them, and they that are great exercise authority upon them. 20:26 But it shall not be so among you:** but whosoever will be great among you, let him be your minister;

The humble submissive service to God and man, is the true lesson of the Passover foot washing.

If we faithfully and zealously serve our God by learning and keeping all of his Word; in due time he will exalt us: If we seek the chief seats for ourselves we will be rejected by God the Father and Jesus Christ as unfit to receive a kingdom; which we would then lead into the same kind of internal strife.

1 Samuel 26:13 Then David went over to the other side, and stood on the top of an hill afar off; a great space being between them: **26:14** And David cried to the people, and to Abner the son of Ner, saying, Answerest thou not, Abner? Then Abner answered and said, Who art thou that criest to the king? **26:15** And David said to Abner, Art not thou a valiant man? and who is like to thee in Israel? wherefore then hast thou not kept thy lord the king? for there came one of the people in to destroy the king thy lord.

David rebuked Abner.

26:16 This thing is not good that thou hast done. As the LORD liveth, ye are worthy to die, because ye have not kept your master, **the LORD's anointed.** And now see where the king's spear is, and the cruse of water that was at his bolster.

Saul responded

26:17 And Saul knew David's voice, and said, Is this thy voice, my son David? And David said, It is my voice, my lord, O king.

David then pronounces a curse on those who had cast him out; and the same curse is pronounced on those who serve their own idols and seek to cast the faithful out of the Synagogues [assemblies] today seeking to turn us aside from our zeal for the Word of God.

26:18 And he said, Wherefore doth my lord thus pursue after his servant? for what have I done? or what evil is in mine hand? **26:19** Now therefore, I pray thee, let my lord the king hear the words of his servant. If the LORD have stirred thee up against me, let him accept an offering: but if they be the children of men, cursed be they before the LORD; for they have driven me out this day from abiding in the inheritance of the LORD, saying, Go, serve other gods.

David then describes himself in humility as nothing and refuses to shed Saul's blood.

26:20 Now therefore, let not my blood fall to the earth before the face of the LORD: for the king of Israel is come out to seek a flea, as when one doth hunt a partridge in the mountains.

The main lesson in all these trials is that we must not try to exalt ourselves. We must wait on the Master Potter to form us into what he desires to see in us, to form us and teach us and train us to be good kings and priests who will receive an everlasting priesthood and kingdom.

God could have struck down Saul at any moment, yet he let Saul live so that he could use Saul to teach David how not to be a king, and to continually test David's loyalty to live by every Word of God, so that God could be absolutely certain that David would not turn out to be another Saul.

David was a king in training and te New Covenant Spiritual Ekklesia are also kings in training.

This is the same reason that Jesus Christ has allowed wicked men to take over today's Spiritual Ekklesia; to TEST our loyalty to God as opposed to any loyalty to men which is idolatry; and by teaching us a lesson of loyalty and zeal to keep the whole Word of God to make us fit to be kings and priests for all eternity.

This is not some game that is going on; the decisions we make, as to who we will follow and the lessons we learn, will determine our fitness to be kings and priests of Jesus Christ and God the Father for all eternity.

The calendar, the new moon's, the sanctity of the Sabbath; are all TESTS, to determine our zeal and loyalty to the Word of God above any zeal for our idols of men.

Saul is again moved by David's words and actions and expressed his remorse.

26:21 Then said Saul, I have sinned: return, my son David: for I will no more do thee harm, because my soul was precious in thine eyes this day: behold, I have played the fool, and have erred exceedingly.

David then sends back Saul's possessions.

26:22 And David answered and said, Behold the king's spear! and let one of the young men come over and fetch it.

Each person will be blessed or cursed by God's judgment in direct proportion to his zeal for the righteousness of learning and living by every Word of God. This applies to US today and to all people for all time.

26:23 The LORD render to every man his righteousness and his faithfulness; for the LORD delivered thee into my hand to day, but I would not stretch forth mine hand against the LORD's anointed.

David then asks Christ to deliver him for his faithfulness to the Word of God.

26:24 And, behold, as thy life was much set by this day in mine eyes, so let my life be much set by in the eyes of the LORD, and let him deliver me out of all tribulation.

26:25 Then Saul said to David, Blessed be thou, my son David: thou shalt both do great things, and also shalt still prevail. So David went on his way, and Saul returned to his place.

1 Samuel 27

David then seeks to escape from Saul and avoid any possible civil war, by going to the Philistines.

1 Samuel 27:1 And David said in his heart, I shall now perish one day by the hand of Saul: there is nothing better for me than that I should speedily escape into the land of the Philistines; and Saul shall despair of me, to seek me any more in any coast of Israel: so shall I escape out of his hand. **27:2** And David arose, and he passed over with the six hundred men that were with him unto Achish, the son of Maoch, king of Gath. **27:3** And David dwelt with Achish at Gath, he and his men, every man with his household, even David with his two wives, Ahinoam the Jezreelitess, and Abigail the Carmelitess, Nabal's wife.

Saul then gives up on David as inaccessible to him

27:4 And it was told Saul that David was fled to Gath: and he sought no more again for him.

Ziklag which sits on the border between Gaza and Judah approximately the modern Israeli town of Sderot was given to David,

27:5 And David said unto Achish, If I have now found grace in thine eyes, let them give me a place in some town in the country, that I may dwell there: for why should thy servant dwell in the royal city with thee? **27:6 Then Achish gave him Ziklag that day: wherefore Ziklag pertaineth unto the kings of Judah unto this day.**

David and his band of 600 dwelt in Ziklag one year and four months, during which time they raided and discomfited the Amalekites, the enemies of Israel.

27:7 And the time that David dwelt in the country of the Philistines was a full year and four months. **27:8** And David and his men went up, and invaded the Geshurites, and the Gezrites, and the Amalekites: for those nations were of old the inhabitants of the land, as thou goest to Shur, even unto the land of Egypt.

David killed many Amalekites and brought back their spoil, deceiving Achish by claiming that the spoil was from raids on Judah. This was a military deception to allow David to continue to fight the enemies of Israel while maintaining a refuge from the king of Israel, a very peculiar situation.

27:9 And David smote the land, and left neither man nor woman alive, and took away the sheep, and the oxen, and the asses, and the camels, and the apparel, and returned, and came to Achish. **27:10** And Achish said, Whither have ye made a road to day? And David said, Against the south of Judah, and against the south of the Jerahmeelites, and against the south of the Kenites.

While he dwelt in Ziklag David continually fought the enemies of Israel, and left none alive to tell about it.

27:11 And David saved neither man nor woman alive, to bring tidings to Gath, saying, Lest they should tell on us, saying, So did David, and so will be his manner all the while he dwelleth in the country of the Philistines.

Achish believed David and thought that David had spoiled Judah and that David was now utterly estranged from Israel, when in fact David was fighting the enemies of Judah.

27:12 And Achish believed David, saying, He hath made his people Israel utterly to abhor him; therefore he shall be my servant for ever.

1 Samuel 28

Achish believing that David was anathema to Israel, called David to fight against Israel alongside the Philistines.

1 Samuel 28:1 And it came to pass in those days, that the Philistines gathered their armies together for warfare, to fight with Israel. And Achish said unto David, Know thou assuredly, that thou shalt go out with me to battle, thou and thy men.

Achish knowing how much spoil David had gained by killing the Amalekites [but thinking that spoil had been taken from Israel] thought that David and Israel were permanently estranged and offered to make David his own body guard.

28:2 And David said to Achish, Surely thou shalt know what thy servant can do. And Achish said to David, Therefore will I make thee keeper of mine head for ever.

Saul facing the battle and not having Samuel to consult and the priests now supporting David, sought someone to consult God for him, and was deceived and tempted into consulting a witch to produce Samuel from the dead.

28:3 Now Samuel was dead, and all Israel had lamented him, and buried him in Ramah, even in his own city. And Saul had put away those that had familiar spirits, and the wizards, out of the land. **28:4** And the Philistines gathered themselves together, and came and pitched in Shunem: and Saul gathered all Israel together, and they pitched in Gilboa. **28:5** And when Saul saw the host of the Philistines, **he was afraid, and his heart greatly trembled**.

Saul tried to consult God, but had been rejected; and since he did not seek God in heartfelt sincere repentance, God would not hear him.

Many who do look into the Word of God at the first, receive no answer because they are not sincerely repentantly submissive to learn and to live by every Word of God.

Saul received no answer because he was not sincerely and faithfully following and living by the Word of God and he was doing what was right in his own eyes like the majority of today's Spiritual Ekklesia. Many love their organizational idols and have no love for the truth, therefore the truth is withheld.

> **2 Thessalonians 2:10** And with all deceivableness of unrighteousness in them that perish; because they received not the love of the truth, that they might be saved. **2:11** And for this cause God shall send them strong delusion, that they should believe a lie: **2:12** That they all might be damned who believed not the truth, but had pleasure in unrighteousness.

Because many follow our idols of men and do not sincerely and zealously follow and live by every Word of God; they are deceived about the beginning of the tribulation and will be rejected by Jesus Christ into the furnace of correction (Rev 3:15-22).

1 Samuel 28:6 And when Saul enquired of the LORD, the LORD answered him not, neither by dreams, nor by Urim, nor by prophets.

At this point we might exclaim how terrible it is to seek out a familiar spirit [demon] about the future or anything else, yet we do exactly the same thing in today's Spiritual Ekklesia! What do I mean with that statement? I mean that whenever we study the teachings and false traditions of men and apply them to keep them, instead of living by every Word of God; we are turning our backs on the Word of God to follow doctrines of familiar [demonic] spirits.

How many of you consult horoscopes in the local papers? How many Assemblies have turned aside from what Jesus Christ commanded us to preach, to a worldly business model organization and outreach? How many organizations use the Nicolaitane [Babylonian Mysteries] government system for church leadership?

Do we not realize that learning false doctrine and false prophecy to follow it, is turning our backs on the Word of God to embrace the ways of the enemy of God?

To willfully seek out the teachings of the enemy to do them, in place of any zeal for the Word of God; is an act of disloyalty to God and his Word, it is rebellion and mutiny against God and his Word.

God's Word says that to obey or follow any person contrary to the whole Word and teachings of God; is idolatry and rebellion against Almighty God. If we follow anyone contrary to the whole Word of God, we will be rejected from our calling.

> **1 Samuel 15:23** For rebellion is as the sin of witchcraft, and stubbornness [to keep our own ways and not submit to God] is as iniquity and idolatry. Because thou hast rejected the word of the Lord, he hath also rejected thee from being king.

1 Samuel 28:7 Then said Saul unto his servants, Seek me a woman that hath a familiar spirit, that I may go to her, and enquire of her. And his servants said to him, Behold, there is a woman that hath a familiar spirit at Endor.

28:8 And Saul disguised himself, and put on other raiment, and he went, and two men with him, and they came to the woman by night: and he said, I pray thee, divine unto me by the familiar spirit, and bring me him up, whom I shall name unto thee. **28:9** And the woman said unto him, Behold, thou knowest what Saul hath done, how he hath cut off those that have familiar spirits, and the wizards, out of the land: wherefore then layest thou a snare for my life, to cause me to die? **28:10** And Saul sware to her by the LORD, saying, As the LORD liveth, there shall no punishment happen to thee for this thing.

A demon appears to them in the form of Samuel and the woman is given recognition of who Saul really was by the demon.

28:11 Then said the woman, Whom shall I bring up unto thee? And he said, Bring me up Samuel. **28:12** And when the woman saw Samuel, she cried with a loud voice: and the woman spake to Saul, saying, Why hast thou deceived me? for thou art Saul.

Saul demands to know what the woman has seen. Today very many are filled with such curiosity that they seek out the teachings of Satan instead of seeking out the truth from the Word of God. She says that she sees an old man and Saul is deceived and jumps to the conclusion that this is Samuel.

Saul bows before an apparition. We also bow before our organizational idols of men: How very many still bow down to some man and keep the words of men contrary to scripture?

28:13 And the king said unto her, Be not afraid: for what sawest thou? And the woman said unto Saul, I saw gods ascending out of the earth. **28:14** And he said unto her, What form is he of? And she said, An old man cometh up; and he is covered with a mantle. And Saul perceived that it was Samuel, and he stooped with his face to the ground, and bowed himself.

Saul then asks the demon what he should do; we still have an opportunity to do what Saul should have done! We should run to God and sincerely repent, committing ourselves to learning and zealously keeping the whole Word of God with all our beings forever! We must love God enough to DO what God says!

28:15 And [the demon appearing as] Samuel said to Saul, Why hast thou disquieted me, to bring me up? And Saul answered, I am sore distressed; for the Philistines make war against me, and God is departed from me, and answereth me no more, neither by prophets, nor by dreams: therefore I have called thee, that thou mayest make known unto me what I shall do.

This evil spirit then tells Saul the truth! Yes evil spirits sometimes speak the truth; but we are to seek God and we are not to turn our backs on God's Word to follow after demons. Every false religion is a mix of truth and error, which is what makes it so enticing and so deceitful, for Satan presents himself as an angel of light.

28:16 Then said Samuel, Wherefore then dost thou ask of me, seeing the LORD is departed from thee, and is become thine enemy? **28:17** And the LORD hath done to him, as he spake by me: for the LORD hath rent the kingdom out of thine hand, and given it to thy neighbour, even to David: **28:18 Because thou obeyedst not the voice of the LORD,** nor executedst his fierce wrath upon Amalek, therefore hath the LORD done this thing unto thee this day.

Brethren, the whole of scripture repeats over and over and over again that we are to obey the Word of God above ALL others, including those who claim to be prophets or apostles (Deu 13).

28:19 Moreover the LORD will also deliver Israel with thee into the hand of the Philistines: and to morrow shalt thou and thy sons be with me [dead]: the LORD also shall deliver the host of Israel into the hand of the Philistines.

Saul was fasting for an answer and yet he would not turn from his own ways to sincerely repent before God.

A fast which is not fasting in sincere repentance and commitment to go and sin no more, is simply a pointless exercise.

WHY fast for spiritual growth, when we will not accept what God is teaching us in his Word? We need to fast the fast of sincere repentance and turn to the Word of God to learn and to keep it in wholehearted Christ-like zeal; then we will begin to grow spiritually!

28:20 Then Saul fell straightway all along on the earth, and was sore afraid, because of the words of Samuel: and there was no strength in him; for he had eaten no bread all the day, nor all the night. **28:21** And the woman came unto Saul, and saw that he was sore troubled, and said unto him, Behold, thine handmaid hath obeyed thy voice, and I have put my life in my hand, and have hearkened unto thy words which thou spakest unto me.

The woman then advises Saul to break his fast because he had fainted, but he refuses her because his heart is very heavy.

28:22 Now therefore, I pray thee, hearken thou also unto the voice of thine handmaid, and let me set a morsel of bread before thee; and eat, that thou mayest have strength, when thou goest on thy way.

When Saul's servants also entreat him, Saul relents and eats.

28:23 But he refused, and said, I will not eat. But his servants, together with the woman, compelled him; and he hearkened unto their voice. So he arose from the earth, and sat upon the bed. **28:24** And the woman had a fat calf in the house; and she hasted, and killed it, and took flour, and kneaded it, and did bake unleavened bread thereof: **28:25** And she brought it before Saul, and before his servants; and they did eat. Then they rose up, and went away that night.

1 Samuel 29

The last battle of Saul

1 Samuel 29:1 Now the Philistines gathered together all their armies to Aphek: and the Israelites pitched by a fountain which is in Jezreel. **29:2** And the lords of the Philistines passed on by hundreds, and by thousands: but David and his men passed on in the rereward with Achish.

The leaders of the Philistines questioned the presence of David and his band.

29:3 Then said the princes of the Philistines, What do these Hebrews here? And Achish said unto the princes of the Philistines, Is not this David, the servant of Saul the king of Israel, which hath been with me these days, or these years, and I have found no fault in him since he fell unto me unto this day?

The leaders of the Philistines rejected the presence of David and his band.

29:4 And the princes of the Philistines were wroth with him; and the princes of the Philistines said unto him, Make this fellow return, that he may go again to his place which thou hast appointed him, and let him not go down with us to battle, lest in the battle he be an adversary to us: for wherewith should he reconcile himself unto his master? should it not be with the heads of these men? **29:5** Is not this David, of whom they sang one to another in dances, saying, Saul slew his thousands, and David his ten thousands?

Achish is still deceived into thinking that David is an enemy of Israel and a friend of the Philistines, but the other Philistine leaders are more prudent than Achish.

29:6 Then Achish called David, and said unto him, Surely, as the LORD liveth, thou hast been upright, and thy going out and thy coming in with me in the host is good in my sight: for I have not found evil in thee since the day of thy coming unto me unto this day: nevertheless the lords favour thee not. **29:7** Wherefore now return, and go in peace, that thou displease not the lords of the Philistines.

David asks why he is being sent away and Achish gives him the answer.

29:8 And David said unto Achish, But what have I done? and what hast thou found in thy servant so long as I have been with thee unto this day, that I may not go fight against the enemies of my lord the king? **29:9** And Achish answered and said to David, I know that thou art good in my sight, as an angel of God: notwithstanding the princes of the Philistines have said, He shall not go up with us to the battle.

David then departed in the morning while the Philistines went up to battle at Jezreel.

29:10 Wherefore now rise up early in the morning with thy master's servants that are come with thee: and as soon as ye be up early in the morning, and have light, depart. **29:11** So David and his men rose up early to depart in the morning, to return into the land of the Philistines. And the Philistines went up to Jezreel.

1 Samuel 30

The Amalekites attacked and destroyed Ziklag in the absence of David and his band; yet God protected the people and saved them alive.

1 Samuel 30:1 And it came to pass, when David and his men were come to Ziklag on the third day, that the Amalekites had invaded the south, and Ziklag, and smitten Ziklag, and burned it with fire; **30:2** And had taken the women captives, that were therein: **they slew not any, either great or small, but carried them away,** and went on their way.

David and his men discovered the fall of Ziklag and the loss of their families and wept sore.

30:3 So David and his men came to the city, and, behold, it was burned with fire; and **their wives, and their sons, and their daughters, were taken captives. 30:4** Then David and the people that were with him lifted up their voice and wept, until they had no more power to weep. **30:5** And David's two wives were taken captives, Ahinoam the Jezreelitess, and Abigail the wife of Nabal the Carmelite.

David seeks God, as we all should do in both good times and bad

30:6 And David was greatly distressed; for the people spake of stoning him, because the soul of all the people was grieved, every man for his sons and for his daughters: but **David encouraged himself in the LORD his God.**

God told David to pursue and liberate his loved ones

30:7 And David said to Abiathar the priest, Ahimelech's son, I pray thee, bring me hither the ephod. And Abiathar brought thither the ephod to David. **30:8** And David enquired at the LORD, saying, Shall I pursue after this troop? shall I overtake them? And he answered him, **Pursue: for thou shalt surely overtake them, and without fail recover all.**

30:9 So David went, he and the six hundred men that were with him, and came to the brook Besor, where those [200 men could not continue] that were left behind stayed. **30:10** But David pursued, he and four hundred men: for two hundred abode behind, which were so faint that they could not go over the brook Besor.

They found a faint Egyptian and made inquiries of him

30:11 And they found an Egyptian in the field, and brought him to David, and gave him bread, and he did eat; and they made him drink water; **30:12** And they gave him a piece of a cake of figs, and two clusters of raisins: and when he had eaten, his spirit came again to him: for he had eaten no bread, nor drunk any water, three days and three nights.

The Egyptian explains that Amalek invaded Judah while the Israelites and Philistines were fighting in the north of Judah.

30:13 And David said unto him, To whom belongest thou? and whence art thou? And he said, I am a young man of Egypt, servant to an Amalekite; and my master left me, because three days agone I fell sick. **30:14** We made an invasion upon the south of the Cherethites, and upon the coast which belongeth to Judah, and upon the south of Caleb; and we burned Ziklag with fire.

David asks this Egyptian to guide him to the camp of the Amalekites.

30:15 And David said to him, Canst thou bring me down to this company? And he said, Swear unto me by God, that thou wilt neither kill me, nor deliver me into the hands of my master, and I will bring thee down to this company.

They caught the Amalekites partying and drunken

30:16 And when he had brought him down, behold, they were spread abroad upon all the earth, eating and drinking, and dancing, because of all the great spoil that they had taken out of the land of the Philistines, and out of the land of Judah.

Only 400 escaped the slaughter by David and his band, and all those that had been taken captive were recovered.

This crisis was a test to build up the faith of David that God keeps his promises and will deliver all who put their trust in him. Very often we are tested with trials, and if we trust in God and diligently seek him to keep his Word; he will keep his promises and deliver us in the resurrection to eternal spirit.

30:17 And David smote them from the twilight even unto the evening of the next day: and there escaped not a man of them, save four hundred young men, which rode upon camels, and fled. **30:18** And David recovered all that the Amalekites had carried away: and David rescued his two wives. **30:19** And there was nothing lacking to them, neither small nor great, neither sons nor daughters, neither spoil, nor any thing that they had taken to them: David recovered all. **30:20** And David took all the flocks and the herds, which they drave before those other cattle, and said, This is David's spoil.

David then made a law that the spoil should be shared equally between the fighters and those supporting them from the rear.

30:21 And David came to the two hundred men, which were so faint that they could not follow David, whom they had made also to abide at the brook Besor: and they went forth to meet David, and to meet the people that were with him: and when David came near to the people, he saluted them.

30:22 Then answered all the wicked men and men of Belial, of those that went with David, and said, Because they went not with us, we will not give them ought of the spoil that we have recovered, save to every man his wife and his children, that they may lead them away, and depart.

30:23 Then said David, Ye shall not do so, my brethren, with that which the LORD hath given us, who hath preserved us, and delivered the company that came against us into our hand. **30:24** For who will hearken unto you in this matter? but **as his part is that goeth down to the battle, so shall his part be that tarrieth by the stuff:** they shall part alike.

30:25 And it was so from that day forward, that he made it a statute and an ordinance for Israel unto this day [the day this was written].

David then sent a portion of his goods to the elders of Judah; this coming while Saul was still king was a gesture of immense kindness that would have made an impression on Judah encouraging their acceptance of David as the new king when the time came.

David had long ago been anointed king by Samuel, yet all of his subsequent life from his "calling" was about teaching him the attributes of a godly king and preparing him for the kingdom.

This is a lesson for us, that the called out and anointed to be kings and priests of the New Covenant, are also being trained up as they wait and endure many things patiently, to be proper godly kings in the spiritual Promised Land of eternity. We are not only being trained by our studies and the trials that beset us, we are also being continual TESTED as to our unswerving loyalty to the whole Word of God.

Why do the faithful suffer?

Because the Master Potter is forming our clay into his own image, so that we learn to be like him through internalizing his Word and his very Nature!

Because the Master Builder is molding us into a spiritual character house that will last for all eternity!

Because we are being trained up and being continually tested as to our fitness to receive a kingdom and to rule it righteously forever!

When we are being buffeted and tried, it is to help us to learn and grow spiritually; to help us to become more like God through learning the habit of unshakably standing on the whole Word of God, no matter what anyone else says or does!

The scriptures contain much about David and many of his own writings; because he is prime example of growing up into a righteous king for us to learn from. David made many mistakes as we also do; that is not the issue for everyone makes mistakes; the issue is how we deal with our mistakes!

Do we just justify ourselves and continue in our errors and sins like many Assemblies in today's Spiritual Ekklesia do in their lack of zeal for the sanctity of the Sabbath etc etc? Or do we diligently study and then sincerely repent, change and go forward in the light of the truth of God's Word?

David was a magnificent example for us; not because he was perfect, but because he had a perfect attitude of clinging always to the Word of God and of quickly repenting whenever he found himself in sin. That is an example that we should all follow.

30:26 And when David came to Ziklag, he sent of the spoil unto the elders of Judah, even to his friends, saying, Behold a present for you of the spoil of the enemies of the LORD; **30:27** To them which were in Bethel, and to them which were in south Ramoth, and to them which were in Jattir, **30:28** And to them which were in Aroer, and to them which were in Siphmoth, and to them which were in Eshtemoa, **30:29** And to them which were in Rachal, and to them which were in the cities of the Jerahmeelites, and to them which were in the cities of the Kenites, **30:30** And to them which were in Hormah, and to them which were in Chorashan, and to them which were in Athach, **30:31** And to them which were in Hebron, and to all the places where David himself and his men were wont to haunt.

1 Samuel 31

After David was sent away by the captains of the Philistines; they engaged Saul and Israel in battle, and the Philistines defeated Israel and the sons of Saul were killed; even beloved Jonathan.

1 Samuel 31:1 Now the Philistines fought against Israel: and the men of Israel fled from before the Philistines, and fell down slain in mount Gilboa. **31:2** And the Philistines followed hard upon Saul and upon his sons; and the Philistines slew Jonathan, and Abinadab, and Melchishua, Saul's sons.

Saul was also grievously wounded

31:3 And the battle went sore against Saul, and the archers hit him; and he was sore wounded of the archers. **31:4** Then said Saul unto his armourbearer, Draw thy sword, and thrust me through therewith; lest these uncircumcised come and thrust me through, and abuse me. But **his armourbearer would not; for he was sore afraid**. Therefore Saul took a sword, and fell upon it. **31:5** And when his armourbearer saw that Saul was dead, he fell likewise upon his sword, and died with him.

31:6 So Saul died, and his three sons, and his armourbearer, and all his men, that same day together.

Then Judah abandoned their cities that were close to the Philistines [modern Gaza].

31:7 And when the men of Israel that were on the other side of the valley, and they that were on the other side Jordan, saw that the men of Israel fled, and that Saul and his sons were dead, they forsook the cities, and fled; and the Philistines came and dwelt in them.

When the Philistines came to take the spoil they found Saul and his sons, and they rejoiced for Saul had done them much hurt during his rule.

31:8 And it came to pass on the morrow, when the Philistines came to strip the slain, that they found Saul and his three sons fallen in mount Gilboa. **31:9** And they cut off his head, and stripped off his armour, and sent into the land of the Philistines round about, to publish it in the house of their idols, and among the people. **31:10** And they put his armour in the house of Ashtaroth: and they fastened his body to the wall of Bethshan.

Then the men of Jabeshgilead rescued the bodies of Saul and his sons in a valiant deed; for this city was very loyal to Saul.

31:11 And when the inhabitants of Jabeshgilead heard of that which the Philistines had done to Saul; **31:12** All the valiant men arose, and went all night, and took the body of Saul and the bodies of his sons from the wall of Bethshan, and came to Jabesh, and burnt them there. **31:13** And they took their bones, and buried them under a tree at Jabesh, and fasted seven days.

Second Samuel

2 Samuel 1

The story of Saul and David is an allegory of the kingship of Satan and Satan's struggle to avoid being replaced by Messiah and the called out of God, after having disqualified himself by his failure to obey God.

An Amalekite tries to ingratiate himself with David by claiming the murder of king Saul and receives his proper reward.

2 Samuel 1:1 Now it came to pass after the death of Saul, when David was returned from the slaughter of the Amalekites, and David had abode two days in Ziklag; **1:2** It came even to pass on the third day, that, behold, a man came out of the camp from Saul with his clothes rent, and earth upon his head: and so it was, when he came to David, that he fell to the earth, and did obeisance. **1:3** And David said unto him, From whence comest thou? And he said unto him, Out of the camp of Israel am I escaped. **1:4** And David said unto him, How went the matter? I pray thee, tell me.

When the news of Saul's death is told, David asks for confirmation.

And he answered, That the people are fled from the battle, and many of the people also are fallen and dead; and Saul and Jonathan his son are dead also. **1:5** And David said unto the young man that told him, How knowest thou that Saul and Jonathan his son be dead?

The man identifies himself as an Amalekite [a people that Christ had condemned to extinction as a type of sin, for their terrible cruelty] and tells a story.

1:6 And the young man that told him said, As I happened by chance upon mount Gilboa, behold, Saul leaned upon his spear; and, lo, the chariots and horsemen followed hard after him. **1:7** And when he looked behind him, he saw me, and called unto me. And I answered, Here am I. **1:8** And he said unto me, Who art thou? And I answered him, I am an Amalekite.

This man lied, claiming to have killed Saul, hoping for a good reward from David.

1:9 He said unto me again, Stand, I pray thee, upon me, and slay me: for anguish is come upon me, because my life is yet whole in me.

1:10 So I stood upon him, and slew him, because I was sure that he could not live after that he was fallen: and I took the crown that was upon his head, and the bracelet that was on his arm, and have brought them hither unto my lord.

David and his band then mourned greatly for Saul and his sons. In spite of all that Saul had done, David loved Saul and Jonathan dearly. This is an example for us that we should not despise the sinful, but we should love the person while hating the path of self-destruction that they have chosen.

If we truly loved the brethren, we would tell them the truth in the hope of saving them.

> **Ezekiel 33:11** Say unto them, **As I live, saith the Lord God, I have no pleasure in the death of the wicked; but that the wicked turn from his way and live: turn ye, turn ye from your evil ways; for why will ye die, O house of Israel?**

Brethren, let me ask you: If God's Word says something and anyone were to then say that it is all right if you don't obey God; are they really loving you by encouraging you to remain on the path to destruction? or does God want us to Cry Aloud and Spare Not; as he has commanded us to do (Isaiah 58:1)?

My friends, I tell you the truth that no person who falters in his zeal to learn and to live by every Word of God will be resurrected to spirit to rule others. That is the truth, no person who exalts men and the traditions of men above the Word of God is fit for a part in the priesthood and kingship of Jesus Christ. I warn you out of love, in the hope that everyone will turn to live by every Word of God and that they might be saved and inherit eternal life.

> **Isaiah 58:1** Cry aloud, spare not, lift up thy voice like a trumpet, and shew my people their transgression, and the house of Jacob their sins.

> Even the law says the same thing: **Leviticus 19:17** Thou shalt not hate thy brother in thine heart: thou shalt in any wise rebuke thy neighbour, and not suffer sin upon him.

2 Samuel 1:11 Then David took hold on his clothes, and rent them; and likewise all the men that were with him: **1:12** And they mourned, and wept, and fasted until even, for Saul, and for Jonathan his son, and for the people of the LORD, and for the house of Israel; because they were fallen by the sword.

David then turned to demand who this man was.

1:13 And David said unto the young man that told him, Whence art thou? And he answered, I am the son of a stranger, an Amalekite.

David immediately had the Amalekite killed for smiting the Lord's anointed.

In the New Covenant dispensation how do we know who the LORD's anointed is? The LORD's spiritually anointed will be anointed by God's Holy Spirit and he will live by every Word of God and will teach all peoples to do likewise. He will not respect persons or the traditions of men above the Word of God, he will never shrink back from rebuking sin or false doctrine and if he is found in error himself he will quickly change; sincerely repenting, loving and accepting the truth: God's Word is Truth.

1:14 And David said unto him, How wast thou not afraid to stretch forth thine hand to destroy the LORD's anointed? **1:15** And David called one of the young men, and said, Go near, and fall upon him. And he smote him that he died. **1:16** And David said unto him, Thy blood be upon thy head; for thy mouth hath testified against thee, saying, I have slain the LORD's anointed.

Today in the New Covenant dispensation, anyone who is not zealous to live by every Word of God and teaches tolerance for sin is just as guilty and deserving of death as that young man; such wicked men will be cast into the fire of great tribulation by Almighty God.

1:17 And David lamented with this lamentation over Saul and over Jonathan his son: **1:18** (Also he bade them teach the children of Judah the use of the bow: behold, it is written in the book of Jasher.)

David's loving lament for Saul his enemy.

Brethren, in the spiritual context it is a great sin to rejoice at the fall of our enemies, rather let us warn them and seek that they might repent and be saved.

1:19 The beauty of Israel is slain upon thy high places: how are the mighty fallen! **1:20** Tell it not in Gath, publish it not in the streets of Askelon; lest the daughters of the Philistines rejoice, lest the daughters of the uncircumcised triumph.

1:21 Ye mountains of Gilboa, let there be no dew, neither let there be rain, upon you, nor fields of offerings: for there the shield of the mighty is vilely cast away, the shield of Saul, as though he had not been anointed with oil.

1:22 From the blood of the slain, from the fat of the mighty, the bow of Jonathan turned not back, and the sword of Saul returned not empty.

1:23 Saul and Jonathan were lovely and pleasant in their lives, and in their death they were not divided: they were swifter than eagles, they were stronger than lions.

1:24 Ye daughters of Israel, weep over Saul, who clothed you in scarlet, with other delights, who put on ornaments of gold upon your apparel.

1:25 How are the mighty fallen in the midst of the battle! O Jonathan, thou wast slain in thine high places.

1:26 I am distressed for thee, my brother Jonathan: very pleasant hast thou been unto me: thy love to me was wonderful, passing the love of women.

1:27 How are the mighty fallen, and the weapons of war perished!

Jesus Christ and God the Father are distressed over the final death of every sinner. Speaking of the final death in the lake of fire, God is not willing that any should perish; that is why the true Lamb of God gave his life in willing sacrifice for the sincerely repented sins of the world.

2 Samuel 2

David does not act on his own but asks the one who became Jesus Christ what he should do and is told to go to Hebron.

2 Samuel 2:1 And it came to pass after this, that David enquired of the LORD, saying, Shall I go up into any of the cities of Judah? And the LORD said unto him, Go up. And David said, Whither shall I go up? And he said, Unto Hebron.

David then took his family and all his men up to Hebron.

2:2 So David went up thither, and his two wives also, Ahinoam the Jezreelitess, and Abigail Nabal's wife the Carmelite. **2:3** And his men that were with him did David bring up, every man with his household: and they dwelt in the cities of Hebron.

The people of Judah accepted David and proclaimed him their king; and told him of the deed of the people of Jabeshgilead.

2:4 And the men of Judah came, and there they anointed David king over the house of Judah. And they told David, saying, That the men of Jabeshgilead were they that buried Saul.

David then declared peace with the people of Jabeshgilead who had afore time betrayed him to Saul.

Likewise the time will come when all the true called out will be reconciled to God and to one another. Even those who think themselves enemies today will in the near future see the light and be reconciled. Note that when the word Lord is in full capitals it is a direct reference to YHVH.

2:5 And David sent messengers unto the men of Jabeshgilead, and said unto them, Blessed be ye of the LORD, that ye have shewed this kindness unto your lord, even unto Saul, and have buried him. **2:6** And now the LORD shew kindness and truth unto you: and I also will requite you this kindness, because ye have done this thing. **2:7** Therefore now let your hands be strengthened, and be ye valiant: for your master Saul is dead, and also the house of Judah have anointed me king over them.

Abner, Saul's chief of staff, then took the last surviving son of Saul and made him king over Israel, which was his duty to his master Saul.

2:8 But Abner the son of Ner, captain of Saul's host, took Ishbosheth the son of Saul, and brought him over to Mahanaim; **2:9** And made him king over Gilead, and over the Ashurites, and over Jezreel, and over Ephraim, and over Benjamin, and over all Israel. **2:10** Ishbosheth Saul's son was forty years old when he began to reign over Israel, and reigned two years. But the house of Judah followed David.

David remained as king of Judah only, for seven years and six months.

2:11 And the time that David was king in Hebron over the house of Judah was seven years and six months.

Then Abner of Saul and Joab of David met and their men fought; Israel fighting against Judah.

2:12 And Abner the son of Ner, and the servants of Ishbosheth the son of Saul, went out from Mahanaim to Gibeon. **2:13** And Joab the son of Zeruiah, and the servants of David, went out, and met together by the pool of Gibeon: and they sat down, the one on the one side of the pool, and the other on the other side of the pool.

2:14 And Abner said to Joab, Let the young men now arise, and play [fight] before us. And Joab said, Let them arise.

2:15 Then there arose and went over by number twelve of Benjamin, which pertained to Ishbosheth the son of Saul, and twelve of the servants of David. **2:16** And they caught every one his fellow by the head, and thrust his sword in his fellow's side; so they fell down together: wherefore that place was called Helkathhazzurim, which is in Gibeon. **2:17** And there was a very sore battle that day; and Abner was beaten, and the men of Israel, before the servants of David.

Abner fled and was chased by Asahel.

2:18 And there were three sons of Zeruiah there, Joab, and Abishai, and Asahel: and Asahel was as light of foot as a wild roe. **2:19** And Asahel pursued after Abner; and in going he turned not to the right hand nor to the left from following Abner. **2:20** Then Abner looked behind him, and said, Art thou Asahel? And he answered, I am.

Abner a mighty man of war, then told Asahel to turn aside and fight another, but Asahel would not stop his pursuit of Abner.

2:21 And Abner said to him, Turn thee aside to thy right hand or to thy left, and lay thee hold on one of the young men, and take thee his armour. But Asahel would not turn aside from following of him.

Asahel would not turn back and so was slain by Abner against the will of Abner.

2:22 And Abner said again to Asahel, Turn thee aside from following me: wherefore should I smite thee to the ground? how then should I hold up my face to Joab thy brother? **2:23** Howbeit he refused to turn aside: wherefore Abner with the hinder end of the spear smote him under the fifth rib, that the spear came out behind him; and he fell down there, and died in the same place: and it came to pass, that as many as came to the place where Asahel fell down and died stood still.

Joab and Abishai then continued the pursuit, being made more determined because of the death of Asahel their brother.

2:24 Joab also and Abishai pursued after Abner: and the sun went down when they were come to the hill of Ammah, that lieth before Giah by the way of the wilderness of Gibeon.

The tribe of Benjamin then supported Abner of Israel against Judah because Saul and his son were from Benjamin.

2:25 And the children of Benjamin gathered themselves together after Abner, and became one troop, and stood on the top of an hill.

Abner then called out for a truce, and Joab answers that if he had not sought peace he would have been dead by morning and Joab's men would then go home in victorious peace: Nevertheless Joab accepted the truce.

2:26 Then Abner called to Joab, and said, Shall the sword devour for ever? knowest thou not that it will be bitterness in the latter end? how long shall it be then, ere thou bid the people return from following their brethren? **2:27** And Joab said, As God liveth, unless thou hadst spoken, surely then in the morning the people had gone up every one from following his brother. **2:28** So Joab blew a trumpet, and all the people stood still, and pursued after Israel no more, neither fought they any more.

Then the two captains, Abner of Israel and Joab of Judah; withdrew their men from the battle.

2:29 And Abner and his men walked all that night through the plain, and passed over Jordan, and went through all Bithron, and they came to Mahanaim. **2:30** And Joab returned from following Abner: and when he had gathered all the people together, there lacked of David's servants nineteen men and Asahel. **2:31** But the servants of David had smitten of Benjamin, and of Abner's men, so that three hundred and threescore [360] men died.

2:32 And they took up Asahel, and buried him in the sepulchre of his father, which was in Bethlehem. And Joab and his men went all night, and they came to Hebron at break of day.

2 Samuel 3

The next two chapters are tales of betrayal by men who were associated with David and which could have gone very badly for David. The death of Abner could have angered Israel and brought the armies of Israel against David and Judah in a great war, but instead God worked things out for the best for David.

David did that which was right and God moved Israel towards joining David. This is a lesson for us that if we are diligent and faithful to be zealous to KEEP the Word of God in all our doings; God will deliver us even if we must suffer for a time like Joseph did.

Romans 8:28 And we know that all things work together for good to them that love God, to them who are the called according to his purpose.

We also see David letting his love for Mi-chal [pronounced Me-khal] turn him aside from obeying God; for he knew that God had said that Saul would be cut off and yet he loved Mi-chal, and if she had conceived by him the house of Saul and of David would have been joined in the child. Further the law also forbids taking back a wife who has left and married another.

We can also say that David's faith and patience were being tested as he was given a taste of kingship over Judah but was not given the full kingship over all Israel which was promised to him.

This speaks to the testing and building of our own faith and patience as we struggle to overcome and to faithfully, fully internalize the whole Word of God to become like God and worthy of our calling.

For two thousand years those who love God enough to keep his Word have been saying "next year, next year; soon, soon." Our Lord counsels us to patiently maintain our zeal for the whole Word of God.

Because of the Joab / Abner confrontation, there was conflict between Judah and Israel for almost seven years.

2 Samuel 3:1 Now there was long war between the house of Saul and the house of David: but David waxed stronger and stronger, and the house of Saul waxed weaker and weaker.

David's wives and sons in Hebron according to 2 Samuel 3

Chart wiki The mother's name	The son's name
Ahinoam the Yizre'elite	His first born was Amnon.
Abigail – the wife of Naval the Karmelite	His second was Kil'av.
Maacah – the daughter of Talmay – King of Geshur	The third – Absalom[2]
Haggith	The fourth – Adoniyya.
Abital	The fifth – Shefatya.
Eglah	The sixth Yitre'am.

3:2 And unto David were sons born in Hebron: and his firstborn was Amnon, of Ahinoam the Jezreelitess; **3:3** And his second, Chileab, of Abigail the wife of Nabal the Carmelite; and the third, Absalom the son of Maacah the daughter of Talmai king of Geshur; **3:4** And the fourth,

Adonijah the son of Haggith; and the fifth, Shephatiah the son of Abital; **3:5** And the sixth, Ithream, by Eglah David's wife. These were born to David in Hebron.

3:6 And it came to pass, while there was war between the house of Saul and the house of David, that Abner made himself strong for the house of Saul.

The son of Saul angers his champion Abner by accusing him of taking his father's concubine; which accusation causes Abner to turn away from Saul to David.

3:7 And Saul had a concubine, whose name was Rizpah, the daughter of Aiah: and Ishbosheth said to Abner, Wherefore hast thou gone in unto my father's concubine? **3:8** Then was Abner very wroth for the words of Ishbosheth, and said, Am I a [dead dog] dog's head, which against Judah do shew kindness this day unto the house of Saul thy father, to his brethren, and to his friends, and have not delivered thee into the hand of David, that thou chargest me to day with a fault concerning this woman?

Abner then reveals that he knows that God had given the kingdom to David and swears to deliver the kingdom to David.

3:9 So do God to Abner, and more also, except, as the LORD hath sworn to David, even so I do to him; **3:10** To translate the kingdom from the house of Saul, and to set up the throne of David over Israel and over Judah, from Dan even to Beersheba.

After the outburst of Abner, the son of Saul feared Abner

3:11 And he could not answer Abner a word again, because he feared him.

David then demanded that his wife Mi-chal be restored to him.

3:12 And Abner sent messengers to David on his behalf, saying, Whose is the land? saying also, Make thy league with me, and, behold, my hand shall be with thee, to bring about all Israel unto thee. **3:13** And he said, Well; I will make a league with thee: but one thing I require of thee, that is, Thou shalt not see my face, except thou first bring Michal Saul's daughter, when thou comest to see my face.

Ishbosheth returns David's wife to him to seal the deal for his abdication and the unifying of the kingdom under David.

3:14 And David sent messengers to Ishbosheth Saul's son, saying, Deliver me my wife Michal, which I espoused to me for an hundred foreskins of the Philistines. **3:15** And Ishbosheth sent, and took her from her husband, even from Phaltiel the son of Laish.

3:16 And her husband went with her along weeping behind her to Bahurim. Then said Abner unto him, Go, return. And he returned.

Abner then led Israel to join Judah and David.

3:17 And Abner had communication with the elders of Israel, saying, Ye sought for David in times past to be king over you: **3:18** Now then do it: for the LORD hath spoken of David, saying, By the hand of my servant David I will save my people Israel out of the hand of the Philistines, and out of the hand of all their enemies.

Abner then went to David to speak to him about uniting the kingdom

3:19 And Abner also spake in the ears of Benjamin: and Abner went also to speak in the ears of David in Hebron all that seemed good to Israel, and that seemed good to the whole house of Benjamin.

A pact is made with Abner

3:20 So Abner came to David to Hebron, and twenty men with him. And David made Abner and the men that were with him a feast. **3:21** And Abner said unto David, I will arise and go, and will gather all Israel unto my lord the king, that they may make a league with thee, and that thou mayest reign over all that thine heart desireth. And David sent Abner away; and he went in peace.

Joab hears that David has let Abner go in peace and is outraged because Abner had killed his brother Asahel.

3:22 And, behold, the servants of David and Joab came from pursuing a troop, and brought in a great spoil with them: but Abner was not with David in Hebron; for he had sent him away, and he was gone in peace. **3:23** When Joab and all the host that was with him were come, they told Joab, saying, Abner the son of Ner came to the king, and he hath sent him away, and he is gone in peace.

Joab then lies, telling David that Abner had come to deceive him.

3:24 Then Joab came to the king, and said, What hast thou done? behold, Abner came unto thee; why is it that thou hast sent him away, and he is quite gone? **3:25** Thou knowest Abner the son of Ner, that he came to deceive thee, and to know thy going out and thy coming in, and to know all that thou doest.

Joab then sought Abner to kill him.

3:26 And when Joab was come out from David, he sent messengers after Abner, which brought him again from the well of Sirah: but David knew it not. **3:27** And when Abner was returned to Hebron, Joab took him aside in the gate to speak with him quietly, and smote him there under the fifth rib, that he died, for the blood of Asahel his brother.

David then cursed Joab for his treachery in that he had lied and had broken the truce to kill Abner.

3:28 And afterward when David heard it, he said, I and my kingdom are guiltless before the LORD for ever from the blood of Abner the son of Ner: **3:29** Let it rest on the head of Joab, and on all his father's house; and let there not fail from the house of Joab one that hath an issue, or that is a leper, or that leaneth on a staff [is lame], or that falleth on the sword [commits suicide], or that lacketh bread.

David then held a state funeral for Abner the chief of staff of Saul; for Abner had been a champion of Israel against the Philistines and Amalekites.

3:30 So Joab, and Abishai his brother slew Abner, because he had slain their brother Asahel at Gibeon in the battle. **3:31** And David said to Joab, and to all the people that were with him, Rend your clothes, and gird you with sackcloth, and mourn before Abner. And king David himself followed the bier. **3:32** And they buried Abner in Hebron: and the king lifted up his voice, and wept at the grave of Abner; and all the people wept.

David then eulogizes Abner with what can only be described as a condemnation of Joab and Abishai as wicked men.

3:33 And the king lamented over Abner, and said, Died Abner as a fool dieth? **3:34** Thy hands were not bound, nor thy feet put into fetters: **as a man falleth before wicked men, so fellest thou.** And all the people wept again over him.

They fasted the day of the funeral.

3:35 And when all the people came to cause David to eat meat while it was yet day, David sware, saying, So do God to me, and more also, if I taste bread, or ought else, till the sun be down.

Israel noticed David's respect for Abner which did much to win Israel over to David.

3:36 And all the people took notice of it, and it pleased them: as whatsoever the king did pleased all the people. **3:37** For all the people and all Israel understood that day that it was not of the king to slay Abner the son of Ner.

David then reveals that he is powerless to punish Joab and Abishai for this killing, because they were powerful leaders [princes] in the land.

3:38 And the king said unto his servants, Know ye not that there is a prince and a great man fallen this day in Israel? **3:39** And I am this day weak, though anointed king; and these men the sons of Zeruiah be too hard [too strong] for me: the LORD shall reward the doer of evil according to his wickedness.

2 Samuel 4

Abner was a very mighty man in Israel and his death caused the king of Israel the son of Saul to fear David greatly, and all Israel was unsettled and disposed to David.

2 Samuel 4:1 And when Saul's son heard that Abner was dead in Hebron, his hands were feeble, and all the Israelites were troubled.

Saul was of Benjamin and Jonathan's son Ish-bosheth, had two friends who were captains in his army who were Benjamites.

4:2 And Saul's son had two men **that were captains of bands**: the name of the one was **Baanah,** and the name of the other **Rechab,** [they were] the sons of Rimmon a Beerothite, of the children of Benjamin: (for Beeroth also was reckoned to Benjamin. **4:3** And the Beerothites fled to Gittaim, and were sojourners there until this day.)

Now remember the covenant between David and Jonathan that David would hold the sons of Jonathan in high regard.

4:4 And Jonathan, Saul's son, had a son that was lame of his feet. He was five years old when the tidings came of Saul and Jonathan out of Jezreel, **and his nurse took him up, and fled: and it came to pass, as she made**

haste to flee, that he fell, and became lame. And his name was Mephibosheth.

The Benjamite captains of these two bands of Ish-bosheth, came to him as he was at rest and murdered him.

4:5 And the sons of Rimmon the Beerothite, [his sons were] **Rechab and Baanah,** went, and came about the heat of the day to the house of Ishbosheth, who lay on a bed at noon. **4:6** And they came thither into the midst of the house, as though they would have fetched wheat; and they smote him under the fifth rib: and Rechab and Baanah his brother escaped.

These two Benjamite assassins then took the head of Ish-bosheth the son of Saul a man of Benjamin to David, thinking that they would receive a great reward.

4:7 For when they came into the house, he lay on his bed in his bedchamber, and they smote him, and slew him, and beheaded him, and took his head, and gat them away through the plain all night. **4:8** And they brought the head of Ishbosheth unto David to Hebron, and said to the king, Behold the head of Ishbosheth the son of Saul thine enemy, which sought thy life; and the LORD hath avenged my lord the king this day of Saul, and of his seed.

David then pronounces sentence on those two murderers, and buries the head of Ish-bosheth with his captain Abner.

4:9 And David answered Rechab and Baanah his brother, the sons of Rimmon the Beerothite, and said unto them, As the LORD liveth, who hath redeemed my soul out of all adversity, **4:10** When one told me, saying, Behold, Saul is dead, thinking to have brought good tidings, I took hold of him, and slew him in Ziklag, who thought that I would have given him a reward for his tidings: **4:11** How much more, when wicked men have slain a righteous person in his own house upon his bed? shall I not therefore now require his blood of your hand, and take you away from the earth? **4:12** And David commanded his young men, and they slew them, and cut off their hands and their feet, and hanged them up over the pool in Hebron. But they took the head of Ishbosheth, and buried it in the sepulchre of Abner in Hebron.

2 Samuel 5

David becomes king of a united Israel

2 Samuel 5:1 Then came all the tribes of Israel to David unto Hebron, and spake, saying, Behold, we are thy bone and thy flesh. **5:2** Also in time past, when Saul was king over us, thou wast he that leddest out and broughtest in Israel: and the LORD said to thee, Thou shalt feed my people Israel, and thou shalt be a captain over Israel. **5:3** So all the elders of Israel came to the king to Hebron; and king David made a league with them in Hebron before the LORD: and they anointed David king over Israel.

5:4 David was thirty years old when he began to reign, and he reigned forty years. **5:5** In Hebron **he reigned over Judah seven years and six months:** and **in Jerusalem he reigned thirty and three years over all Israel and Judah.**

David went up in peace to Jerusalem and the Jebusite inhabitants rejected him.

5:6 And the king and his men went to Jerusalem unto the Jebusites, the inhabitants of the land: which spake unto David, saying, Except thou take away the blind and the lame, thou shalt not come in hither: thinking, David cannot come in hither.

David takes the city, Jerusalem

5:7 Nevertheless David took the strong hold of Zion: the same is the city of David. **5:8** And David said on that day, Whosoever getteth up to the gutter, [the watercourse, the city then getting its water from, was a spring and stream outside the walls] and smiteth the Jebusites, and the lame and the blind [a euphemism for the wicked, as physical types of spiritual blindness and inability to walk in God's Word] that are hated of David's soul, he shall be chief and captain. Wherefore they said, [because the law said that the blind and lame may not enter the Holy Place] The blind and the lame shall not come into the house.

David makes Jerusalem his capital

5:9 So David dwelt in the fort, and called it the city of David. And David built round about from Millo and inward. **5:10** And David went on, and grew great, and the LORD God of hosts was with him.

Hiram king of Tyre recognized David as king and built a palace for David. With his acceptance by all Israel and international recognition, David was established on his throne.

5:11 And Hiram king of Tyre sent messengers to David, and cedar trees, and carpenters, and masons: and they built David an house.

5:12 And David perceived that the LORD had established him king over Israel, and that he had exalted his kingdom for his people Israel's sake.

David multiplies his wives

5:13 And David took him more concubines and wives out of Jerusalem, after he was come from Hebron: and there were yet sons and daughters born to David.

David's sons born in Jerusalem (1 Chronicles 3:5-8 · 1 Chronicles 14:3-7). Considering that the sons are usually given in birth order, Solomon was David's fourth son born in Jerusalem.

5:14 And these be the names of those that were born unto him in Jerusalem; **Shammuah, and Shobab, and Nathan, and Solomon, 5:15** Ibhar also, and Elishua, and Nepheg, and Japhia, **5:16** And Elishama, and Eliada, and Eliphalet.

The Philistines seeing a growing threat from Israel go up to battle.

5:17 But when the Philistines heard that they had anointed David king over Israel, all the Philistines came up to seek David; and David heard of it, and went down to the hold. **5:18** The Philistines also came and spread themselves in the valley of Rephaim.

David inquires of God and then goes up to the battle knowing that God has burst out before him upon the Philistines like a mighty rush of water bursts forth from a broken dam.

5:19 And David enquired of the LORD, saying, Shall I go up to the Philistines? wilt thou deliver them into mine hand? And the LORD said unto David, Go up: for I will doubtless deliver the Philistines into thine hand. **5:20** And David came to Baalperazim, and David smote them there, and said, **The LORD hath broken forth upon mine enemies before me, as the breach** [of a dam] **of waters.** Therefore he called the name of that place Baalperazim. [place of breaking forth]

The Philistines were defeated and fled leaving behind their gods.

5:21 And there they left their images, and David and his men burned them.

The Philistines again made ready for battle, and David sought and received instructions from the one who later became flesh as Jesus Christ.

5:22 And the Philistines came up yet again, and spread themselves in the valley of Rephaim. **5:23** And when David enquired of the LORD, he said, Thou shalt not go up; but fetch a compass behind them, and come upon them over against the mulberry trees. **5:24** And let it be, when thou hearest the sound of a [wind of the going forth of God] going in the tops of the mulberry trees, that then thou shalt bestir thyself: for then shall the LORD go out before thee, to smite the host of the Philistines.

David obeys God

5:25 And David did so, as the LORD had commanded him; and smote the Philistines from Geba until thou come to Gazer.

2 Samuel 6

David desired to bring the Ark to Jerusalem; to have both the king and the religion centered in the same city.

2 Samuel 6:1 Again, David gathered together all the chosen men of Israel, thirty thousand. **6:2** And David arose, and went with all the people that were with him from Baale of Judah, to bring up from thence the ark of God, whose name is called by the name of the LORD of hosts that dwelleth between the cherubims.

Here they followed the actions of the Philistines without seeking out the Word of God on the matter.

Today the Ekklesia does the same thing; seeking to worship God by our own ways and traditions; instead of doing what God has commanded us to do.

6:3 And they set the ark of God upon a new cart, and brought it out of the house of Abinadab that was in Gibeah: and Uzzah and Ahio, the sons of Abinadab, drave the new cart. **6:4** And they brought it **out of the house of Abinadab which was at Gibeah,** accompanying the ark of God: and Ahio went before the ark. **6:5** And David and all the house of Israel played before the LORD on all manner of instruments made of fir wood, even on harps, and on psalteries, and on timbrels, and on cornets, and on cymbals.

With great rejoicing before the Lord they went up with the Ark, but NOT as God had commanded them. Therefore even though they were rejoicing in God, they were rebelling against God to do what they thought was right, rather than doing what God had commanded.

Then this man who was seeking to please God was killed for doing what he thought was right instead of doing what God said was right. This is a powerful lesson for us today; that God expects us to be zealous to learn and to live by every Word of God, and NOT to rely on what we think is right.

Because we in today's Spiritual Ekklesia delight in zeal for our own ways and false traditions, and we decry and reject any zeal for learning and living by every Word of God in any practical terms; we shall also be corrected by Jesus Christ (Rev 3:16-22, Laodicea).

6:6 And when they came to Nachon's threshingfloor, Uzzah put forth his hand to the ark of God, and took hold of it; for the oxen shook it. **6:7** And the anger of the LORD was kindled against Uzzah; and God smote him there for his error; and there he died by the ark of God.

6:8 And David was displeased, because the LORD had made a breach upon Uzzah: and he called the name of the place Perezuzzah to this day [the breach of Uzzah, a place where God "burst forth upon Uzzah, so that he died,"].

David then feared to proceed any further with moving the Ark to Jerusalem until he had studied the matter out. David learned his lesson, he learned to do things God's way; today we must also learn this same lesson.

6:9 And David was afraid of the LORD that day, and said, How shall the ark of the LORD come to me? **6:10** So David would not remove the ark of the LORD unto him into the city of David: but David carried it aside into the house of Obededom the Gittite. **6:11** And the ark of the LORD continued in the house of Obededom the Gittite three months: and the LORD blessed Obededom, and all his household.

During three months David was searching the scriptures for the right way to move the Ark and then he understood that the presence of the Ark was to be a blessing and not a curse; if only we would do as God commands and learn and live by every Word of God, he would dwell within us and be a blessing to us.

David then brought the Ark to Jerusalem; transporting it as God's Word commanded.

We need to understand that being in the presence of God is a blessing to all those who are diligent to learn and to live by every Word of God, but coming into the presence of God is destruction to the unrepentant sinner who exalts his own ways above the Word of God.

We need to understand that even those who are sincerely thinking that they are doing right yet acting contrary to the Word of God; will be corrected. We are to search the scriptures and we are to learn to live by every Word of God and not by our own assumptions and suppositions.

I have no doubt of the sincerity of many who stand on their own false ways and mistakenly claim to be godly; yet they are facing strong correction for worshiping God by their own ways and not worshiping God according to HIS Word, submitting to and obeying the whole Word of God.

God is a tremendous blessing to all those who live in true godliness, rejoicing and eagerly internalizing every Word of God to learn it and keep it, spiritually growing to become like God.

6:12 And it was told king David, saying, The LORD hath blessed the house of Obededom, and all that pertaineth unto him, because of the ark of God. So David went and brought up the ark of God from the house of Obededom into the city of David with gladness.

David offered sacrifices before the Ark of God as it was transported, and the Ark was brought with great rejoicing to the city of Jerusalem.

6:13 And it was so, that when they that bare the ark of the LORD had gone six paces, he sacrificed oxen and fatlings.

David was filled with so much joy at the presence of the Ark [throne] of God, that he could not contain and leaped and danced for joy before the Ark of God! Leaping and Shouting for Joy as the trumpets sounded before the Ark [Throne] OF GOD!

Unlike those, who like Mi-chal look down their noses in contempt for those who rejoice in joyous zeal for the Eternal: Each of us should also REJOICE over the whole Word of God, and God's presence in those who are zealous to learn and keep his Word!

6:14 And David danced before the LORD with all his might; and David was girded with a linen ephod [a priestly garment]. **6:15** So David and all the house of Israel brought up the ark of the LORD with shouting, and with the sound of the trumpet.

Mi-chal saw David rejoicing before the Ark and thought that he acted unseemly for a king, and she began to despise him as being without her conception of regal dignity. Much of the Ekklesia today is like Mi-chal who had her own ideas of human dignity, instead of being exuberantly zealous for the Word of God.

6:16 And as the ark of the LORD came into the city of David, Michal Saul's daughter looked through a window, and saw king David leaping and dancing before the LORD; and she despised him in her heart.

After the Ark was captured by the Philistines, King Saul moved the tabernacle to Nob, near his home town of Gibeah, but after he massacred the priests there (1 Samuel 21-22), it was moved to Gibeon, where it remained until the Temple was built. (1 Chronicles 16:39; 21:29; 2 Chronicles 1:2–6, 13).

The Ark was located in Kiriath-Jearim (1 Chronicles 13:5-6) just prior to David's moving the ark to Jerusalem where it was placed "inside the tent David had pitched for it" (2 Samuel 6:17; 1 Chronicles 15:1), not in the tabernacle, which remained at Gibeon.

The altar of the tabernacle at Gibeon was used for sacrificial worship (1 Chronicles 16:39; 21:29; 1 Kings 3:2-4), until Solomon finally brought the structure and its furnishings to Jerusalem to furnish and dedicate the Temple. (1 Kings 8:4)

6:17 And they brought in the ark of the LORD, and set it in his place, **in the midst of the tabernacle that David had pitched for it:** and David offered burnt offerings and peace offerings before the LORD.

Then David blessed the people in the name of the Lord God of Abraham, Isaac and Jacob.

6:18 And as soon as David had made an end of offering burnt offerings and peace offerings, he blessed the people in the name of the LORD of hosts.

David then fed all of the people before the Lord. This is a picture of the resurrected David in the coming kingdom as king over all Israel, feeding them with the Word of God.

6:19 And he dealt among all the people, even among the whole multitude of Israel, as well to the women as men, to every one a cake of bread, and a good piece of flesh, and a flagon of wine. So all the people departed every one to his house.

Mi-chal rebukes David out of her haughty pride and her own idea of what is proper for a king likely gotten from her father Saul, and David rebuked her.

6:20 Then David returned to bless his household. And Michal the daughter of Saul came out to meet David, and said, How glorious was the king of Israel to day, who uncovered himself to day [humbled himself and took off his royal robes to wear a priestly ephod] in the eyes of the handmaids of his servants, as one of the vain fellows shamelessly uncovereth himself [dressing as a common priest and not a king]!

6:21 And David said unto Michal, It was before the LORD, which chose me before thy father, and before all his house, to appoint me ruler over the people of the LORD, over Israel: therefore will I play before the LORD.

David openly declares that he will be humble and rejoice before God, and that he will be honored by God for doing so.

6:22 And I will yet be more vile than thus, and will be base [lowly and humble] in mine own sight: and of the maidservants which thou hast spoken of, of them shall I be had in honour.

This is a picture of how those zealous for God will be exalted to be kings and priests of God for eternity, bearing much fruit; while those who despise zeal and exuberant enthusiasm to learn and live by every Word of God, and to rejoice in our Mighty One, preferring their own pride; will not bear any godly fruit. David then refused Mi-chal to come to him as her husband for the rest of her life and the Word of God to Saul was fulfilled that no descendant of his would sit on the throne.

6:23 Therefore Michal the daughter of Saul had no child unto the day of her death.

2 Samuel 7

David began to think about building a temple for the Ark

2 Samuel 7:1 And it came to pass, when the king sat in his house, and the LORD had given him rest round about from all his enemies; **7:2** That the king said unto Nathan the prophet, See now, I dwell in an house of cedar, but the ark of God dwelleth within curtains. **7:3** And Nathan said to the king, Go, do all that is in thine heart; for the LORD is with thee.

The word of YHVH [who later became flesh as Jesus Christ: Hebrew: Yeshua Messiah] did not come directly to David but to Nathan.

7:4 And it came to pass that night, that the word of the LORD came unto Nathan, saying,

7:5 Go and tell my servant David, Thus saith the LORD, Shalt thou build me an house for me to dwell in? **7:6** Whereas I have not dwelt in any house since the time that I brought up the children of Israel out of Egypt, even to this day, but have walked in a tent and in a tabernacle.

7:7 In all the places wherein I have walked with all the children of Israel spake I a word with any of the tribes of Israel, whom I commanded to feed my people Israel, saying, Why build ye not me an house of cedar? **7:8** Now therefore so shalt thou say unto my servant David, Thus saith the LORD of hosts, I took thee from the sheepcote, from following the sheep, to be ruler over my people, over Israel: **7:9** And I was with thee whithersoever thou wentest, and have cut off all thine enemies out of thy sight, and have made thee a great name, like unto the name of the great men that are in the earth.

God's promise of a fixed Temple at Jerusalem to be built by Solomon and a prophecy that after Messiah comes Israel will be given permanent peaceful possession of the land.

7:10 Moreover I will appoint a place for my people Israel, and will plant them, that they may dwell in a place of their own, and move no more; neither shall the children of wickedness afflict them any more, as beforetime,

God had never asked for a fixed house before, but had required a movable tabernacle [meeting tent].

7:11 And as since the time that I commanded judges [rulers, non-dynastic kings] to be over my people Israel, and have caused thee to rest from all thine enemies.

Because David had wanted to build a Temple for God, God promised that God will build the house [family] of David and that David's son Solomon would build a Temple for God.

Very soon now Jesus Christ will come and he will build the Ezekiel Temple; and he will rule all humanity under God the Father, forever.

. . . Also the LORD telleth thee that he will make thee an house. **7:12** And when thy days be fulfilled, and thou shalt sleep with thy fathers [after David dies], I will set up thy seed after thee, which shall proceed out of thy bowels, and I will establish his kingdom. **7:13** He [Solomon] shall build an house for my name, and **I will stablish the throne of his kingdom for ever.**

This promise of an eternal kingdom was not about the line of Solomon, which Solomonic line was conditional on Solomon living by every Word of God (1 Chron 28:7, 2 Chron 7:17, 1 Kings 9:4, see below), but concerned the throne of David which David would receive in the resurrection.

We are also called out to be kings and priests and if we turn aside to our own ways and traditions contrary to the whole Word of God, we shall also be corrected.

Just like God chastened the Mosaic Covenant kings for their sins, God our Father will surely chasten the New Covenant called out, for our idolatry and sins if we will not repent on our own.

7:14 I will be his father, and he shall be my son. If he commit iniquity, I will chasten him with the rod of men, and with the stripes of the children of men: **7:15** But my mercy shall not depart away from him, as I took it from Saul, whom I put away before thee.

Take careful note here that God does NOT say that Solomon's kingdom or lineage would endure forever, the promise is that God would not abandon Solomon himself. This is a promise that Solomon would be king and would build the Jerusalem Temple; and second that God would not abandon Solomon.

God means what God says; and forever means far more than a mere physical lineage of rulers; forever means for all eternity!

Now God makes a third promise directly to David and it does NOT say that David's physical lineage would be established: rather God promised that David's throne would be established FOREVER.

7:16 And **thine house and thy kingdom shall be established for ever before thee: thy throne shall be established for ever** [for eternity]. **7:17** According to all these words, and according to all this vision, so did Nathan speak unto David.

1. God promised David that his son Solomon would be given the throne of Israel,
2. That God would be like a father to Solomon and would correct him, but would not abandon him if he sinned, and then
3. God promised David an eternal throne.

So far so good, but this scripture must be taken in the context with other scriptures on the same subject; making the promise of a line of kings descending from Solomon ABSOLUTELY CONDITIONAL on Solomon living by every Word of God (1 Chron 28:7, 2 Chron 7:17, 1 Kings 9:4, see below).

> **1 Chronicles 28:1** And David assembled all the princes of Israel, the princes of the tribes, and the captains of the companies that ministered to the king by course, and the captains over the thousands, and captains over the hundreds, and the stewards over all the substance and possession of the king, and of his sons, with the

officers, and with the mighty men, and with all the valiant men, unto Jerusalem.

28:2 Then David the king stood up upon his feet, and said, Hear me, my brethren, and my people: As for me, I had in mine heart to build an house of rest for the ark of the covenant of the Lord, and for the footstool of our God, and had made ready for the building: **28:3** But God said unto me, Thou shalt not build an house for my name, because thou hast been a man of war, and hast shed blood.

28:4 Howbeit the Lord God of Israel chose me before all the house of my father **to be king over Israel for ever**: for he hath chosen Judah to be the ruler; and of the house of Judah, the house of my father; and among the sons of my father he liked me to make me king over all Israel:

28:5 And of all my sons, (for the Lord hath given me many sons,) he hath chosen Solomon my son to sit upon the throne of the kingdom of the Lord over Israel. **28:6** And he said unto me, Solomon thy son, he shall build my house and my courts: for I have chosen him to be my son, and I will be his father.

The promise to David was unconditional because David had already proved himself, but the promise to Solomon was very much conditional!

28:7 Moreover **I will establish his kingdom for ever, IF he be constant to do my commandments and my judgments,** as at this day. [most of David's line were not constant to keep God's commandments except Hezekiah, Jehoshaphat, Josiah and a few others temporarily]

28:8 Now therefore in the sight of all Israel the congregation of the Lord, and in the audience of our God, **keep and seek for all the commandments of the Lord your God**: that ye may possess this good land, and leave it for an inheritance for your children after you for ever.

28:9 And thou, **Solomon my son, know thou the God of thy father, and serve him with a perfect heart and with a willing mind:** for the Lord searcheth all hearts, and understandeth all the imaginations of the thoughts: **if thou seek him, he will be found of thee; but if thou forsake him, he will cast thee off for ever. 28:10** Take heed now; for the Lord hath chosen thee to build an house for the sanctuary: be strong, and do it.

This is a very conditional promise by God to Solomon.

> **1 Kings 9:4 And IF thou wilt walk before me, as David thy father walked, in integrity of heart, and in uprightness, to do according to all that I have commanded thee, and wilt keep my statutes and my judgments: 9:5 Then I will establish the throne of thy kingdom** [the throne of Solomon, as opposed to David's throne] **upon Israel for ever,** as I promised to David thy father, saying, There shall not fail thee a man upon the throne of Israel.
>
> **9:6** But if ye shall at all turn from following me, ye or your children, and will not keep my commandments and my statutes which I have set before you, but go and serve other gods, and worship them: **9:7** Then will I cut off Israel out of the land which I have given them; and this house, which I have hallowed for my name, will I cast out of my sight; and Israel shall be a proverb and a byword among all people:
>
> **9:8** And at this house, which is high, every one that passeth by it shall be astonished, and shall hiss; and they shall say, Why hath the Lord done thus unto this land, and to this house? **9:9** And they shall answer, Because they forsook the Lord their God, who brought forth their fathers out of the land of Egypt, and have taken hold upon other gods, and have worshipped them, and served them: therefore hath the Lord brought upon them all this evil.

Notice that David's throne was already established forever, the promise will be fulfilled by the resurrected David's rule over a united Israel for all eternity; but Solomon's throne and dynasty was absolutely CONDITIONAL on his living by every Word of God.

How can this be and what does this mean? This is so important that God repeated the warning to Solomon when the Temple was dedicated.

> **2 Chronicles 7:17** And as for thee, **if thou wilt walk before me, as David thy father walked, and do according to all that I have commanded thee, and shalt observe my statutes and my judgments; 7:18 Then will I stablish the throne of thy kingdom**, according as I have covenanted with David thy father, saying, There shall not fail thee a man to be ruler in Israel.
>
> **7:19** But if ye turn away, and forsake my statutes and my commandments, which I have set before you, and shall go and serve other gods, and worship them; **7:20** Then will I pluck them up by the

> roots out of my land which I have given them; and this house, which I have sanctified for my name, will I cast out of my sight, and will make it to be a proverb and a byword among all nations.
>
> **7:21** And this house, which is high, shall be an astonishment to every one that passeth by it; so that he shall say, Why hath the Lord done thus unto this land, and unto this house? **7:22** And it shall be answered, Because they forsook the Lord God of their fathers, which brought them forth out of the land of Egypt, and laid hold on other gods, and worshipped them, and served them: therefore hath he brought all this evil upon them.

Notice that David's throne was already established forever [for all eternity through the resurrection of David], but Solomon's throne was absolutely CONDITIONAL on his living by every Word of God.

How can this be and what does this mean?

The answer is that David was already promised to be resurrected to eternal life and to receive an eternal kingdom, because he had already proved that he was zealous to live by every Word of God.

God promised David a resurrection to spirit so that he could personally rule the united house of Israel forever. While the promise to Solomon was a conditional promise [which failed because of Solomon's sins] concerned the physical line of Solomon!

Messiah the Christ will come as King of all kings and with him will come a resurrected David as king over the once again united whole house of Israel!

Paul wrote of David in Hebrews 11, that David had died NOT having received the promises and that David would be resurrected to spirit with all of God's faithful.

> **Hebrews 11:32** And what shall I more say? for the time would fail me to tell of Gedeon, and of Barak, and of Samson, and of Jephthae; of **David also**, and Samuel, and of the prophets:

The promise of an eternal throne made to David, was a promise of a resurrection to eternal life, to sit upon the throne of a united Israel FOREVER!

David was a man after God's own heart (Acts 13:22) because he NEVER worshiped other gods; and because whenever he sinned, he quickly and sincerely repented just as soon as he realized that he had sinned.

Speaking of the post resurrection millennium: **Hosea 3:5** Afterward shall the children of Israel return, and **seek the Lord their God, and David their king**; and shall fear the Lord and his goodness in the latter days.

When Christ comes, he will set a resurrected David back upon his throne, to rule all Israel FOREVER, thus fulfilling God's promise to David!

Ezekiel 34:23 And I will set up one shepherd over them, and he shall feed them, **even my servant David;** he shall feed them, and he shall be their shepherd. **34:24** And I the Lord will be their God, and my servant David a prince among them; I the Lord have spoken it.

Ezekiel 37:24 And **David my servant shall be king over them**; and they all shall have one shepherd: they shall also walk in my judgments, and observe my statutes, and do them [thus showing that the whole law and every Word of God will also be kept forever!]. **37:25** And they shall dwell in the land that I have given unto Jacob my servant, wherein your fathers have dwelt; and they shall dwell therein, even they, and their children, and their children's children for ever: and my servant David shall be their prince for ever.

Jeremiah 33:17 For thus saith the Lord; David shall never want a man to sit upon the throne of the house of Israel;

How is this promise to be fulfilled? Solomon turned away from God and was disqualified, therefore God's promise to David will be fulfilled by the resurrection of David himself!

Quoting Amos 9:11 Luke writes in **Acts 15:16 After this I will return, and will build again the tabernacle of David, which is fallen down**; and I will build again the ruins thereof, and I will set it up:

Amos 9:11 In that day will I raise up **the tabernacle of David** [the Davidic line] **that is fallen**, and close up the breaches thereof; and I will raise up his ruins, and I will build it as in the days of old:

After the coming of Christ, Israel will again be united and will turn to the Eternal, and the resurrected David will be king over all Israel; and God's promise of a perpetual Davidic throne over Israel will be fulfilled!

Jeremiah 30:9 But they shall serve the Lord their God, and **David their king, whom I will raise up unto them**.

See "The Dynasty of David" article at theshininglight.info site.

David responded to God

2 Samuel 7:18 Then went king David in, and sat before the LORD, and he said, Who am I, O Lord GOD? and what is my house, that thou hast brought me hitherto? **7:19** And this was yet a small thing in thy sight, O Lord GOD; but thou hast spoken also of thy servant's house for a great while to come. And is this the manner of man, O Lord GOD? **7:20** And what can David say more unto thee? for thou, Lord GOD, knowest thy servant.

7:21 For thy word's sake, and according to thine own heart, hast thou done all these great things, to make thy servant know them.

7:22 Wherefore thou art great, O LORD God: for there is none like thee, neither is there any God beside thee, according to all that we have heard with our ears.

David acknowledged that God had delivered physical Israel out of Egypt and had given them that land.

The Spiritual Ekklesia must acknowledge that we have been called out of the bondage of spiritual Egypt [bondage to Satan, sin and death] and delivered by God Almighty; and that we are to overcome all sin to take possession of an eternal Promised Land in which we shall be kings and priests forever if we overcome and faint not.

What people in all the earth is like those who are faithful and passionately zealous to follow God, and to live by every Word of God to learn it and to keep it?

Not that the Spiritual Ekklesia are great in themselves; but that God will exalt them IF they are completely submissive and dedicatedly loyal to love and follow the Rock of Salvation with wholehearted sincerity, forever; abundantly faithful to follow the Great and Mighty God of Abraham, Isaac, Jacob and Moses!

Yet like physical Israel, today Spiritual Israel has fallen very far away from their God.

7:23 And what one nation in the earth is like thy people, even like Israel, whom God went to redeem for a people to himself, and to make him a name, and to do for you great things and terrible, for thy land, before thy people, which thou redeemedst to thee from Egypt, from the nations and their gods? **7:24** For thou hast confirmed to thyself thy people Israel to be a people unto thee for ever: and thou, LORD, art become their God.

7:25 And now, O LORD God, the word that thou hast spoken concerning thy servant, and concerning his house, establish it for ever, and do as thou hast said.

May God bring us back to him in sincere repentance and be merciful to us.

7:26 And **let thy name be magnified for ever**, saying, The LORD of hosts is the God over Israel: and let the house of thy servant David be established before thee.

Jesus Christ promised to build the house of David and he has promised to build God's faithful into a holy priesthood and give them offices in his eternal kingdom.

> **1 Peter 2:9** But ye are a chosen generation, a royal priesthood, an holy nation, a peculiar [special] people; that ye should shew forth the praises of him who hath called you out of darkness [sin] into his marvellous light [godliness];

2 Samuel 7:27 For thou, O LORD of hosts, God of Israel, hast revealed to thy servant, saying, I will build thee an house: therefore hath thy servant found in his heart to pray this prayer unto thee. **7:28** And now, O Lord GOD, thou art that God, and thy words be true, and thou hast promised this goodness unto thy servant:

7:29 Therefore now let it please thee to bless the house of thy servant, that it may **continue for ever before thee**: for thou, O Lord GOD, hast spoken it: and with thy blessing let the house of thy servant be blessed for ever.

2 Samuel 8

David destroyed the enemies of Israel and subjugated the full extent of the land promised to Israel.

2 Samuel 8:1 And after this it came to pass that David smote the Philistines, and subdued them: and David took Methegammah out of the hand of the Philistines. **8:2** And he smote Moab, and measured them with a line, casting them down to the ground; even with two lines measured he to put to death, and with one full line to keep alive. And so **the Moabites became David's servants, and brought gifts** [tribute].

David carried his campaign right to the Euphrates, building a kingdom for his son Solomon so that Solomon could be a man of peace.

8:3 David smote also Hadadezer, the son of Rehob, king of Zobah, as he went to recover his border at the river Euphrates. **8:4** And David took from him a thousand chariots, and seven hundred horsemen, and twenty thousand footmen: and David houghed all the chariot horses, but reserved of them for an hundred chariots.

> **Hough** hamstring, i.e., sever the "tendon of Achilles" the hock of the foot of the hinder legs of captured horses (Joshua 11:6, 2 Samuel 8:4, 1 Chronicles 18:4), so as to render them useless for battle.

David also defeated Damascus and Syria.

8:5 And when the Syrians of Damascus came to succour Hadadezer king of Zobah, David slew of the Syrians two and twenty thousand men. **8:6** Then David put garrisons in Syria of Damascus: and the Syrians became servants to David, and brought gifts [tribute]. And the LORD preserved David whithersoever he went.

David gained much spoil and riches and also gained many allies among those who had been oppressed by the kings he defeated.

8:7 And David took the shields of gold that were on the servants of Hadadezer, and brought them to Jerusalem. **8:8** And from Betah, and from Berothai, cities of Hadadezer, king David took exceeding much brass.

8:9 When Toi king of Hamath heard that David had smitten all the host of Hadadezer, **8:10** Then Toi sent Joram his son unto king David, to salute him, and to bless him, because he had fought against Hadadezer, and smitten him: for Hadadezer had wars with Toi. And Joram brought with him vessels of silver, and vessels of gold, and vessels of brass:

David dedicated this immense wealth to the building of the Temple of God.

8:11 Which also king David did dedicate unto the LORD, with the silver and gold that he had dedicated of all nations which he subdued; **8:12** Of Syria, and of Moab, and of the children of Ammon, and of the Philistines, and of Amalek, and of the spoil of Hadadezer, son of Rehob, king of Zobah.

8:13 And David gat him a name [great reputation] when he returned from smiting of the Syrians in the valley of salt, being eighteen thousand men.

8:14 And he put garrisons in Edom; throughout all Edom put he garrisons, and all they of **Edom became David's servants.** And the LORD preserved David whithersoever he went.

8:15 And David reigned over all Israel; and David executed judgment and justice unto all his people.

8:16 And Joab the son of Zeruiah was over the host; and Jehoshaphat the son of Ahilud was recorder; **8:17** And Zadok the son of Ahitub, and Ahimelech the son of Abiathar, were the [chief] priests; and Seraiah was the scribe; **8:18** And Benaiah the son of Jehoiada was over both the Cherethites and the Pelethites; and David's sons were chief rulers.

Hundreds of years later God inspired the prophets to record that these same areas and countries, including Moab, Edom and Syria will be ruled by, serve and pay tribute to the millennial Davidic kingdom of a returned and united Israel under the resurrected king David. The nations of Israel will also continue to overspread the same areas that they have today, as well as many returning to Palestine.

In a very few years we will see Jesus Christ ruling in Jerusalem as King over all the earth, and the resurrected David ruling a once again united Israel including the same territory that he ruled anciently.

2 Samuel 9

David is kind to the family of Saul for Jonathan's sake.

2 Samuel 9:1 And David said, Is there yet any that is left of the house of Saul, that I may shew him kindness for Jonathan's sake? **9:2** And there was of the house of Saul a servant whose name was Ziba. And when they had called him unto David, the king said unto him, Art thou Ziba? And he said, Thy servant is he.

9:3 And the king said, Is there not yet any of the house of Saul, that I may shew the kindness of God unto him? And Ziba said unto the king, Jonathan hath yet a son, which is lame on his feet. **9:4** And the king said unto him, Where is he? And Ziba said unto the king, Behold, he is in the house of Machir, the son of Ammiel, in Lodebar. **9:5** Then king David sent, and fetched him out of the house of Machir, the son of Ammiel, from Lodebar.

9:6 Now when Mephibosheth, the son of Jonathan, the son of Saul, was come unto David, he fell on his face, and did reverence. And David said, Mephibosheth. And he answered, Behold thy servant! **9:7** And David said unto him, Fear not: for I will surely shew thee kindness for Jonathan thy father's sake, and will restore thee all the land of Saul thy father; and thou shalt eat bread at my table continually.

David restored to Mephibo-sheth all his rightful inheritance according to the law of God, from the property of his grandfather Saul.

9:8 And he bowed himself, and said, What is thy servant, that thou shouldest look upon such a dead dog as I am?

Then David commissioned Saul's servant Ziba to oversee the lands, while David took care of Mephibo-sheth the son of his beloved friend Jonathan personally.

9:9 Then the king called to Ziba, Saul's servant, and said unto him, I have given unto thy master's son all that pertained to Saul and to all his house.

Ziba was himself a wealthy man having 20 servants and 15 sons; and he committed himself to do as David had said.

9:10 Thou therefore, and thy sons, and thy servants, shall till the land for him, and thou shalt bring in the fruits, that thy master's son may have food to eat: but Mephibosheth thy master's son shall eat bread alway at my table. Now Ziba had fifteen sons and twenty servants. **9:11** Then said Ziba unto the king, According to all that my lord the king hath commanded his servant, so shall thy servant do. As for Mephibosheth, said the king, he shall eat at my table, as one of the king's sons.

Jonathan the faithful to God, called his son **Mephibo-sheth:** "exterminator of shame"; i.e., "destroyer of idols".

Mephibo-sheth had one son of his own and they were cared for personally by David.

9:12 And **Mephibosheth had a young son, whose name was Micha**. And all that dwelt in the house of Ziba were servants unto Mephibosheth. **9:13** So Mephibosheth dwelt in Jerusalem: for he did eat continually at the king's table; and was lame on both his feet.

2 Samuel 10

In Israel it was not lawful to mourn for the dead by making cuttings in the beard or flesh, but it was the custom in Ammon to do so. David thinking to do the dead king honor; instead, provoked a diplomatic incident by committing what was to the Ammonites an insult to the dead, his representatives not cutting their beards in mourning.

2 Samuel 10:1 And it came to pass after this, that the king of the children of Ammon died, and Hanun his son reigned in his stead. **10:2** Then said David, I will shew kindness unto Hanun the son of Nahash, as his father shewed kindness unto me. And David sent to comfort him by the hand of his servants for his father. And David's servants came into the land of the children of Ammon.

The new king of Ammon's servants were angered by this apparent affront and declared that David's servants were not there to mourn [because they did not follow the Ammonite customs of mourning] but had come to spy out the land.

10:3 And the princes of the children of Ammon said unto Hanun their lord, Thinkest thou that David doth honour thy father, that he hath sent comforters unto thee? hath not David rather sent his servants unto thee, to search the city, and to spy it out, and to overthrow it?

They cut the beards of David's representatives in half and also cut off the lower half of their garments, sending them home in shame, and doing an insult to David who was by that time a great and mighty king.

This was an act of returning great evil for a perceived evil; and precipitated a serious animosity between the two nations bringing enormous bloodshed.

We are instructed to return good for evil and if the new king of Ammon had treated these men with respect in spite of a perceived affront to his pride, much bloodshed would have been avoided.

10:4 Wherefore Hanun took David's servants, and shaved off the one half of their beards, and cut off their garments in the middle, even to their buttocks, and sent them away.

David protected his servants from shame and was most outraged.

10:5 When they told it unto David, he sent to meet them, because the men were greatly ashamed: and the king said, Tarry at Jericho until your beards be grown, and then return.

Then the king of Ammon realized the magnitude of his error and was greatly afraid, and hired the Syrians to fight David for him.

10:6 And when the children of Ammon saw that they stank before David, the children of Ammon sent and hired the Syrians of Ammon hired Bethrehob and the Syrians of Zoba, twenty thousand footmen, and of king Maacah a thousand men, and of Ishtob twelve thousand men.

David sent his army out to the battle

10:7 And when David heard of it, he sent Joab, and all the host of the mighty men. **10:8** And the children of Ammon came out, and put the battle in array at the entering in of the gate: and the Syrians of Zoba, and of Rehob, and Ishtob, and Maacah, were by themselves in the field.

Joab selected the best of the army to stand against Syria having much respect for them as fighters, and the remainder of the army he gave to his brother Abishai to fight the Ammonites.

10:9 When Joab saw that the front of the battle was against him before and behind, he chose of all the choice men of Israel, and put them in array against the Syrians: **10:10** And the rest of the people he delivered into the hand of Abishai his brother, that he might put them in array against the children of Ammon.

It appears that Abishai was outnumbered and Joab encouraged his brother.

10:11 And he said, If the Syrians be too strong for me, then thou shalt help me: but if the children of Ammon be too strong for thee, then I will come and help thee.

Let all those of today's spiritual Israel be of a good courage to follow our Lord, and he will give us victory over sin and Satan.

10:12 Be of good courage, and let us play the men for our people, and for the cities of our God: and the LORD do that which seemeth him good.

The hired enemy was driven from the battlefield and the army of Israel returned home.

10:13 And Joab drew nigh, and the people that were with him, unto the battle against the Syrians: and they fled before him. **10:14** And when the children of Ammon saw that the Syrians were fled, then fled they also before Abishai, and entered into the city. So Joab returned from the children of Ammon, and came to Jerusalem.

The Syrians were not about to give up and they brought together a much greater army.

10:15 And when the Syrians saw that they were smitten before Israel, they gathered themselves together. **10:16** And Hadarezer sent, and brought out the Syrians that were beyond the river: and they came to Helam; and Shobach the captain of the host of Hadarezer went before them.

David himself then gathered all the men of Israel and went out to battle destroying the enemy host.

10:17 And when it was told David, he gathered all Israel together, and passed over Jordan, and came to Helam. And the Syrians set themselves in array against David, and fought with him. **10:18** And the Syrians fled before Israel; and David slew the men of seven hundred chariots of the Syrians, and forty thousand horsemen, and smote Shobach the captain of their host, who died there.

Then Syria and Ammon made peace with David and served Israel and her king David, just as they will serve Israel and her resurrected king David in the millennium.

The prophets tell us that with the coming of Christ, David shall be raised up and will again rule a united Israel; and at that time Syria, Turkey, the Philistines in Gaza, Amman and Moab, and the remainder of the Palestinians will serve Israel.

Then the land of Israel will be restored as it was during the reign of David and Solomon, from the Wadi el Arish of Egypt, to the Euphrates.

Very soon now during the tribulation these nations will be devastated by the armies of Asia as they come up against Jerusalem; and being humbled they will be glad to look for their deliverance to Messiah the Christ coming as the King of the world and to David his servant, resurrected to be king over a united Israel.

10:19 And when all the kings that were servants to Hadarezer saw that they were smitten before Israel, **they made peace with Israel, and served them.** So the Syrians feared to help the children of Ammon any more.

Ahithophel, Bathsheba and Absalom

The next several chapters concern Bathsheba and David's sin against Uriah; the rebellion of Absalom and the turning of Ahithophel's loyalty to David into hatred.

> To properly understand these events it is necessary to realize that **Bathsheba is the daughter of Eliam** one of David's thirty mighty men (2 Samuel 11:3 & 23:34).
>
> **Eliam was the son of Ahithophel** who was David's chief adviser, making Bathsheba the granddaughter of one of David's chief counselors, and the daughter of one of his Mighty Men and the wife of another, Bathsheba's husband Uriah the Hittite who was also one of David's thirty commanders or mighty men (2 Samuel 23:39).
>
> **Bathsheba [Hebrew: Bat-Sheva,** daughter of an oath**]:** Probably Bathsheba was in awe of the king, and feared his position and authority; not daring to cry out against him.

Our Sin Today: Herein lies a great lesson for us all; should we fear and submit to the supposed authority of men, even supposed men of God; or should we first fear, respect and obey the Word of God, above the words of men?

David was a mighty man of God and yet he made many mistakes.

Do not assume that the spiritual leaders in today's Ekklesia cannot make mistakes or even go astray like Saul; prove all things by God's Word before obeying and following them. One of the biggest issues for those within the brotherhood is that they have been purposefully indoctrinated into the fear of men for decades.

Brethren, we are to fear God and do HIS will, and we are not fear any man.

David's sin: We see that while David committed adultery and murder, another great often overlooked sin was the abuse of the office and position entrusted to him [and to the leaders and elders today] by God.

Our sin today: When spiritual leaders and elders teach people to follow the traditions of men and turn the brethren away from living by every Word of God to follow themselves, demanding loyalty to their own ways above loyalty to God's Word; they are also abusing their office and position like Eli's sons.

2 Samuel 11

Then after Passover when the old year had ended, Israel went up to destroy Ammon. The city of Rabbah being modern Ammon, Jordan.

2 Samuel 11:1 And it came to pass, **after the year was expired** [spring], at the time when kings go forth to battle, that David sent Joab, and his servants with him, and all Israel; and they destroyed the children of Ammon, and besieged Rabbah. But David tarried still at Jerusalem.

In those days it was very common for people to go up on their flat rooftops in the cool of the evening to find relief from the heat of the house. David may well have previously met Bathsheba fully covered, but may not have recognized her at a distance, and naked. This incident may have been very late at night and Bathsheba may have felt that she was alone, since David was already in his bed and restless had risen to walk upon his roof top.

11:2 And it came to pass in an eveningtide, that David arose from off his bed, and walked upon the roof of the king's house: and from the roof he saw a woman washing herself; and the woman was very beautiful to look upon.

BOTH Eliam and Uriah were among David's 30 senior commanders and well known to him.

11:3 And David sent and enquired after the woman. And one said, Is not this Bathsheba, the **daughter of Eliam**, **the wife of Uriah** the Hittite [and the granddaughter of David's chief adviser Ahithophel]? **11:4** And David sent messengers, and took her; and she came in unto him, and he lay with her; for **she was purified from her uncleanness:** and she returned unto her house. **11:5** And the woman conceived, and sent and told David, and said, I am with child.

David became an adulterer and knowingly so, for he had been told of her husband BEFORE he sent for her and betrayed his friend. David departed from the Word of God and had lusted after and stolen what belonged to another.

Today we of spiritual Israel commit spiritual adultery when we turn away from the Husband of our baptismal espousal to follow others; instead of zealously learning and passionately living by every Word of God.

11:6 And David sent to Joab, saying, Send me Uriah the Hittite. And Joab sent Uriah to David. **11:7** And when Uriah was come unto him, David demanded of him how Joab did, and how the people did, and how the war prospered. **11:8** And David said to Uriah, Go down to thy house, and wash thy feet. And Uriah departed out of the king's house, and there followed him a mess of meat from the king. **11:9** But Uriah slept at the door of the king's house with all the servants of his lord, and went not down to his house.

Uriah was such a loyal dedicated man that he could not take his ease and rest while his comrades were in the field.

11:10 And when they had told David, saying, Uriah went not down unto his house, David said unto Uriah, Camest thou not from thy journey? why then didst thou not go down unto thine house? **11:11** And Uriah said unto David, The ark, and Israel, and Judah, abide in tents; and my lord Joab, and the servants of my lord, are encamped in the open fields; shall I then go into mine house, to eat and to drink, and to lie with my wife? as thou livest, and as thy soul liveth, I will not do this thing.

Then David got him drunk and sent him home to his wife, but he still would not go.

11:12 And David said to Uriah, Tarry here to day also, and to morrow I will let thee depart. So Uriah abode in Jerusalem that day, and the morrow. **11:13** And when David had called him, he did eat and drink before him; and he made him drunk: and at even he went out to lie on his bed with the servants of his lord, but went not down to his house.

David then ordered the murder of his most faithful and loyal officer to try and cover up his own sin.

It is important to understand that God allowed the murder of the righteous Uriah because God was working with David and that God will raise up Uriah in his time and will save him also. God is wiser than any one of us can begin to comprehend and God is working everything out for the ultimate good of everyone, even for those who must suffer for righteousness sake in this life.

In the same way many leaders and elders in today's Spiritual Ekklesia are trying to spiritually murder the faithful for their zeal for God; by pressuring them to turn from their zeal for the Word of God to follow themselves and their false traditions.

11:14 And it came to pass in the morning, that David wrote a letter to Joab, and sent it by the hand of Uriah. **11:15** And he wrote in the letter, saying, Set ye Uriah in the forefront of the hottest battle, and retire ye from him, that he may be smitten, and die.

Joab the mighty man, a man strong enough to have stood up to David, obeyed David and carried out the murder instead of taking a stand for godliness or standing up for his officer; he did not even send back to question or confirm the order.

11:16 And it came to pass, when Joab observed the city, that he assigned Uriah unto a place where he knew that valiant men [where the enemy was strong] were. **11:17** And the men of the city went out, and fought with Joab: and there fell some of the people of the servants of David; and Uriah the Hittite died also.

Then Joab sent a messenger with news of the loss of some of the army, and told the messenger to mention Uriah.

11:18 Then Joab sent and told David all the things concerning the war; **11:19** And charged the messenger, saying, When thou hast made an end of telling the matters of the war unto the king, **11:20** And if so be that the king's wrath arise, and he say unto thee, Wherefore approached ye so nigh unto the city when ye did fight? knew ye not that they would shoot from the wall? **11:21** Who smote Abimelech the son of Jerubbesheth? did not a woman cast a piece of a millstone upon him from the wall, that he died in Thebez? why went ye nigh the wall? then say thou, Thy servant Uriah the Hittite is dead also.

11:22 So the messenger went, and came and shewed David all that Joab had sent him for. **11:23** And the messenger said unto David, Surely the men prevailed against us, and came out unto us into the field, and we were upon them even unto the entering of the gate. **11:24** And the shooters shot from off the wall upon thy servants; and some of the king's servants be dead, and thy servant Uriah the Hittite is dead also.

David then approved of the deed

11:25 Then David said unto the messenger, Thus shalt thou say unto Joab, Let not this thing displease thee, for the sword devoureth one as well as another: make thy battle more strong against the city, and overthrow it: and encourage thou him.

Bathsheba who probably did not consent to her rape and did not cry out simply because there was no escape from the king and no one would have dared to help her; mourned for her husband Uriah.

Bathsheba may have been a righteous woman like her husband Uriah for Solomon tells us in Proverbs that he was taught many of his proverbs by his mother Bathsheba.

11:26 And when the wife of Uriah heard that Uriah her husband was dead, she mourned for her husband.

David then took her to wife, but God was greatly displeased with him.

11:27 And when the mourning was past, David sent and fetched her to his house, and she became his wife, and bare him a son. But the thing that David had done displeased the LORD.

2 Samuel 12

The one who later gave up his Godhood to become flesh as Jesus Christ then sent Nathan the prophet to David to rebuke him for his sins.

Nathan gets David's attention by using a parable that David could identify with.

2 Samuel 12:1 And the LORD sent Nathan unto David. And he came unto him, and said unto him, There were two men in one city; the one rich, and the other poor. **12:2** The rich man had exceeding many flocks and herds:

12:3 But the poor man had nothing, save one little ewe lamb, which he had bought and nourished up: and it grew up together with him, and with his children; it did eat of his own meat, and drank of his own cup, and lay in his bosom, and was unto him as a daughter.

12:4 And there came a traveller unto the rich man, and he [the rich man] spared to take of his own flock and of his own herd, to dress for the wayfaring man that was come unto him; but took the poor man's lamb, and dressed it for the man that was come to him.

At this point David, not yet seeing his own deed, was rightly angered at the attitude of the rich man in stealing the little that the poor man had.

12:5 And David's anger was greatly kindled against the man; and he said to Nathan, As the LORD liveth, the man that hath done this thing shall surely die: **12:6** And he shall restore the lamb fourfold, because he did this thing, and because he had no pity.

Nathan then declared that David was the rich sinner and explained his sin to him.

Notice that David had the power of life and death and yet Nathan feared God more than the mighty David, and faithfully delivered God's strong rebuke to David.

The first lesson here is that we are called to follow God the Father and Jesus Christ and to keep the whole Word of God; no matter what any man says and regardless of the titles they claim, or the power they may seem to have.

It is far better to be cast out of the assemblies for being faithful to the whole Word of God, than to remain in corporate church assemblies and be separated from God by fearing men more than we love God!

12:7 And Nathan said to David, Thou art the man. Thus saith the LORD God of Israel, I anointed thee king over Israel, and I delivered thee out of the hand of Saul; **12:8** And I gave thee thy master's house, and thy master's wives into thy bosom, and gave thee the house of Israel and of Judah; and if that had been too little, I would moreover have given unto thee such and such things.

12:9 Wherefore hast thou despised the commandment of the LORD, to do evil in his sight? thou hast killed Uriah the Hittite with the sword, and hast taken his wife to be thy wife, and hast slain him with the sword of the children of Ammon.

Then Jesus Christ cursed the house of David with continual bloodshed and declares that his own wives will be publicly violated. The following chapters record the fulfillment of that curse.

The revenge of Ahithophel; remember that Ahithophel the chief adviser to David who later counseled Absalom to violate his father's wives; was also the grandfather of Bathsheba who was violated by David.

12:10 Now therefore the sword shall never depart from thine house; because thou hast despised me, and hast taken the wife of Uriah the Hittite to be thy wife. **12:11** Thus saith the LORD, Behold, I will raise up evil against thee out of thine own house, and I will take thy wives before thine eyes, and give them unto thy neighbour, and he shall lie with thy wives in the sight of this sun. **12:12** For thou didst it secretly: but I will do this thing before all Israel, and before the sun.

Christ forgives the repentant David, but takes the life of the child.

12:13 And David said unto Nathan, I have sinned against the LORD. And Nathan said unto David, The LORD also hath put away thy sin; thou shalt not die. **12:14** Howbeit, because by this deed thou hast given great occasion to the enemies of the LORD to blaspheme, the child also that is born unto thee shall surely die.

David fasted for the child in sorrowful repentance.

12:15 And Nathan departed unto his house. And the LORD struck the child that Uriah's wife bare unto David, and it was very sick. **12:16** David therefore besought God for the child; and David fasted, and went in, and lay all night upon the earth. **12:17** And the elders of his house arose, and went to him, to raise him up from the earth: but he would not, neither did he eat bread with them.

12:18 And it came to pass on the seventh day, that the child died. And the servants of David feared to tell him that the child was dead: for they said, Behold, while the child was yet alive, we spake unto him, and he would not hearken unto our voice: how will he then vex himself, if we tell him that the child is dead? **12:19** But when David saw that his servants whispered, David perceived that the child was dead: therefore David said unto his servants, Is the child dead? And they said, He is dead.

David arises and accepts the judgment of God when it is clearly final.

12:20 Then David arose from the earth, and washed, and anointed himself, and changed his apparel, and came into the house of the LORD, and worshipped: then he came to his own house; and when he required, they set bread before him, and he did eat.

David's servants ask him for an explanation of his actions.

12:21 Then said his servants unto him, What thing is this that thou hast done? thou didst fast and weep for the child, while it was alive; but when the child was dead, thou didst rise and eat bread.

David says that the dead child was dead and that he himself will also die, and he accepts the judgment of the Eternal.

Brethren, the Eternal is the final judge of all men; why fear men and not fear the judgment of God; why follow men and break the Word of God who is our final Judge?

12:22 And he said, While the child was yet alive, I fasted and wept: for I said, Who can tell whether GOD will be gracious to me, that the child may live? **12:23** But now he is dead, wherefore should I fast? can I bring him back again? I shall go to him, but he shall not return to me.

12:24 And David comforted Bathsheba his wife, and went in unto her, and lay with her: and she bare a son, and **he called his name Solomon: and the LORD loved him.**

>**Solomon** means peace, and the name was given to the child to reflect the reconciliation and peace between David and God through sincere repentance and acceptance by the Eternal.
>
>Variations: Salem, Shalom, Shlomo, Sulayman and Zalman.
>
>**Jedidiah** "Friend of God" or "Beloved of God:" Jedidiah was the "blessing" name given by God through the prophet Nathan.

12:25 And he sent by the hand of Nathan the prophet; and he **called his name** [Nathan was inspired by God to name the child] **Jedidiah, because of the LORD.**

Amman is punished for their insult to David, and for hiring armies against Israel and for their grave sins.

The local gods, like Baal and Molech were different titles for the same god, which was the sun god; the sun being chosen by Satan as his physical representation.

These people threw their own children as sacrifices alive into the fire of Molech.

12:26 And Joab fought against Rabbah [modern Ammon] of the children of Ammon, and took the royal city.

Joab informs David that Rabbah is about to fall and bids him come and take credit for the final victory. This is a very courteous gesture to the king, for it is a coveted glory for any commander to take a large city.

12:27 And Joab sent messengers to David, and said, I have fought against Rabbah, and have taken the city of waters. **12:28** Now therefore gather the rest of the people together, and encamp against the city, and take it: lest I take the city, and it be called after my name.

12:29 And David gathered all the people together, and went to Rabbah, and fought against it, and took it.

12:30 And he took their king's crown from off his head, the weight whereof was a talent [a talent is from 50 to as much as 75 pounds] of gold with the precious stones: and it was set on David's head. And he brought forth the spoil of the city in great abundance.

And he brought out the princes of the children of Ammon, the counselors of Hattun, who had advised the king of Ammon to use David's ambassadors in so shameful a manner and others that expressed their pleasure and satisfaction in that offense: and put them under saws, and under harrows of iron, and under axes of iron; whereby they were cut asunder, as some were later killed by the Romans and others; their flesh torn to pieces, and they were put to extreme pain and agony, and so died most miserably (1 Chronicles 20:3).

12:31 And he brought forth the people that were therein, and put them under saws, and under harrows of iron, and under axes of iron [David had them beaten with iron staves], and made them pass through the brick-kiln [David then threw the chief men into the fire [of the brick kiln], just like they had done to their own children in burning them alive to their god Molech.] and thus did he unto all the cities of the children of Ammon. So David and all the people returned unto Jerusalem.

> **1 kings 11:5** "they caused the chief men to pass through Malcem [the fire of Milcom or Molech], the abomination of the children of Ammon."

They had made their own children to pass through the fire and burnt them alive; and now they themselves were made to pass through the fire and burnt alive, as a righteous punishment for their barbarous and wicked idolatry.

2 Samuel 13

The curse for the sin against Uriah came quickly to David's house with his children knowing of their father's sins, thinking that they could also take liberties with the Word of God.

Such is the power of a bad example; it causes others to also become lax: While a good example of zeal for the righteousness of the whole Word of God, causes others to see the rightness and goodness of the Word of God.

People like sheep tend to be followers; and our examples speak far louder than words. Children will follow the example they see, rather then keep what is spoken to them; so will the brethren.

Amnon David's son, lusted after David's daughter by another mother, Tamer.

2 Samuel 13:1 And it came to pass after this, that Absalom the son of David had a fair sister, whose name was Tamar; and Amnon the son of David loved her.

Amnon allowed himself to lust after that which he could not lawfully have. Jesus tells us that to nurse temptation in our hearts is the root that leads ultimately to the sinful act. As soon as we are tempted, we must reject the temptation right out of our minds immediately, and replace it with something positive to dwell on.

13:2 And Amnon was so vexed, that he fell sick for his sister Tamar; for she was a virgin; and Amnon thought it hard for him to do anything to her.

Amnon allowed his cousin Jonadab to entice him into sin. Yet Amnon could have said no and rebuked his cousin. Stay upon the Word of God and reject any enticement to turn aside.

Such enticement to sin is of particular strength if it comes from someone we love or respect. Do not allow a church leader or elder or friend to entice us into any kind of sin; including calling the Sabbath holy and then encouraging us to pollute it.

13:3 But Amnon had a friend, whose name was Jonadab, the son of Shimeah David's brother: and Jonadab was a very subtil man. **13:4** And he said unto him, Why art thou, being the king's son, lean from day to day? wilt thou not tell me? And Amnon said unto him, I love Tamar, my brother Absalom's sister.

This is no greater evil than what the leaders and elders of the Ekklesia do today, teaching us to commit spiritual adultery against our espoused Husband, Jesus Christ, by following others contrary to any part of the whole Word of God.

13:5 And Jonadab said unto him, Lay thee down on thy bed, and make thyself sick: and when thy father cometh to see thee, say unto him, I pray thee, let my sister Tamar come, and give me meat, and dress the meat in my sight, that I may see it, and eat it at her hand.

Amnon followed the advice of his friend just like so many brethren today have followed their elders and leaders into the sin of exalting them and their false traditions above the Word of God: which is spiritual adultery.

13:6 So Amnon lay down, and made himself sick: and when the king was come to see him, Amnon said unto the king, I pray thee, let Tamar my sister come, and make me a couple of cakes in my sight, that I may eat at her hand.

David then visits his "sick" son and sends for Tamar.

13:7 Then David sent home to Tamar, saying, Go now to thy brother Amnon's house, and dress him meat. **13:8** So Tamar went to her brother Amnon's house; and he was laid down. And she took flour, and kneaded it, and made cakes in his sight, and did bake the cakes.

When the food was ready he caused all to leave them except Tamar herself.

13:9 And she took a pan, and poured them out before him; but he refused to eat. And Amnon said, Have out all men from me. And they went out every man from him. **13:10** And Amnon said unto Tamar, Bring the meat into the chamber, that I may eat of thine hand. And Tamar took the cakes which she had made, and brought them into the chamber to Amnon her brother.

Tamar rejects him and struggles and argues until he forces her.

This is a good example that are we to struggle against evil and the enticement to sin by exalting men and corporate entities or any other idol above the Word of God and our espoused spiritual Husband.

13:11 And when she had brought them unto him to eat, he took hold of her, and said unto her, Come lie with me, my sister.

She tried to convince him to let her go by saying [probably falsely] that the king would assent if he asked their father David first. I do not believe this for a second and I think Amnon did not believe it either. This was a mere desperate argument to try to restrain Amnon, which argument failed.

13:12 And she answered him, Nay, my brother, do not force me; for no such thing ought to be done in Israel: do not thou this folly. **13:13** And I, whither shall I cause my shame to go? and as for thee, thou shalt be as one of the fools in Israel. Now therefore, I pray thee, speak unto the king; for he will not withhold me from thee. **13:14** Howbeit he would not hearken unto her voice: but, being stronger than she, forced her, and lay with her.

Then Amnon his lust satisfied suddenly had a case of guilt, and instead of accepting the blame for forcing her, he turned against Tamar.

13:15 Then Amnon hated her exceedingly; so that the hatred wherewith he hated her was greater than the love wherewith he had loved her. And Amnon said unto her, Arise, be gone. **13:16** And she said unto him, There is no cause: this evil in sending me away is greater than the other that thou didst unto me. But he would not hearken unto her.

I find it strange that Tamar would not run from this man who had so abused her, yet Amnon had to have his servant force her out.

Is it not the same today, that many abused people become loyal to their oppressors? This "Stockholm Syndrome" drives many in today's Ekklesia to be faithful to abusive leaders.

People with abusing spouses or parents tend to deal with this in one of two main ways;

1. They blame themselves and try even harder to please their abusers,

2. They fight back and or seek a way out, sometimes by murder, sometimes by flight, sometimes by suicide and sometime by escaping through alcohol or drugs or other addictions.

I imagine it is the same in abusive groups, which is why they often try so hard to put everyone on a guilt trip often blaming everyone for their own failings; this only causes most of the abused to seek all the harder to please their abusers [Stockholm Syndrome].

13:17 Then he called his servant that ministered unto him, and said, Put now this woman out from me, and bolt the door after her.

13:18 And she had a garment of divers colours upon her: for with such robes were the king's daughters that were virgins apparelled. Then his servant brought her out, and bolted the door after her.

Then Tamar went out mourning

13:19 And Tamar put ashes on her head, and rent her garment of divers colours that was on her, and laid her hand on her head, and went on crying.

And so the curse of Christ moved in the house of David, because David's sins had set an example for his own children to turn them to do the same kinds of evil.

13:20 And Absalom her brother said unto her, Hath Amnon thy brother been with thee? but hold now thy peace, my sister: he is thy brother; regard not this thing. So Tamar remained desolate in her brother Absalom's house.

David was furious but did little to correct Amnon, and Absalom despised his brother for the rape of his sister and determined to destroy him.

13:21 But when king David heard of all these things, he was very wroth. **13:22** And Absalom spake unto his brother Amnon neither good nor bad: for Absalom hated Amnon, because he had forced his sister Tamar.

Absalom invited all of his brothers and his father to his sheep shearing which would have been hard work followed by a big feast.

13:23 And it came to pass after two full years, that Absalom had sheepshearers in Baalhazor, which is beside Ephraim: and Absalom invited all the king's sons. **13:24** And Absalom came to the king, and said, Behold now, thy servant hath sheepshearers; let the king, I beseech thee, and his servants go with thy servant.

David said no for he did not want his whole family to be indebted to Absalom for his feast.

13:25 And the king said to Absalom, Nay, my son, let us not all now go, lest we be chargeable unto thee. And he pressed him: howbeit he would not go, but blessed him.

Then Absalom managed to cause David to allow Amnon to go.

13:26 Then said Absalom, If not, I pray thee, let my brother Amnon go with us. And the king said unto him, Why should he go with thee? **13:27** But Absalom pressed him, that **he let Amnon and all the king's sons go with him.**

Then Absalom commanded his servants to kill Amnon when he was drunk and incapacitated with wine from the sheep shearing feast.

13:28 Now Absalom had commanded his servants, saying, Mark ye now when Amnon's heart is merry with wine, and when I say unto you, Smite Amnon; then kill him, fear not: have not I commanded you? be courageous, and be valiant. **13:29** And the servants of Absalom did unto Amnon as Absalom had commanded. Then all the king's sons arose, and every man gat him up upon his mule, and fled.

When David heard a rumor that all his sons were dead he began to mourn greatly.

13:30 And it came to pass, while they were in the way, that tidings came to David, saying, Absalom hath slain all the king's sons, and there is not one of them left. **13:31** Then the king arose, and tare his garments, and lay on the earth; and all his servants stood by with their clothes rent.

Then the very Jonadab who had enticed Amnon into his sin comforted David saying that only the wicked son was dead.

13:32 And Jonadab, the son of Shimeah David's brother, answered and said, Let not my lord suppose that they have slain all the young men the king's sons; for Amnon only is dead: for by the appointment of Absalom this hath been determined from the day that he forced his sister Tamar. **13:33** Now therefore let not my lord the king take the thing to his heart, to think that all the king's sons are dead: for Amnon only is dead.

Absalom then fled to the north to Talmai the king of Geshur his maternal grandfather..

13:34 But Absalom fled. And the young man that kept the watch lifted up his eyes, and looked, and, behold, there came much people by the way of the hill side behind him.

Jonadab the person responsible for all of this, was busy trying to ingratiate himself to David; office politics at its worst.

13:35 And Jonadab said unto the king, Behold, the king's sons come: as thy servant said, so it is. **13:36** And it came to pass, as soon as he had made an end of speaking, that, behold, the king's sons came, and lifted up their voice and wept: and the king also and all his servants wept very sore.

David loved Absalom and understood that he had actually done the right thing by killing the sister rapist. David himself should have executed justice and did not.

Because this may seem like dry ancient history to many I would like to ask you to lean back, close your eyes and imagine: How you would feel if your son raped your daughter and then was killed by your other son?

Can you even begin to imagine the agony of spirit that David was going through as he learned his lesson concerning his own sins with Bathsheba and his betrayal of the responsibilities that Jesus Christ had placed on his shoulders by making him king?

We too have been called out to become kings, and we must prove our loyalty to Jesus Christ and the whole Word of God, just like David as king was expected to do.

Our own following of others contrary to the Word of our God, is spiritual adultery. When we turn aside to follow others away from the Husband of our baptismal commitment, we are throwing the crown we were called to, into the dirt; we are despising our calling to learn and to live by every Word of God.

Think about that the next time some elder bids you to break the sanctity of the Sabbath by participating in some catered meal.

When we sin we need to repent just as sincerely and wholeheartedly as David did, and we need to STOP committing the sin, learn our lesson and go forward to live by every Word of God in future.

13:37 But Absalom fled, and went to Talmai, the son of Ammihud, king of Geshur. And David mourned for his son every day. **13:38** So Absalom fled, and went to Geshur, and was there three years.

David had accepted that Amnon was dead, but he missed Absalom knowing that he was still alive.

13:39 And the soul of king David longed to go forth unto Absalom: for he [David knew that if anyone else had raped their sister, then David would have done exactly what Absalom had done] was comforted concerning Amnon, seeing he was dead.

2 Samuel 14

Joab teaches David by the mouth of a woman

Joab knew that David mourned for Absalom and that what Absalom had done was right in slaying the wicked.

2 Samuel 14:1 Now Joab the son of Zeruiah perceived that the king's heart was toward Absalom. **14:2** And Joab sent to Tekoah, and fetched thence a wise woman, and said unto her, I pray thee, feign thyself to be a mourner, and put on now mourning apparel, and anoint not thyself with oil, but be as a woman that had a long time mourned for the dead: **14:3** And come to the king, and speak on this manner unto him. So Joab put the words in her mouth.

The woman appeals for justice to David with the words of Joab in a parable, like Nathan had spoken in a parable.

14:4 And when the woman of Tekoah spake to the king, she fell on her face to the ground, and did obeisance, and said, Help, O king. **14:5** And the king said unto her, What aileth thee? And she answered, I am indeed a widow woman, and mine husband is dead. **14:6** And thy handmaid had two sons, and they two strove together in the field, and there was none to part them, but the one smote the other, and slew him.

14:7 And, behold, the whole family is risen against thine handmaid, and they said, Deliver him that smote his brother, that we may kill him, for the life of his brother whom he slew; and we will destroy the heir also: and so they shall quench my coal which is left, and shall not leave to my husband neither name nor remainder upon the earth.

The king then tells her to return home while he contemplates his judgment.

14:8 And the king said unto the woman, Go to thine house, and I will give charge concerning thee. **14:9** And the woman of Tekoah said unto the king, My lord, O king, the iniquity be on me, and on my father's house: and the king and his throne be guiltless.

David then tells her to send anyone who bothers her again in the matter, to him.

14:10 And the king said, Whoever saith ought unto thee, bring him to me, and he shall not touch thee any more.

She asks David to remember the law of God, that justice should reign in the land and not vengeance.

14:11 Then said she, I pray thee, let the king remember the LORD thy God, that thou wouldest not suffer the revengers of blood to destroy any more, lest they destroy my son. And he said, As the LORD liveth, there shall not one hair of thy son fall to the earth.

She then asks if she may speak on, and she begins to speak of Absalom.

14:12 Then the woman said, Let thine handmaid, I pray thee, speak one word unto my lord the king. And he said, Say on.

She asks David why he wishes vengeance against his beloved Absalom and not justice; because Absalom has only done what was right, to destroy wickedness when the king would not do so.

14:13 And the woman said, Wherefore then hast thou thought such a thing against the people of God? for the king doth speak this thing [David made his judgment about her story, while he is at fault in his own deeds] as one which is faulty, in that the king doth not fetch home again his banished [Absalom].

She tells David that all will die in the flesh; but that God desires mercy and not vengeance. She appeals to David to forgive his son Absalom.

14:14 For we must needs die, and are as water spilt on the ground, which cannot be gathered up again; **neither doth God respect any person: yet**

doth he devise means, [a way of salvation, that reconciles the repentant to God] **that his banished be not** [forever] **expelled from him**.

She then declares that David is righteous and will discern the right thing to do; to forgive his son so that God might be with David.

14:15 Now therefore that I am come to speak of this thing unto my lord the king, it is because the people have made me afraid: and thy handmaid said, I will now speak unto the king; it may be that the king will perform the request of his handmaid.

14:16 For the king will hear, to deliver his handmaid out of the hand of the man that would destroy me and my son together out of the inheritance of God. **14:17** Then thine handmaid said, **The word of my lord the king shall now be comfortable: for as an angel of God, so is my lord the king to discern good and bad: therefore the LORD thy God will be with thee.**

David discerns the hand of Joab in this woman.

Joab as chief of staff of David's armies could not rebuke David due to his position and used the woman to counsel the king of Israel.

14:18 Then the king answered and said unto the woman, Hide not from me, I pray thee, the thing that I shall ask thee. And the woman said, Let my lord the king now speak. **14:19** And the king said, Is not the hand of Joab with thee in all this? And the woman answered and said, As thy soul liveth, my lord the king, none can turn to the right hand or to the left from ought that my lord the king hath spoken: for thy servant Joab, he bade me, and he put all these words in the mouth of thine handmaid: **14:20** To fetch about this form of speech hath thy servant Joab done this thing: and my lord is wise, according to the wisdom of an angel of God, to know all things that are in the earth.

David is moved to forgive his son and calls Joab to bring Absalom home.

14:21 And the king said unto Joab, Behold now, I have done this thing: go therefore, bring the young man Absalom again. **14:22** And Joab fell to the ground on his face, and bowed himself, and thanked the king: and Joab said, To day thy servant knoweth that I have found grace in thy sight, my lord, O king, in that the king hath fulfilled the request of his servant.

Absalom came home but his father still would not see him.

14:23 So Joab arose and went to Geshur, and brought Absalom to Jerusalem. **14:24** And the king said, Let him turn to his own house, and let him not see my face. So Absalom returned to his own house, and saw not the king's face.

Absalom was much loved by the people, but was badly treated by his father David. At this point the direction this was heading should be clear.

Absalom who had killed the wicked, was loved and despised at the same time by his father, who could not look upon him for sorrow over what had been done; and by excluding this popular son David offended his son deeply. Absalom felt hated by his father and loved by the people.

Absalom was a strong, virile and good looking man, very impressive to the people; while David the king was growing old.

14:25 But in all Israel there was none to be so much praised as Absalom for his beauty: from the sole of his foot even to the crown of his head there was no blemish in him. **14:26** And when he polled his head, (for it was at every year's end that he polled it: because the hair was heavy on him, therefore he polled it:) he weighed the hair of his head at two hundred shekels after the king's weight.

Absalom named his daughter Tamar after his sister. Oh how they must have been close and loved each other and their father David. What a terrible tragedy has befallen the family of David because of his sin of adultery with Bathsheba against Uriah. The Greek tragedies have nothing on this terrible tragedy of the family of David.

14:27 And unto Absalom there were born three sons, and one daughter, whose name was Tamar: she was a woman of a fair countenance. **14:28** So Absalom dwelt two full years in Jerusalem, and saw not the king's face.

Absalom sends for Joab to ask to be invited to see his father David, but Joab will not come to him.

14:29 Therefore Absalom sent for Joab, to have sent him to the king; but he would not come to him: and when he sent again the second time, he would not come.

Absalom was desperate to see his father David and reconcile with him, so desperate that he risked conflict with Joab to get his attention.

14:30 Therefore he said unto his servants, See, Joab's field is near mine, and he hath barley there; go and set it on fire. And Absalom's servants set the field on fire.

Joab rushes to the house of Absalom to demand why his field had been attacked.

14:31 Then Joab arose, and came to Absalom unto his house, and said unto him, Wherefore have thy servants set my field on fire?

Absalom demands that Joab bring him to his father, David the king.

14:32 And Absalom answered Joab, Behold, I sent unto thee, saying, Come hither, that I may send thee to the king, to say, Wherefore am I come from Geshur? it had been good for me to have been there still: now therefore let me see the king's face; and if there be any iniquity in me, let him kill me.

A temporary reconciliation is made, but the emotional pain remains because David loved the wicked dead more than the righteous son.

Absalom, feeling rejected by his father for doing the right thing by his sister and thrusting wickedness out of the royal family and the nation; began to consider himself more worthy to rule than his father, who had refused to deal with the wickedness of Amnon.

14:33 So Joab came to the king, and told him: and when he had called for Absalom, he came to the king, and bowed himself on his face to the ground before the king: and the king kissed Absalom.

2 Samuel 15

Absalom gets political and works to gain a personal following

2 Samuel 15:1 And it came to pass after this, that Absalom prepared him chariots and horses, and fifty men to run before him. **15:2** And Absalom rose up early, and stood beside the way of the gate: and it was so, that when any man that had a controversy came to the king for judgment, then Absalom called unto him, and said, Of what city art thou? And he said, Thy servant is of one of the tribes of Israel.

David was neglecting his responsibilities and did not appoint judges and justice for the people and this was a legitimate grievance. David should also have been aware that Absalom was undermining and usurping him, by exalting himself and not making recommendations to the king, and should have taken steps to correct this situation before the rebellion developed.

Isn't this exactly what many leaders and elders are doing when they say follow me, and they condemn any zeal to live by every Word of God our KING? Such elders are fomenting rebellion against the King of kings!

15:3 And Absalom said unto him, See, thy matters are good and right; but there is no man deputed of the king to hear thee. **15:4** Absalom said moreover, Oh that I were made judge in the land, that every man which hath any suit or cause might come unto me, and I would do him justice!

15:5 And it was so, that when any man came nigh to him to do him obeisance, he put forth his hand, and took him, and kissed him.

Absalom enticed the hearts of Israel to follow him in place of following the king; just like so many of today's elders have stolen the hearts of the brethren to follow themselves instead of living by every Word of God the GREAT KING.

15:6 And on this manner did Absalom to all Israel that came to the king for judgment: so Absalom stole the hearts of the men of Israel.

Absalom then requests to go to Hebron [where David had been made king of Judah].

15:7 And it came to pass after forty [not forty years later, since David's entire reign was only forty years, but properly four years after Absalom had returned to Jerusalem] years, that Absalom said unto the king, I pray thee, let me go and pay my vow, which I have vowed unto the LORD, in Hebron. **15:8** For thy servant vowed a vow while I abode at Geshur in Syria, saying, If the LORD shall bring me again indeed to Jerusalem, then I will serve the LORD. **15:9** And the king said unto him, Go in peace. So he arose, and went to Hebron.

David's entire reign was only forty years.

> **2 Samuel 5:4** David was thirty years old when he began to reign, and he reigned forty years. **5:5** In Hebron **he reigned over Judah seven years and six months:** and **in Jerusalem he reigned thirty and three years over all Israel and Judah.**

David's entire kingship was only 40 years and he ruled for some time after the death of Absalom!

The forty years mentioned below is clearly a scribal error and is a reference to FOUR years after the beginning of Absalom's political usurpation.

2 Samuel 15:10 But Absalom sent spies throughout all the tribes of Israel, saying, As soon as ye hear the sound of the trumpet, then ye shall say, Absalom reigneth in Hebron.

200 men accompanied Absalom to Hebron not knowing of the conspiracy, this company was used to deceive the others gathering there that Absalom was a man of authority, while Israel was being called to Hebron to declare Absalom king without realizing what was happening.

15:11 And with Absalom went two hundred men out of Jerusalem, that were called; and they went in their simplicity, and they knew not any thing.

Ahithophel David's chief adviser and the grandfather of Bathsheba entered the picture, joining the rebellion of Absalom. Here the tragedy of Tamar and Absalom was joined with the tragedy of Bathsheba and Uriah as David's chief adviser joins David's son in a conspiracy against him in accordance with the prophecy and curse of God for David's evil deeds.

As more and more people began to come to Absalom, David was forced to flee for his life.

15:12 And Absalom sent for Ahithophel the Gilonite, David's counsellor, from his city, even from Giloh, while he offered sacrifices. And the conspiracy was strong; for the people increased continually with Absalom.

15:13 And there came a messenger to David, saying, The hearts of the men of Israel are after Absalom. **15:14** And David said unto all his servants that were with him at Jerusalem, Arise, and let us flee; for we shall not else escape from Absalom: make speed to depart, lest he overtake us suddenly, and bring evil upon us, and smite the city with the edge of the sword.

David's servants remained loyal to him

15:15 And the king's servants said unto the king, Behold, thy servants are ready to do whatsoever my lord the king shall appoint.

Besides his many wives David also had many concubines, ten of which he left at Jerusalem.

15:16 And the king went forth, and all his household after him. And the **king left ten women, which were concubines, to keep the house**. **15:17** And the king went forth, and all the people after him, and tarried in a place that was far off.

The original 600 men who had been with him from the days of Saul remained faithful to David.

15:18 And all his servants passed on beside him; and all the Cherethites, and all the Pelethites, and all the Gittites, **six hundred men which came after him from Gath**, passed on before the king.

The foreigner Ittai was also loyal to David

15:19 Then said the king to Ittai the Gittite, Wherefore goest thou also with us? return to thy place, and abide with the king: for thou art a stranger, and also an exile.

David's friend Ittai had come to visit only the day before and was caught up in the turmoil.

15:20 Whereas thou camest but yesterday, should I this day make thee go up and down with us? seeing I go whither I may, return thou, and take back thy brethren: mercy and truth be with thee. **15:21** And Ittai answered the king, and said, As the LORD liveth, and as my lord the king liveth, surely in what place my lord the king shall be, whether in death or life, even there also will thy servant be.

Then David fled with his six hundred men, his family and friends and with the priests and Ark of YHVH.

15:22 And David said to Ittai, Go and pass over. And Ittai the Gittite passed over, and all his men, and all the little ones that were with him. **15:23** And all the country wept with a loud voice, and all the people passed over: the king also himself passed over the brook Kidron, and all the people passed over, toward the way of the wilderness.

15:24 And lo Zadok also, and all the Levites were with him, bearing the ark of the covenant of God: and they set down the ark of God; and Abiathar went up, until all the people had done passing out of the city.

Then David commanded Zadok to return with the Ark into Jerusalem, and placed himself voluntarily in the hands of God.

15:25 And the king said unto Zadok, Carry back the ark of God into the city: if I shall find favour in the eyes of the LORD, he will bring me again, and shew me both it, and his habitation: **15:26** But if he thus say, I have no delight in thee; behold, here am I, let him do to me as seemeth good unto him. **15:27** The king said also unto Zadok the priest, Art not thou a seer? return into the city in peace, and your two sons with you, Ahimaaz thy son, and Jonathan the son of Abiathar.

David tells the priests that he will remain in the wilderness until they send for him.

15:28 See, I will tarry in the plain of the wilderness, until there come word from you to certify me. **15:29** Zadok therefore and Abiathar carried the ark of God again to Jerusalem: and they tarried there.

David then covered his head and removed his shoes in abject submission before God, and went out weeping in mourning and weeping in submissive repentance the others also weeping; for they knew that this was from God fulfilling the curse for David's sin against Uriah, so many years before.

15:30 And David went up by the ascent of mount Olivet, and wept as he went up, and had his head covered, and he went barefoot: and all the people that was with him covered every man his head, and they went up, weeping as they went up.

Ahithophel, whose counsel was wise beyond the understanding of most men, had joined with Absalom and David knew he was bested; so he prayed to God for deliverance.

15:31 And one told David, saying, Ahithophel is among the conspirators with Absalom. And David said, O LORD, I pray thee, turn the counsel of Ahithophel into foolishness.

While David worshiped [remember the Hebrew meaning of that word which is to OBEY God] his friend Hushai came to him and it was decided that Hushai would return to Absalom to secretly defeat any further moves against David.

15:32 And it came to pass, that when David was come to the top of the mount, where he worshipped God, behold, Hushai the Archite came to meet him with his coat rent, and earth upon his head:

The aged Hushai would be a burden to David on the run, but could aid him by taking a place in the court of Absalom and keeping the priests informed; the priests could then send their son's as messengers to keep David informed.

15:33 Unto whom David said, If thou passest on with me, then thou shalt be a burden unto me: **15:34** But if thou return to the city, and say unto Absalom, I will be thy servant, O king; as I have been thy father's servant hitherto, so will I now also be thy servant: then mayest thou for me defeat the counsel of Ahithophel.

15:35 And hast thou not there with thee Zadok and Abiathar the priests? therefore it shall be, that **what thing soever thou shalt hear out of the king's house, thou shalt tell it to Zadok and Abiathar the priests**. **15:36** Behold, **they have there with them their two sons, Ahimaaz Zadok's son, and Jonathan Abiathar's son; and by them ye shall send unto me every thing that ye can hear.**

15:37 So Hushai David's friend came into the city, and Absalom came into Jerusalem.

2 Samuel 16

Ziba the servant of Saul's son who had been given charge over all the estate of Saul, brings food and transportation for David.

2 Samuel 16:1 And when David was a little past the top of the hill [of olives], behold, Ziba the servant of Mephibosheth met him, with a couple of asses saddled, and upon them two hundred loaves of bread, and an hundred bunches of raisins, and an hundred of summer fruits, and a bottle of wine. **16:2** And the king said unto Ziba, What meanest thou by these? And Ziba said, **The asses be for the king's household to ride on; and the bread and summer fruit for the young men to eat; and the wine, that such as be faint in the wilderness may drink.**

> **Subplot:** While Ziba helps David to flee, Mephibo-sheth thinks that by remaining in Jerusalem he can subvert Absalom and take the kingdom for himself.

16:3 And the king said, And where is thy master's son? And Ziba said unto the king, Behold, **he abideth at Jerusalem: for he said, To day shall the house of Israel restore me the kingdom of my father.**

Then David challenged Ziba to asertain if he is loyal to Mephibo-sheth and is hoping that David will flee away and never return. Ziba then pledges his loyalty to David.

16:4 Then said the king to Ziba, Behold, thine are all that pertained unto Mephibosheth [David then gives Ziba the possessions of the disloyal Mephibo-sheth]. **And Ziba said, I humbly beseech thee that I may find grace in thy sight, my lord, O king.**

All of Saul's descendants are dead except Mephibo-sheth; and Shimei a more distant relative of Saul also hates David for the kingdom's departure from Saul.

16:5 And when king David came to Bahurim, behold, thence came out a man of the family of the house of Saul, whose name was **Shimei, the son of Gera: he came forth, and cursed still as he came. 16:6** And he cast stones at David, and at all the servants of king David: and all the people and all the mighty men were on his right hand and on his left.

Shemia cursed David for Saul's sake, yet these things had come upon David for Uriah and Bathsheba. This Shemai was a very rich and a powerful chieftain of Benjamin as we shall see, and this matter was political in support of the attempt to take the kingdom by Mephibo-sheth, Saul's son.

16:7 And thus said Shimei when he cursed, Come out, come out, thou bloody man, and thou man of Belial: **16:8** The LORD hath returned upon thee all the blood of the house of Saul, in whose stead thou hast reigned; and the LORD hath delivered the kingdom into the hand of Absalom thy son: and, behold, thou art taken in thy mischief, because thou art a bloody man.

Abishai the brother of Joab then asked David to let him kill this man, and David acknowledged that this curse was because of his own sins against God.

16:9 Then said Abishai the son of Zeruiah unto the king, Why should this dead dog curse my lord the king? let me go over, I pray thee, and take off his head.

16:10 And the king said, What have I to do with you, ye sons of Zeruiah? so let him curse, because the LORD hath said unto him, Curse David. Who shall then say, Wherefore hast thou done so?

David says that his own son Absalom seeks his life and he cares for nothing. David extends mercy to Shemai in the hope that God will extend mercy to him.

16:11 And David said to Abishai, and to all his servants, Behold, my son, which came forth of my bowels, seeketh my life: how much more now may this Benjamite do it? let him alone, and let him curse; for the LORD hath bidden him. **16:12** It may be that the LORD will look on mine affliction, and that the LORD will requite me good for his cursing this day.

Shemai chased them across the Mount of Olives cursing and throwing stones as they went. Shemai was doubtless taking his vengeance and rejoicing over what he saw to be retribution for Saul and rejoicing over the thought that Saul was being restored by his descendant Mephibo-sheth.

16:13 And as David and his men went by the way, Shimei went along on the hill's side over against him, and cursed as he went, and threw stones at him, and cast dust.

David and his band came to Jordan and rested and refreshed there.

16:14 And the king, and all the people that were with him, came weary, and refreshed themselves there.

Absalom comes up from Hebron to Jerusalem

16:15 And Absalom, and all the people the men of Israel, came to Jerusalem, and Ahithophel with him.

David's friend Hushai then appeared and declared "God save the king" which words were intended to be mistaken as loyalty to Absalom; but Hushai meant them as words for the rightful king David.

16:16 And it came to pass, when Hushai the Archite, David's friend, was come unto Absalom, that Hushai said unto Absalom, God save the king, God save the king.

Absalom then asks Hushai if this was loyalty to his friend David [Absalom might well have asked himself if his actions were the actions of a loyal son]; Hushai then wisely replied that he was loyal to God. Absalom thinking that he was God's choice, was ignorant that Hushai had meant that David was God's choice.

Let today's brethren beware of this kind of double speak from leaders and elders today, and demand straight answers from them. Many say that we should be loyal to God while meaning and demanding that we be loyal to them because they consider themselves as having God's authority.

16:17 And Absalom said to Hushai, Is this thy kindness to thy friend? why wentest thou not with thy friend? **16:18** And Hushai said unto Absalom, Nay; but whom the LORD, and this people, and all the men of Israel, choose, his will I be, and with him will I abide. **16:19** And again, whom should I serve? should I not serve in the presence of his son? as I have served in thy father's presence, so will I be in thy presence.

Then Absalom asked for advice from his counselors; and Ahithophel gave his evil counsel to revenge his family against David's rape of Bathsheba and murder of her husband, thereby causing the prophecy of God by Nathan to be further fulfilled.

16:20 Then said Absalom to Ahithophel, Give counsel among you what we shall do.

16:21 And Ahithophel said unto Absalom, Go in unto thy father's concubines, which he hath left to keep the house; and all Israel shall hear that thou art abhorred of thy father: then shall the hands of all that are with thee be strong. **16:22** So they spread Absalom a tent upon the top of the house; and Absalom went in unto his father's concubines in the sight of all Israel.

Atithophel was considered to be very wise and his advice was followed, fulfilling the prophecy.

> **2 Samuel 12:11** Thus saith the Lord, Behold, I will raise up evil against thee out of thine own house, and **I will take thy wives before thine eyes, and give them unto thy neighbour, and he shall lie with thy wives in the sight of this sun. 12:12** For thou didst it secretly: but I will do this thing before all Israel, and before the sun.

2 Samuel 16:23 And the counsel of Ahithophel, which he counselled in those days, was as if a man had enquired at the oracle of God: so was all the counsel of Ahithophel [respected] both with David and with Absalom.

2 Samuel 17

Ahithophel then advised an immediate attack to slay David, and Absalom was pleased; being full of bitter hatred over his treatment by his father David over his execution of the sister rapist Amnon.

2 Samuel 17:1 Moreover Ahithophel said unto Absalom, Let me now choose out twelve thousand men, and I will arise and pursue after David this night: **17:2** And I will come upon him while he is weary and weak handed, and will make him afraid: and all the people that are with him shall flee; and I will smite the king only: **17:3** And I will bring back all the people unto thee: the man whom thou seekest is as if all returned: so all the people shall be in peace.

Absalom was pleased but asked for a second opinion from Hushai

17:4 And the saying pleased Absalom well, and all the elders of Israel. **17:5** Then said Absalom, Call now Hushai the Archite also, and let us hear likewise what he saith. **17:6** And when Hushai was come to Absalom, Absalom spake unto him, saying, Ahithophel hath spoken after this manner: shall we do after his saying? if not; speak thou.

Hushai advises that David will lodge with his mighty men and not with the civilians, and being a strong and experienced man of war enraged by this rebellion; David will not be easily taken.

17:7 And Hushai said unto Absalom, The counsel that Ahithophel hath given is not good at this time. **17:8** For, said Hushai, thou knowest thy father and his men, that they be mighty men, and they be chafed in their minds, as a bear robbed of her whelps in the field: and thy father is a man of war, and will not lodge with the people.

Hushai warns: When David's small band manages to kill some of Absalom's men they will lose heart and flee away.

17:9 Behold, he is hid now in some pit, or in some other place: and it will come to pass, when some of them be overthrown at the first, that whosoever heareth it will say, There is a slaughter among the people that follow Absalom. **17:10** And he also that is valiant, whose heart is as the heart of a lion, shall utterly melt: for all Israel knoweth that thy father is a mighty man, and they which be with him are valiant men.

Hushai counsels that Absalom gather together a large army before going after David.

17:11 Therefore I counsel that all Israel be generally gathered unto thee, from Dan even to Beersheba, as the sand that is by the sea for multitude; and that thou go to battle in thine own person. **17:12** So shall we come upon him in some place where he shall be found, and we will light upon him as the dew falleth on the ground: and of him and of all the men that are with him there shall not be left so much as

one. **17:13** Moreover, if he be gotten into a city, then shall all Israel bring ropes to that city, and we will draw it into the river, until there be not one small stone found there.

Hushai's counsel is accepted and it buys time for David.

17:14 And Absalom and all the men of Israel said, The counsel of Hushai the Archite is better than the counsel of Ahithophel. For the LORD had appointed to defeat the good counsel of Ahithophel, to the intent that the LORD might bring evil upon Absalom.

Hushai then sends word to David to hide himself quickly and not camp in the open plain that night lest Absalom change his mind and attack him in the open.

17:15 Then said Hushai unto Zadok and to Abiathar the priests, Thus and thus did Ahithophel counsel Absalom and the elders of Israel; and thus and thus have I counselled. **17:16** Now therefore send quickly, and tell David, saying, Lodge not this night in the plains of the wilderness, but speedily pass over [Jordan]; lest the king be swallowed up, and all the people that are with him.

A woman was sent with a message for the sons of the priests who were in hiding

17:17 Now Jonathan and Ahimaaz stayed by Enrogel; for they might not be seen to come into the city: and a wench went and told them; and they went and told king David.

The messengers were betrayed and almost caught on their mission to David, having to hide in a woman's well.

17:18 Nevertheless a lad saw them, and told Absalom: but they went both of them away quickly, and came to a man's house in Bahurim, which had a well in his court; whither they went down. **17:19** And the woman took and spread a covering over the well's mouth, and spread ground corn thereon; and the thing was not known. **17:20** And when Absalom's servants came to the woman to the house, they said, Where is Ahimaaz and Jonathan? And the woman said unto them, They be gone over the brook of water. And when they had sought and could not find them, they returned to Jerusalem.

17:21 And it came to pass, after they were departed, that they came up out of the well, and went and told king David, and said unto David, Arise, and pass quickly over the water [river Jordan]: for thus hath Ahithophel counselled against you.

David then crossed Jordan with his own army and escaped to the east.

17:22 Then David arose, and all the people that were with him, and they passed over Jordan: by the morning light there lacked not one of them that was not **gone over Jordan**.

At that point the wise Ahithophel knew that the cause of Absalom was lost and that he would die a traitor, so he hanged himself.

17:23 And when Ahithophel saw that his counsel was not followed, he saddled his ass, and arose, and gat him home to his house, to his city, and put his household in order, and hanged himself, and died, and was buried in the sepulchre of his father.

17:24 Then David came to Mahanaim. And Absalom passed over Jordan, he and all the men of Israel with him.

Absalom took the cousin of Joab to be his captain in place of Joab who was loyal to David.

17:25 And Absalom made **Amasa captain** of the host instead of Joab: which Amasa was a man's son, whose name was Ithra an Israelite, that went in to Abigail the daughter of Nahash, sister to Zeruiah Joab's mother.

Amasa was the son of an Abigail (2 Sam 17:25), who was the sister of King David (1 Chr 2:16,17) and Zeruiah [was the mother of Joab]. Hence, Amasa was a nephew to David and a cousin of Joab, as well as a cousin to Absalom.

The two armies camped in the Golan

17:26 So Israel and Absalom pitched in the land of Gilead.

Then friends of David brought them supplies.

17:27 And it came to pass, when David was come to Mahanaim, that Shobi the son of Nahash of Rabbah of the children of Ammon, and Machir the son of Ammiel of Lodebar, and Barzillai the Gileadite of Rogelim,

17:28 Brought beds, and basons, and earthen vessels, and wheat, and barley, and flour, and parched corn, and beans, and lentiles, and parched pulse, **17:29** And honey, and butter, and sheep, and cheese of kine, for David, and for the people that were with him, to eat: for they said, The people is hungry, and weary, and thirsty, in the wilderness.

All of this fulfilled the prophecy by Nathan, and punished David for his sins. The one who later became Jesus Christ was allowing David to experience a lesson that he would never forget; so that he would never again depart from the Word of God for all eternity.

We are also being taught the very same lesson that we are to be passionately loyal to live by every Word of God!

Those who idolize men and corporate entities to commit spiritual adultery with them by turning aside from the Word of God to follow them; are being taught the same lesson! Just as David suffered, we will also suffer for our spiritual adultery in the imminent great tribulation.

We are all being taught a lesson of loyalty to God to prepare us for a righteous kingship if we do learn the lesson of absolute and total loyalty to God and to zealously learn and to live by every Word of God; regardless of the trials or temptations to do otherwise!

2 Samuel 18

Ahithophel's vengeful and wicked counsel to Absalom regarding his father's concubines fails, so that the action of Absalom far from bringing more followers to Absalom out of fear of David; engendered revulsion against Absalom and many in Israel rallied to go over to David; so that David now had thousands with him in the Golan.

2 Samuel 18:1 And David numbered the people that were with him, and set captains of thousands, and captains of hundreds over them.

David divides his army into three parts

18:2 And David sent forth a third part of the people under the hand of **Joab,** and a third part under the hand of Abishai the son of **Zeruiah**, Joab's brother, and a third part under the hand of **Ittai** the Gittite. And the king said unto the people, I will surely go forth with you myself also.

The people will not let David [now older] go out to the battle

18:3 But the people answered, Thou shalt not go forth: for if we flee away, they will not care for us; neither if half of us die, will they care for us: but now thou art worth ten thousand of us: therefore now it is better that thou succour [command us from a headquarters in the city] us out of the city. **18:4** And the king said unto them, What seemeth you best I will do. And the king stood by the gate side, and all the people came out by hundreds and by thousands.

David asks for care to save Absalom alive

18:5 And the king commanded Joab and Abishai and Ittai, saying, Deal gently for my sake with the young man, even with Absalom. And all the people heard when the king gave all the captains charge concerning Absalom.

The battle was great

18:6 So the people went out into the field against Israel: and the battle was in the wood of Ephraim; **18:7** Where the people of Israel were slain before the servants of David, and there was there a great **slaughter that day of twenty thousand men**.

More people became lost in the forest and perished, then were killed in the fight. You can imagine running in panic through an unfamiliar forest and falling into pits, dead falls [entanglements of fallen trees], quicksand and other dangers.

18:8 For the battle was there scattered over the face of all the country: and the wood devoured more people that day than the sword devoured.

Absalom became entangled in a tree branch by his head

18:9 And Absalom met the servants of David. And Absalom rode upon a mule, and the mule went under the thick boughs of a great oak, and his head caught hold of the oak, and he was taken up between the heaven and the earth; and the mule that was under him went away. **18:10** And a certain man saw it, and told Joab, and said, Behold, I saw Absalom hanged in an oak.

Joab sought to take the life of Absalom, knowing that for future peace Absalom had to die for his rebellion as an example to all rebels in spite of the feelings of David for his son.

David's failure to mete out justice on his sister raping son brought on these quarrels between David and Absalom, and Joab knew that mercy to the rebel would bring on more rebellion unless justice was done.

18:11 And Joab said unto the man that told him, And, behold, thou sawest him, and why didst thou not smite him there to the ground? and I would have given thee ten shekels of silver, and a girdle.

Joab's soldier refused to disobey king David, forcing Joab to take personal action.

18:12 And the man said unto Joab, Though I should receive a thousand shekels of silver in mine hand, yet would I not put forth mine hand against the king's son: for in our hearing the king charged thee and Abishai and Ittai, saying, Beware that none touch the young man Absalom. **18:13** Otherwise I should have wrought falsehood against mine own life: for there is no matter hid from the king, and thou thyself wouldest have set thyself against me.

Joab and his personal aide then slew Absalom.

18:14 Then said Joab, I may not tarry thus with thee. And he took three darts in his hand, and thrust them through the heart of Absalom, while he was yet alive in the midst of the oak. **18:15** And ten young men that bare Joab's armour compassed about and smote Absalom, and slew him.

Joab then stopped the battle because the usurper was dead

18:16 And Joab blew the trumpet, and the people returned from pursuing after Israel: for Joab held back the people. **18:17** And they took Absalom, and cast him into a great pit in the wood, and laid a very great heap of stones upon him: and all [the rebels] Israel fled every one to his tent.

Absalom died childless and had a monument of stone made for himself for that reason.

18:18 Now Absalom in his lifetime had taken and reared up for himself a pillar, which is in the king's dale: for he said, I have no son to keep my name in remembrance: and he called the pillar after his own name: and it is called unto this day, Absalom's place.

Joab delayed the messenger to David in order to send his own messenger to break the news of Absalom's death first.

18:19 Then said Ahimaaz the son of Zadok, Let me now run, and bear the king tidings, how that the LORD hath avenged him of his enemies. **18:20** And Joab said unto him, Thou shalt not bear tidings this day, but thou shalt bear tidings another day: but this day thou shalt bear no tidings, because the king's son is dead.

18:21 Then said Joab to Cushi, Go tell the king what thou hast seen. And Cushi bowed himself unto Joab, and ran. **18:22** Then said Ahimaaz the son of Zadok yet again to Joab, But howsoever, let me, I pray thee, also run after Cushi. And Joab said, Wherefore wilt thou run, my son, seeing that thou hast no tidings ready? **18:23** But howsoever, said he, let me run. And he said unto him, Run.

The son of Zadok Ahimaaz, then outran Cushi to David anyway

Then Ahimaaz ran by the way of the plain, and overran Cushi.

David was in the city and waiting for news

18:24 And David sat between the two gates: and the watchman went up to the roof over the gate unto the wall, and lifted up his eyes, and looked, and behold a man running alone. **18:25** And the watchman cried, and told the king. And the king said, If he be alone, there is tidings in his mouth. And he came apace, and drew near. **18:26** And the watchman saw another man running: and the watchman called unto the porter, and said, Behold another man running alone. And the king said, He also bringeth tidings.

Ahimaaz announced the victory first

18:27 And the watchman said, Me thinketh the running of the foremost is like the running of Ahimaaz the son of Zadok. And the king said, He is a good man, and cometh with good tidings. **18:28** And Ahimaaz called, and said unto the king, All is well. And he fell down to the earth upon his face before the king, and said, **Blessed be the LORD thy God, which hath delivered up the men that lifted up their hand against my lord the king.**

David asks after Absalom

18:29 And the king said, Is the young man Absalom safe? And Ahimaaz answered, When Joab sent the king's servant, and me thy servant, I saw a great tumult, but I knew not what it was. **18:30** And the king said unto him, Turn aside, and stand here. And he turned aside, and stood still.

Cushi then announces the death of Absalom.

18:31 And, behold, Cushi came; and Cushi said, Tidings, my lord the king: for the LORD hath avenged thee this day of all them that rose up against thee. **18:32** And the king said unto Cushi, Is the young man Absalom safe? And Cushi answered, The enemies of my lord the king, and all that rise against thee to do thee hurt, be as that young man is.

David wept over the death of the usurper Absalom his beloved son.

Jesus Christ will not hold back from destroying in the lake of fire all those who reject zeal to live by every Word of God even though he loves them greatly, because he knows that they will continue to rebel and to lead others in rebellion against him and God the Father.

The lack of justice concerning Tamar and the rebellion of Absalom is more than only punishment for Uriah; it is a lesson for David in how to be a king. No king can allow rebellion and law-breaking in his kingdom and expect to have a peaceful stable kingdom; no not even God the Father and Jesus Christ!

It is the duty of a ruler to teach the people to abide by the law and to execute justice honestly and evenhandedly without regard to any person. David had to learn that, and so does the latter day Spiritual Ekklesia.

Those who teach that God will overlook our sins because he loves us, are ignorant, knowing nothing about being kings as they ought to know. God the Father and Jesus Christ cannot afford the kind of emotional overlooking of justice which brought David so much grief.

They MUST and WILL expel all sin, commandment breaking and turning aside from any part of the whole Word of God, because even a speck of rebellion, like leaven, will ultimately infect the whole lump.

Those who wanted to return to Egypt were destroyed in the wilderness and many enemies were brought up to correct Israel when they sinned: So today, Jesus Christ will correct all who take God's Word lightly and turn aside to follow their idols; including idols of men and corporate entities.

Any willful unrepentant sin [breaking the Word of God] is REBELLION against God the Father and Jesus Christ the King of kings, and those who do such things will be corrected, and if still unrepentant they will be destroyed in the final sea of fire.

18:33 And the king was much moved, and went up to the chamber over the gate, and wept: and as he went, thus he said, O my son Absalom, my son, my son Absalom! would God I had died for thee, O Absalom, my son, my son!

David had to learn the hard way that the law of God and Godly justice, trumps personal emotional feelings. We should NOT take any pleasure in the death of the wicked, but rather work to bring them to repentance. However there will be a final day of judgment and all unrepentant sinners will receive the just wages for their conduct from God; which for sin is death, regardless of how much we love them.

Ezekiel 33:11 Say unto them, As I live, saith the Lord God, I have no pleasure in the death of the wicked; but that the wicked turn from his way and live: turn ye, turn ye from your evil ways; for why will ye die, O house of Israel?

Therefore if we really love others; it is our DUTY to: Cry Aloud and Spare Not, rebuking all sin Isaiah 58; in the hope that some might be saved.

2 Samuel 19

David by his sympathy for the sinner, turned the rejoicing of victory over the sin of rebellion against the king into mourning.

Remember the our King is Jesus Christ, and that we are to support him in his dispensing of JUSTICE and his victory over the wicked; instead of becoming emotionally attached to the wicked [Stockholm Syndrome] like David was.

2 Samuel 19:1 And it was told Joab, Behold, the king weepeth and mourneth for Absalom. **19:2** And the victory that day was turned into mourning unto all the people: for the people heard say that day how the king was grieved for his son.

David made the people ashamed of their actions in supporting David and crushing the wicked rebel. We should never be ashamed of the justice of God.

19:3 And the people gat them by stealth that day into the city, as people being ashamed steal away when they flee in battle. **19:4** But the king covered his face, and the king cried with a loud voice, O my son Absalom, O Absalom, my son, my son!

Joab rightly corrects David

Brethren, we should not tolerate any habitual sin [rebellion against any part of the Word of God] in the Ekklesia, nor should we be overlooking or hiding any unrepented sin. All evil should be exposed to the light of day and revealed before all; so that evil might be dealt with and expunged.

19:5 And Joab came into the house to the king, and said, Thou hast shamed this day the faces of all thy servants, which this day have saved thy life, and the lives of thy sons and of thy daughters, and the lives of thy wives, and the lives of thy concubines; **19:6** In that thou lovest thine enemies, and hatest thy friends. For thou hast declared this day, that thou regardest neither princes nor servants: for this day I perceive, that if Absalom had lived, and all we had died this day, then it had pleased thee well.

19:7 Now therefore arise, go forth, and speak comfortably unto thy servants: for I swear by the LORD, if thou go not forth, there will not tarry one with thee this night: and that will be worse unto thee than all the evil that befell thee from thy youth until now.

David had to learn how to be a king; how to rule justly and without compromise, and to reject sympathy for the wicked works of the unrepentant. Even so Jesus Christ will apply his blood of justification ONLY to the Sincerely Repentant, and he will destroy the unrepentant wicked who imagine that forgiveness of past sin is somehow a license to continue in sin and compromise with any part of the whole Word of God.

19:8 Then the king arose, and sat in the gate. [the gate of his refuge city in Golan, to dispense justice] And they told unto all the people, saying, Behold, the king doth sit in the gate. And all the people came before the king: for Israel had fled every man to his tent.

David did not seize the kingdom even though it was his, but waited for Israel to invite him back as their king.

19:9 And all the people were at strife throughout **all the tribes of Israel**, saying, The king saved us out of the hand of our enemies, and he delivered us out of the hand of the Philistines; and now he is fled out of the land for Absalom. **19:10** And Absalom, whom we anointed over us, is dead in battle. Now therefore **why speak ye not a word of bringing the king back?**

David then speaks to Judah by the priests of God

19:11 And king David sent to Zadok and to Abiathar the priests, saying, Speak unto the elders of Judah, saying, Why are ye the last to bring the king back to his house? seeing the speech of all Israel is come to the king, even to his house. **19:12** Ye are my brethren, ye are my bones and my flesh: wherefore then are ye the last to bring back the king?

David then made a political move removing Joab from his office for his disobedience in killing Absalom and offering the job of commander in chief to Amasa of Judah; this brings Judah back into the kingdom and gives David a commander who had been the commander of Absalom's rebellion. David could not have had confidence in Amasa; this was a political appointment to bring Judah into the fold.

19:13 And say ye to Amasa, Art thou not of my bone, and of my flesh? God do so to me, and more also, if thou be not captain of the host before me continually in the room of Joab. **19:14** And he [Amasa] bowed the heart of all the men of Judah, even as the heart of one man; so that they sent this word unto the king, Return thou, and all thy servants. **19:15** So the king returned, and came to Jordan. And Judah came to Gilgal, to go to meet the king, to conduct the king over Jordan.

Shimei of Saul's family then rushes to apologize to David for cursing him over the throne of Saul.

19:16 And Shimei the son of Gera, a Benjamite, which was of Bahurim, hasted and came down with the men of Judah to meet king David. **19:17** And there were a thousand men of Benjamin with him [Shimei], and Ziba [David's loyal man] the servant of the house of Saul, and his fifteen sons and his twenty servants with him; and they went over Jordan before the king.

Shimei repents in fear at the feet of David

19:18 And there went over a ferry boat to carry over the king's household, and to do what he thought good. And Shimei the son of Gera fell down before the king, as he was come over Jordan; **19:19** And said unto the king, Let not my lord impute iniquity unto me, neither do thou remember that which thy servant did perversely the day that my lord the king went out of Jerusalem, that the king should take it to his heart. **19:20** For thy servant doth know that I have sinned: therefore, behold, I am come the first this day of all the house of Joseph to go down to meet my lord the king.

The king forgives Shimei who was begging for his life, deserving to die along with the other rebels.

19:21 But Abishai the son of Zeruiah answered and said, Shall not Shimei be put to death for this, because he cursed the LORD's anointed? **19:22** And David said, What have I to do with you, ye sons of Zeruiah, that ye should this day be adversaries unto me? shall there any man be put to death this day in Israel? for do not I know that I am this day king over Israel? **19:23** Therefore the king said unto Shimei, Thou shalt not die. And the king sware unto him.

Mephibo-sheth who had eaten at the table of David these years; who had hoped to gain the throne, now comes to David.

19:24 And Mephibosheth the son of Saul came down to meet the king, and had neither dressed his feet, nor trimmed his beard, nor washed his clothes, from the day the king departed until the day he came again in peace.

David asked Mephibo-sheth why he had not come to support him, and Mephibo-sheth gives his story in an attempt to save himself, and David spares him for the sake of David's covenant with Jonathan.

19:25 And it came to pass, when he was come to Jerusalem to meet the king, that the king said unto him, Wherefore wentest not thou with me, Mephibosheth? **19:26** And he answered, My lord, O king, my servant deceived me: for thy servant said, I will saddle me an ass, that I may ride thereon, and go to the king; because thy servant is lame. **19:27** And he hath slandered thy servant unto my lord the king; but my lord the king is as an angel of God: do therefore what is good in thine eyes. **19:28** For all of my father's house were but dead men before my lord the king: yet didst thou set thy servant among them that did eat at thine own table. What right therefore have I yet to cry any more unto the king?

David allows Mephibo-sheth to keep his estate

19:29 And the king said unto him, Why speakest thou any more of thy matters? I have said, Thou and Ziba divide the land. **19:30** And Mephibosheth said unto the king, Yea, let him take all, forasmuch as my lord the king is come again in peace unto his own house.

Barzillai a close friend of David who had given him relief during his stay in Gilead came to say his goodbyes.

19:31 And Barzillai the Gileadite came down from Rogelim, and went over Jordan with the king, to conduct him over Jordan. **19:32** Now Barzillai was a very aged man, even fourscore years old: and he had provided the king of sustenance while he lay at Mahanaim; for he was a very great man.

David invites his friend to Jerusalem

19:33 And the king said unto Barzillai, Come thou over with me, and I will feed thee with me in Jerusalem.

Barzillai asks leave to die in his own home and sends his servant Chimham with David.

19:34 And Barzillai said unto the king, How long have I to live, that I should go up with the king unto Jerusalem? **19:35** I am this day fourscore years old: and can I discern between good and evil? can thy servant taste what I eat or what I drink? can I hear any more the voice of singing men and singing women? wherefore then should thy servant be yet a burden unto my lord the king? **19:36** Thy servant will go a little way over Jordan with the king: and why should the king recompense it me with such a reward? **19:37** Let thy servant, I pray thee, turn back again, that I may die in mine own city, and be buried by the grave of my father and of my mother. But behold thy servant Chimham; let him go over with my lord the king; and do to him what shall seem good unto thee.

19:38 And the king answered, Chimham shall go over with me, and I will do to him that which shall seem good unto thee: and whatsoever thou shalt require of me, that will I do for thee. **19:39** And all the people went over Jordan. And when the king was come over, the king kissed Barzillai, and blessed him; and he returned unto his own place.

Then Judah and Israel began to dispute over David the king. Doesn't this remind us of the disciples disputing among themselves over who is to be the greatest under Christ? Is it not the same today with many leader's or elder's claiming to be the greatest?

19:40 Then the king went on to Gilgal, and Chimham went on with him: and all the people of Judah conducted the king, and also half the people of Israel. **19:41** And, behold, all the men of Israel came to the king, and said unto the king, Why have our brethren the men of Judah stolen thee away, and have brought the king, and his household, and all David's men with him, over Jordan?

19:42 And all the men of Judah answered the men of Israel, Because the king is near of kin to us: wherefore then be ye angry for this matter? have we eaten at all of the king's cost? or hath he given us any gift? **19:43** And the men of Israel answered the men of Judah, and said, We have ten parts in the king, and we have also more right in David than ye: why then did ye despise us, that our advice should not be first had in bringing back our king? And the words of the men of Judah were fiercer than the words of the men of Israel.

2 Samuel 20

Part of Benjamin revolts against David: Judah remained with David, while Israel followed Sheba of Benjamin.

2 Samuel 20:1 And there happened to be there a man of Belial, whose name was Sheba, the son of Bichri, a Benjamite: and he blew a trumpet, and said, We have no part in David, neither have we inheritance in the son of Jesse: every man to his tents, O Israel. **20:2** So every man of Israel went up from after David, and followed Sheba the son of Bichri: but the men of Judah clave unto their king, from Jordan even to Jerusalem.

David's ten women who were violated by Absalom were kept celibate until their deaths. This is an example of how the sins of one man can affect many others, and a primary reason why NO sin can be tolerated by a just and godly ruler.

20:3 And David came to his house at Jerusalem; and the king took the ten women his concubines, whom he had left to keep the house, and put them in ward, and fed them, but went not in unto them. So they were shut up unto the day of their death, living in widowhood.

Amasa is commanded to assemble the men of Judah.

Remember that Amasa was made chief by Absalom, and then David made Amasa chief of the army of Israel replacing Joab because Joab killed Absalom; and also to bring about the surrender of the people who had followed Absalom. So Joab was bitter over his own replacement by his cousin Amasa as chief of staff of Israel.

20:4 Then said the king to Amasa, Assemble me the men of Judah **within three days**, and be thou here present. **20:5** So Amasa went to assemble the men of Judah: but he tarried longer than the set time which he had appointed him.

Joab's brother Abashai is given command of the mission.

20:6 And David said to Abishai [the brother of Joab], Now shall Sheba the son of Bichri do us more harm than did Absalom: take thou thy lord's servants [take the army], and pursue after him [quickly], lest he get him fenced cities, and escape us. **20:7** And there went out after him **Joab's men,** and the Cherethites, and the Pelethites, and all the mighty men: and they went out of Jerusalem, to pursue after Sheba the son of Bichri.

20:8 When they were at the great stone which is in Gibeon, Amasa went before them. And Joab's garment that he had put on was girded unto him, and upon it a girdle with a sword fastened upon his loins in the sheath thereof; and as he went forth it fell out.

Joab killed Amasa and then continued the pursuit of Sheba the rebel.

20:9 And Joab said to Amasa, Art thou in health, my brother? And Joab took Amasa by the beard with the right hand to kiss him. **20:10** But Amasa took no heed to the sword that was in Joab's hand: so he smote him therewith in the fifth rib, and shed out his bowels to the ground, and struck him not again; and he died. So Joab and Abishai his brother pursued after Sheba the son of Bichri.

Joab's men then proclaimed Joab the commander in chief in David's name. While on the surface this appears to be a matter of bitterness on the part of Joab; one has to wonder if this act was in the interests of David to remove Amasa who had rebelled with Absalom and could not be trusted.

20:11 And one of Joab's men stood by him, and said, He that favoureth Joab, and he that is for David, let him go after Joab.

The men who saw their chief Amasa wallowing in blood stopped in shock, so that Joab had Amasa removed into a field and covered to hide him.

20:12 And Amasa wallowed in blood in the midst of the highway. And when the man saw that all the people stood still, he removed Amasa out of the highway into the field, and cast a cloth upon him, when he saw that every one that came by him stood still. **20:13** When he was removed out of the highway, all the people went on after Joab, to pursue after Sheba the son of Bichri.

20:14 And he went through all the tribes of Israel **unto Abel, and to Bethmaachah**, and all the Berites: and they were gathered together, and went also after him. **20:15** And they came and besieged him in Abel of Bethmaachah, and they cast up a bank against the city, and it stood in the trench: and all the people that were with Joab battered the wall, to throw it down.

A wise woman saves the city and many lives

20:16 Then cried a wise woman out of the city, Hear, hear; say, I pray you, unto Joab, Come near hither, that I may speak with thee.

Joab listens to the woman. This is an important lesson because not listening to our women is a very foolish thing. Every man should listen to his wife and benefit from her wisdom.

20:17 And when he was come near unto her, the woman said, Art thou Joab? And he answered, I am he. Then she said unto him, Hear the words of thine handmaid. And he answered, I do hear.

20:18 Then she spake, saying, They were wont to speak in old time, saying, They shall surely ask counsel at Abel [Beth-maachah]: and so they ended the matter. **20:19** I am one of them that are peaceable and faithful in Israel: thou seekest to destroy a city and a mother in Israel: why wilt thou swallow up the inheritance of the LORD?

Joab responds

20:20 And Joab answered and said, Far be it, far be it from me, that I should swallow up or destroy. **20:21** The matter is not so: but a man of mount Ephraim, Sheba the son of Bichri by name, hath lifted up his hand against the king, even against David: deliver him only, and I will depart from the city.

The woman then offered a solution and after Sheba was destroyed Joab departed without destroying the people and city.

And the woman said unto Joab, Behold, his head shall be thrown to thee over the wall. **20:22** Then the woman went unto all the people in her wisdom. And they cut off the head of Sheba the son of Bichri, and cast it out to Joab. And he blew a trumpet, and they retired from the city, every man to his tent. And Joab returned to Jerusalem unto the king.

Joab was made Chief of Staff again by David. Why did David restore him to his position and not rebuke him at all? Was Joab's killing of Amasa inspired by David because Amasa had led the army for Absalom?

20:23 Now Joab was over all the host of Israel: and Benaiah the son of Jehoiada was over the Cherethites and over the Pelethites: **20:24** And Adoram was over the tribute: and Jehoshaphat the son of Ahilud was recorder: **20:25** And Sheva was scribe: and Zadok and Abiathar were the priests: **20:26** And Ira also the Jairite was a chief ruler about David.

2 Samuel 21

2 Samuel 21:1 Then there was a famine in the days of David three years, year after year; and David enquired of the LORD. And the LORD answered, It is for Saul, and for his bloody house, because he slew the Gibeonites.

Saul had killed many Gibeonites even though they had a covenant with Israel to be cutters of wood and drawers of water for the tabernacle and the sacrifices. Therefore God had sent famine on the land. One does wonder why this came so long after the deed by Saul, perhaps Jesus was reminding David to make amends for the broken vow of Israel.

21:2 And the king called the Gibeonites, and said unto them; (now the Gibeonites were not of the children of Israel, but of the remnant of the Amorites; and the children of Israel had sworn unto them: and Saul sought to slay them in his zeal to the children of Israel and Judah.)

The Gibeonites humbly declare that they will have no money from Saul or any man of Israel, but demand the sons of Saul. This was part of the curse from the one who later became flesh as Jesus Christ and who had cursed Saul and his descendants for slaughtering many Gibeonites.

21:3 Wherefore David said unto the Gibeonites, What shall I do for you? and wherewith shall I make the atonement, that ye may bless the inheritance of the LORD? **21:4** And the Gibeonites said unto him, We will have no silver nor gold of Saul, nor of his house; neither for us shalt thou kill any man in Israel. And he said, What ye shall say, that will I do for you.

David gives up the sons of Saul

21:5 And they answered the king, The man that consumed us, and that devised against us that we should be destroyed from remaining in any of the coasts of Israel, **21:6 Let seven men of his sons be delivered unto us, and we will hang them up unto the LORD in Gibeah of Saul**, whom the LORD did choose. **And the king said, I will give them.**

21:7 But the king spared Mephibosheth, the son of Jonathan the son of Saul, because of the LORD's oath that was between them, between David and Jonathan the son of Saul.

David gave to them the five sons of his wife Mi-chal by Adriel her second husband, and two other direct sons of Saul. So Saul paid dearly for his transgression against Gibeah, and Mi-chal paid dearly for her mocking of David before the Ark of God, while Adriel paid dearly for taking another man's wife even though she was taken from David by Saul.

21:8 But the king took the **two sons of Rizpah** the daughter of Aiah [Saul's wife], whom she bare unto Saul, **Armoni and Mephibosheth**; and the **five sons of Michal** the daughter of Saul, whom she brought up for [bore to her second husband] Adriel the son of Barzillai the Meholathite:

21:9 And he delivered them into the hands of the Gibeonites, and they hanged them in the hill before the LORD: and they fell all seven together, and were put to death in the days of harvest, in the first days, in the **beginning of barley harvest.**

They were hung on or immediately after the first Sunday Wave Offering day of the Feast of Unleavened Bread.

Rizpah mourned for her sons and for the sons of Saul and protected the bodies from the scavengers until the dew of the morning.

21:10 And Rizpah the daughter of Aiah took sackcloth, and spread it for her upon the rock, from the beginning of harvest until water dropped upon them out of heaven, and suffered neither the birds of the air to rest on them by day, nor the beasts of the field by night.

21:11 And it was told David what Rizpah the daughter of **Aiah, the concubine of Saul**, had done.

David then buried Saul and his sons together, in the tomb of Saul's father Kish.

21:12 And David went and took the bones of Saul and the bones of Jonathan his son from the men of Jabeshgilead, which had stolen [liberated] them from the street of Bethshan, where the Philistines had hanged them, when the Philistines had slain Saul in Gilboa: **21:13** And he brought up from thence the bones of Saul and the bones of Jonathan his son; and they gathered the bones of them that were hanged. **21:14** And the bones of Saul and Jonathan his son buried they in the country of Benjamin in Zelah, in the sepulchre of Kish his father: and they performed all that the king commanded. And after that God was intreated for the land.

David nearly seventy, became weak during a battle with the Philistines

21:15 Moreover the Philistines had yet war again with Israel; and David went down, and his servants with him, and fought against the Philistines: and **David waxed faint. 21:16** And Ishbibenob, which was of the sons of the giant, the weight of whose spear weighed three hundred shekels of brass in weight, he being girded with a new sword, thought to have slain David.

Abishai the brother of Joab saved David

21:17 But Abishai the son of Zeruiah succoured him, and smote the Philistine, and killed him. Then the men of David sware unto him, saying, Thou shalt go no more out with us to battle, that thou quench not the light of Israel.

His commanders then insisted that David was too old to go into battle and would not allow him to go to personally fight any more.

The giants of the Philistines were all slain and giantism was destroyed in the Philistines, so that the descendants of the Philistines who live in Gaza today are ordinary men.

Even though there are nearly a million Palestinian refugees in Gaza today the native people of Gaza are NOT Palestinians who had come from Mesopotamia (2 Kings 17); the native people of Gaza are the modern descendants of the Philistines.

21:18 And it came to pass after this, that there was again a battle with the Philistines at Gob: then Sibbechai the Hushathite slew Saph, which was of the sons of the giant.

21:19 And there was again a battle in Gob with the Philistines, where Elhanan the son of Jaareoregim, a Bethlehemite, slew the brother of Goliath the Gittite, the staff of whose spear was like a weaver's beam.

21:20 And there was yet a battle in Gath, where was a man of great stature, that had on every hand six fingers, and on every foot six toes, four and twenty in number; and he also was born to the giant.

21:21 And when he defied Israel, Jonathan the son of Shimeah the brother of David slew him.

21:22 These four were born to the giant in Gath, and fell by the hand of David, and by the hand of his servants.

2 Samuel 22

A Psalm of David

2 Samuel 22:1 And David spake unto the LORD the words of this song in the day that the LORD had delivered him out of the hand of all his enemies, and out of the hand of Saul:

A song of gratitude and praise by David, to the God of all our comforting..

In all our distress we will be delivered if we trust in our God to follow his Word and depend upon him alone.

22:2 And he said, The LORD is my rock, and my fortress, and my deliverer; **22:3** The God of my rock; in him will I trust: he is my shield, and the horn of my salvation, my high tower, and my refuge, my saviour; thou savest me from violence.

Instead of watering down our zeal to live by every Word of God in order to ease our trials; we should be doing the exact opposite and running to our Mighty One for HIS Deliverance.

22:4 I will call on the LORD, who is worthy to be praised: so shall I be saved from mine enemies.

Our Deliverer will deliver his faithful overcomers out of death and the grave itself!

22:5 When the waves of death compassed me, the floods of ungodly men made me afraid; **22:6** The sorrows of hell compassed me about; the snares of death prevented [held me] me; **22:7** In my distress I called upon the LORD, and cried to my God: and he did hear my voice out of his temple, and my cry did enter into his ears.

This is a history of the deliverance of Israel and Moses, and is a prophecy of what is to come! When God remembers us in the grave he will send Messiah the Christ to shake the heavens and the earth for us, to deliver us from the grave into a resurrection to spirit and granting total victory over the god of rebellion and death, Satan.

22:8 Then the earth shook and trembled; the foundations of heaven moved and shook, because he was wroth. **22:9** There went up a smoke out of his nostrils, and fire out of his mouth devoured: coals were kindled by it. **22:10** He bowed the heavens also, and came down; and darkness was under his feet.

In the darkness of this world, our God is a blazing light of righteousness.

22:11 And he rode upon a cherub, and did fly: and he was seen upon the wings of the wind. **22:12** And he made darkness pavilions round about him, dark waters, and thick clouds of the skies. **22:13** Through the brightness before him were coals of fire kindled.

Our Mighty God thunders his Word and casts out all those who will not seek diligently to learn and live by every Word of God, to internalize every Word of God and to become LIKE HIM!

22:14 The LORD thundered from heaven, and the most High uttered his voice. **22:15** And he sent out arrows, and scattered them; lightning, and discomfited them.

Just like the Red Sea was opened up to expose the dry land, so the graves will be opened up to bring forth the faithful chosen overcomers!

22:16 And the channels of the sea appeared, the foundations of the world were discovered, at the rebuking of the LORD, at the blast of the breath of his nostrils.

The Eternal will deliver his spiritual called out who persevere and overcome, from death itself into eternal life! Evil is too strong for us alone, but the Lord our Deliverer will emancipate us through his own strength so that no flesh may glory.

22:17 He sent from above, he took me; he drew me out of many waters; **22:18** He delivered me from my strong enemy [death], and from them that hated me: for they were too strong for me.

The wicked may persecute the faithful; but if we depend upon our God HE will deliver us because we rely upon HIM!

22:19 They prevented [the wicked fought against] me in the day of my calamity: but the LORD was my stay.

God delights in all those who make the zealous keeping of every Word of God their delight!

22:20 He brought me forth also into a large place: he delivered me, because he delighted in me.

Our reward is directly related to our zeal to learn and to live by every Word of God; which is the righteousness of God.

22:21 The LORD rewarded me according to my righteousness: according to the cleanness of my hands hath he recompensed me. **22:22 For I have kept the ways of the LORD, and have not wickedly departed from my God. 22:23 For all his judgments were before me: and as for his statutes, I did not depart from them. 22:24** I was also upright before him, and have kept myself from mine iniquity.

No, Jesus Christ will not overlook any sin; he will reward every man according to his works.

22:25 Therefore the LORD hath recompensed me according to my righteousness; according to my cleanness in his eye sight.

Consider how the beatitudes of Matthew 5 and many of the teachings of Jesus are quotes from the Psalms.

22:26 With the merciful thou wilt shew thyself merciful, and with the upright man thou wilt shew thyself upright. **22:27** With the pure thou wilt shew thyself pure; and with the froward [stubborn, self-willed] thou wilt shew thyself unsavoury. **22:28** And the afflicted people thou wilt save: but thine eyes are upon the haughty, that thou mayest bring them down.

Jesus Christ is our light (John 1) of righteousness in this dark world, and he taught us that we are to live by every Word of God (Matthew 4:4). If we learn and zealously live by every Word of God, then the light of God will shine within us through the Spirit of God the Father and of Jesus Christ.

22:29 For thou art my lamp, O LORD: and the LORD will lighten my darkness.

The light of the whole Word of God delivers us from all our enemies, and from bondage to Satan, sin and death!

22:30 For by thee I have run through a troop: by my God have I leaped over a wall.

God is perfect and his whole Word is perfect, not just the Ten Commandments but EVERY Word of God. Living by EVERY Word of God converts and delivers the sincerely repentant who are diligent to STOP sinning and go on to sin no more!

22:31 As for God, his way is perfect; the word of the LORD is tried: he is a buckler to all them that trust in him. **22:32** For who is God, save the LORD? and who is a rock, save our God? **22:33** God is my strength and power: and he maketh my way perfect.

In spiritual terms our Mighty One delivers us and teaches us to fight the spiritual battle against sin.

22:34 He maketh my feet like hinds' feet: and setteth me upon my high places. **22:35** He teacheth my hands to war; so that a bow of steel is broken by mine arms. **22:36** Thou hast also given me the shield of thy salvation: and thy gentleness [God's mercy for the sincerely repentant lifts them up from sin and death.] hath made me great.

Carefully thinking through, applying and living by every Word of God, keeps one from slipping into sin.

22:37 Thou hast enlarged my steps under me; so that my feet did not slip.

Through the strength of our God, and our zeal for God and his Word; we will be given victory over sin and death.

22:38 I have pursued mine enemies, and destroyed them; and turned not again until I had consumed them **22:39** And I have consumed them, and wounded them, that they could not arise: yea, they are fallen under my feet.

Our strength to fight sin, which is turning aside from any part of the whole Word of God; comes from Almighty God and not from our own selves.

22:40 For thou hast girded me with strength to battle: them that rose up against me hast thou subdued under me. **22:41** Thou hast also given me the necks of mine enemies, that I might destroy them that hate me.

We can call ourselves godly, we can call on God; but we are not godly and he will not hear us if we are not zealous to learn and to live by every Word of God.

If we love our own pet ideas more than we love the Word of God, we are separated and cut off from God!

If we are absolutely faithful to trust in and follow every Word of God, all sin can be beaten and crushed to nothing under our feet.

22:42 They looked, but there was none to save; even unto the LORD, but he answered them not. **22:43** Then did I beat them as small as the dust of the earth, I did stamp them as the mire of the street, and did spread them abroad.

When the whole earth is repentant in the kingdom of God; all peoples shall know the faithfulness of their changed to spirit kings and will follow their example of faithfulness to God.

22:44 Thou also hast delivered me from the strivings of my people, thou hast kept me to be head of the heathen: a people which I knew not shall serve me. **22:45** Strangers shall submit themselves unto me: as soon as they hear, they shall be obedient unto me.

In God's kingdom most people will turn to the Eternal God and the stranger to godliness [the wicked] will hide themselves.

22:46 Strangers shall fade away, and they shall be afraid out of their close [hiding] places.

22:47 The LORD liveth; and blessed be my rock; and exalted be the God of the rock of my salvation.

God alone delivers his faithful and exalts the righteous.

22:48 It is God that avengeth me, and that bringeth down the people under me. **22:49** And that bringeth me forth from mine enemies: thou also hast lifted me up on high above them that rose up against me: thou hast delivered me from the violent man.

22:50 Therefore I will give thanks unto thee, O LORD, among the heathen [the righteous will thank and glorify God even while living among the wicked], and I will sing praises unto thy name. **22:51** He is the tower of salvation for his king [God is the strength of all those who are chosen to be kings and priests, through their faithfulness to their baptismal commitment to sin no more.]: and sheweth mercy to his anointed, unto David, and to his seed for evermore.

2 Samuel 23

Instructions from God on how to be a godly king; this applies to both physical kings and the spirit kings of the promised spiritual Kingdom of God.

2 Samuel 23:1 Now these be the last words of David. David the son of Jesse said, and the man who was raised up on high, the anointed of the God of Jacob, and the sweet psalmist of Israel, said,

23:2 The Spirit of the LORD spake by me, and his word was in my tongue. **23:3** The God of Israel said, the Rock of Israel spake to me, **He that ruleth over men must be just, ruling in the fear of God.**

God's Word is a light dispelling spiritual darkness (John 1). Those who live by every Word of God will have spiritual sight.

23:4 And he shall be as the light of the morning, when the sun riseth, even a morning without clouds; as the tender grass springing out of the earth by clear shining after rain.

Even though we are now physical: God will raise us up to eternal life and a sure kingdom if we are faithful to him in all things.

23:5 Although my house be not so with God; yet he hath made with me an everlasting covenant, ordered in all things, and sure: for this is all my salvation, and all my desire, although he make it not to grow.

The wicked who tolerate sin and falsely claim that Jesus will also tolerate unrepented sin; will be burned to ashes in the lake of fire.

23:6 But the sons of Belial shall be all of them as thorns thrust away, because they cannot be taken with hands: **23:7** But the man that shall touch them must be fenced with iron and the staff of a spear; and they shall be utterly burned with fire in the same place.

The spiritually called out who are zealous for the Word of God and quick and enthusiastically faithful to follow the Mighty One of Jacob, will be spiritually mighty against sin like the thirty mighty men of David were valiant against physical enemies.

23:8 These be the names of the mighty men whom David had: The Tachmonite that sat in the seat, chief among the captains; the same was **Adino** the Eznite: he lift up his spear against eight hundred, whom he slew at one time.

23:9 And after him was **Eleazar** the son of Dodo the Ahohite, one of the three mighty men with David, when they defied the Philistines that were there gathered together to battle, and the men of Israel were gone away: **23:10** He arose, and smote the Philistines until his hand was weary, and his hand clave [he gripped it so long and so tightly that he could not let it go.] unto the sword: and the LORD wrought a great victory that day; and the people returned after him only to spoil.

23:11 And after him was **Shammah** the son of Agee the Hararite. And the Philistines were gathered together into a troop, where was a piece of ground full of lentiles: and the people fled from the Philistines. **23:12** But he stood in the midst of the ground, and defended it, and slew the Philistines: and **the LORD wrought a great victory.**

23:13 And three of the thirty chief went down, and came to David in the harvest time unto the cave of Adullam: and the troop of the Philistines pitched in the valley of Rephaim. **23:14** And David was then in an hold, and the garrison of the Philistines was then in Bethlehem.

David longed for water and we are to thirst after that spiritual Living Water of the Word of God with all our hearts through all of our lives.

23:15 And David longed, and said, Oh that one would give me drink of the water of the well of Bethlehem, which is by the gate! **23:16** And the three mighty men brake through the host of the Philistines, and drew water out of the well of Bethlehem, that was by the gate, and took it, and brought it to David: nevertheless he would not drink thereof, but poured it out unto the LORD. **23:17** And he said, Be it far from me, O LORD, that I should do this: is not this the blood of the men that went in jeopardy of their lives? therefore he would not drink it. These things did these three mighty men.

David's 30 commanders were divided into ten groups of three each, and Abishai was chief of his own three.

23:18 And **Abishai**, the brother of Joab, the son of Zeruiah, was chief among three. And he lifted up his spear against three hundred, and slew them, and had the name [leadership of his three] among three. **23:19** Was he not most honourable of [his] three? therefore he was their captain: howbeit he attained not unto [the deeds of] the first three [the first three being Adino, Eleazar and Shammah].

23:20 And Benaiah the son of Jehoiada, the son of a valiant man, of Kabzeel, who had done many acts, he slew two lionlike men of Moab: he went down also and slew a lion in the midst of a pit in time of snow: **23:21** And he slew an Egyptian, a goodly man: and the Egyptian had a spear in his hand; but he [Benaiah] went down to him with a staff, and plucked the spear out of the Egyptian's hand, and slew him with his own spear. **23:22** These things did Benaiah the son of Jehoiada, and had the name among [his] three mighty men. **23:23** He was more honourable than the thirty, but he attained not to the first three. And David set him over his guard.

23:24 Asahel the brother of Joab was one of the thirty; **Elhanan** the son of Dodo of Bethlehem, **23:25 Shammah** the Harodite, **Elika** the Harodite, **23:26 Helez** the Paltite, Ira the son of Ikkesh the Tekoite, **23:27 Abiezer** the Anethothite, **Mebunnai** the Hushathite, **23:28 Zalmon** the Ahohite, **Maharai** the Netophathite, **23:29 Heleb** the son of Baanah, a Netophathite, **Ittai** the son of Ribai out of Gibeah of the children of Benjamin, **23:30 Benaiah** the Pirathonite, **Hiddai** of the brooks of Gaash,

23:31 Abialbon the Arbathite, **Azmaveth** the Barhumite, **23:32 Eliahba** the Shaalbonite, of the sons of Jashen, **Jonathan**, **23:33 Shammah** the Hararite, **Ahiam** the son of Sharar the Hararite, **23:34 Eliphelet** the son of Ahasbai, the son of the Maachathite, *Eliam the son of Ahithophel [and father of Bathsheba] the Gilonite*, **23:35 Hezrai** the Carmelite, **Paarai** the

Arbite, **23:36 Igal** the son of Nathan of Zobah, **Bani** the Gadite, **23:37 Zelek** the Ammonite, **Nahari** the Beerothite, armourbearer to Joab the son of Zeruiah, **23:38 Ira** an Ithrite, Gareb an Ithrite, **23:39 Uriah** the Hittite: **thirty and seven in all**.

2 Samuel 24

The being who later became flesh as Jesus Christ was angry with Israel. They had undoubtedly departed from some part of the Word of God to keep their own ways in place of God's Word, for that is the lesson given. David numbered the people to exalt in his own strength; and Christ diminished the people to teach David that we are to rely on God and not on ourselves and our own strength.

If physical Israel angered Christ by compromising with his Word; how much more is Jesus Christ angered by the departure of Spiritual Israel from the Word of God?

2 Samuel 24:1 And again the anger of the LORD was kindled against Israel, and he moved David against them to say, Go, number Israel and Judah.

David commanded Joab to number the people. Remember that Christ had commanded others to number the people at other times. The issue here is that David was trusting in the strength of the people which he had been exalted over and was not trusting in God.

Beware the sin of trusting in men and not in God!

24:2 For the king said to Joab the captain of the host, which was with him, Go now through all the tribes of Israel, from Dan even to Beersheba, and number ye the people, that I may know the number of the people.

Joab protested the counting

24:3 And Joab said unto the king, Now the LORD thy God add unto the people, how many soever they be, an hundredfold, and that the eyes of my lord the king may see it: but why doth my lord the king delight in this thing?

David insisted

24:4 Notwithstanding the king's word prevailed against Joab, and against the captains of the host. And Joab and the captains of the host went out from the presence of the king, to number the people of Israel.

It took nine months and twenty days to count all the people.

24:5 And they passed over Jordan, and pitched in Aroer, on the right side of the city that lieth in the midst of the river of Gad, and toward Jazer: **24:6** Then they came to Gilead, and to the land of Tahtimhodshi; and they came to Danjaan, and about to Zidon, **24:7** And came to the strong hold of Tyre, and to all the cities of the Hivites, and of the Canaanites: and they went out to the south of Judah, even to Beersheba. **24:8** So when they had gone through all the land, they came to Jerusalem at the end of nine months and twenty days.

There were 1,300,000 men of war in Israel.

24:9 And Joab gave up the sum of the number of the people unto the king: and there were in Israel eight hundred thousand valiant men that drew the sword; and the men of Judah were five hundred thousand men.

David then repented and was grieved that he had delighted in his own strength and not in the strength of the Eternal.

24:10 And David's heart smote him after that he had numbered the people.

David repented sincerely from the heart, yet the one who became Jesus Christ still corrected him so that he would learn the lesson thoroughly for all time.

Brethren, here is the answer to why we are not immediately delivered from some trial when we repent. It is very important that we, although forgiven by God, also experience the consequences of our sins and learn the correct lessons from our mistakes.

This is to teach us lessons that will last for eternity and also for us to learn the consequences of our sin thoroughly, so that we can be priests fully able to understand those whom we will be teaching in future.

. . . And David said unto the LORD, I have sinned greatly in that I have done: and now, I beseech thee, O LORD, take away the iniquity of thy servant; for I have done very foolishly.

God then sent his prophet Gad to ask David to make himself a choice as to his punishment.

24:11 For when David was up in the morning, the word of the LORD came unto the prophet Gad, David's seer, saying, **24:12** Go and say unto David, Thus saith the LORD, I offer thee three things; choose thee one of them, that I may do it unto thee.

24:13 So Gad came to David, and told him, and said unto him, Shall seven years of famine come unto thee in thy land? or wilt thou flee three months before thine enemies, while they pursue thee? or that there be three days' pestilence in thy land? now advise, and see what answer I shall return to him that sent me.

David then seeks to place himself fully in the hands of Messiah the Christ; as very many of us will do in the imminent great tribulation, which is coming upon us for the same reason. We shall be cast into tribulation for our pride and self-reliance, and for having no humility [meekness] before God to follow him and faithfully live by every Word of God.

24:14 And David said unto Gad, I am in a great strait: let us fall now into the hand of the LORD; for his mercies are great: and let me not fall into the hand of man.

Then the Being who later became flesh as Jesus Christ killed 70,000 men with a pestilence. Consider that Jesus Christ killed seventy thousand to smash David's idolizing of his own power in his own eyes. Today's Spiritual Ekklesia is also idolizing men and corporate entities, and Jesus Christ will also smash our idols.

Our leaders and elders and our corporate church organizations are going to be SMASHED and CRUSHED into the nothingness of fine dust.

There will be No "Elijah" work by these proud self-centered men who do what they think is right according to the false traditions of men, and reject knowledge of godliness (Hosea 41-6); and hold the table of the Lord in contempt (Mal 1:12) by lifting up their noses at the meat of the whole Word of God being offered to them today.

24:15 So the LORD sent a pestilence upon Israel from the morning even to the time appointed: and there died of the people from Dan even to Beersheba seventy thousand men.

Then the pestilence was stopped at the place which Jesus Christ had chosen for God the Father's Temple.

The Temple today is spiritual, consisting of those who are called of God and in whom God dwells; not any physical building.

24:16 And when the angel stretched out his hand upon Jerusalem to destroy it, the LORD repented him of the evil, and said to the angel that destroyed the people, It is enough: stay now thine hand. And the angel of the LORD was by the threshingplace of Araunah the Jebusite.

David learned his lesson well and repented even more sincerely and deeply. Even so all those people called of God who have departed from any zeal to live by every Word of God to exalt and make idols of their own ways, traditions, men and organizations; will sincerely repent when they find that their fears have come upon them in the tribulation, and their own idols will not be able to save them from the correction of the Eternal.

24:17 And David spake unto the LORD when he saw the angel that smote the people, and said, Lo, I have sinned, and I have done wickedly: but these sheep, what have they done? let thine hand, I pray thee, be against me, and against my father's house.

Gad then told David to build an altar on the spot where the plague had stopped.

24:18 And Gad came that day to David, and said unto him, Go up, rear an altar unto the LORD in the threshingfloor of Araunah the Jebusite. **24:19** And David, according to the saying of Gad, went up as the LORD commanded.

David bought the place from Araunah, even though Araunah is most ready to give it. This shows the repentance and zeal of both David to do as he was told and of Araunah the willing.

24:20 And Araunah looked, and saw the king and his servants coming on toward him: and Araunah went out, and bowed himself before the king on his face upon the ground. **24:21** And Araunah said, Wherefore is my lord the king come to his servant? And David said, To buy the threshingfloor of thee, to build an altar unto the LORD, that the plague may be stayed from the people.

24:22 And Araunah said unto David, Let my lord the king take and offer up what seemeth good unto him: behold, here be oxen for burnt sacrifice, and threshing instruments and other instruments of the oxen for wood. **24:23** All these things did Araunah, as a king, give unto the king. And Araunah said unto the king, The LORD thy God accept thee.

The holy mount was then bought by David for the Eternal for fifty shekels of silver.

24:24 And the king said unto Araunah, Nay; but I will surely buy it of thee at a price: neither will I offer burnt offerings unto the LORD my God of that which doth cost me nothing. So David bought the threshingfloor and the oxen for fifty shekels of silver.

In the millennial kingdom, Messiah the Christ will build a new Temple on this same spot, a glorious Temple; and all nations shall flow to it to worship the Mighty Eternal God and to learn and to live by every Word of God without any compromise or hint of turning aside.

24:25 And David built there an altar unto the LORD, and offered burnt offerings and peace offerings. So the LORD was intreated for the land, and the plague was stayed from Israel.

The story of David is the story of all those called out to God to become priests of the High Priesthood of Melchizedek and kings over all the earth.

Saul, the man of the people was chosen by Christ to be an allegory of Lucifer, who was created and started off perfectly, only to fall away from God.

David was then chosen to replace Saul, as we are called to replace Satan the god-king of this world.

The many trials of David were to prepare him to be king over all Israel for eternity in the resurrection. Our many trials are for the same purpose; to prepare us to be proper godly kings and priests for all eternity.

The many trials of David are consistent with the many trials and testing's of the spiritually called out to replace Satan.

When David relied on God he was always successful in his battles, and when he relied on himself he always failed. This is a lesson for the spiritually called out, that to overcome sin we must always be close to and rely on God our Deliverer, for we cannot overcome sin by our own strength.

David suffered greatly for his sins and so do the spiritually called out, so that the lessons that they are learning will be deeply instilled and will last for eternity.

Even after repentance we may still suffer; this does not mean that we are not forgiven, it means that God is still teaching us the lesson so that it will last for eternity.

The faithful are kings and priests in training, and if we faint not we will receive a kingdom. We must rule that kingdom in true godliness, which means that we must fully internalize every Word of God to learn it and to keep it.

We must not be respecters of persons but we must apply the justice of God's Word to all people equally. That means knowing the whole Word of God and having our eyes open to discern between the wicked willful law breakers and the righteous; and to fully enforce the whole Word of God.

There is NO room in the kingdom of God for willful commandment breaking and compromising with any part of the whole Word of God, and no place for any tolerance of willful sin.

David was a man after God's own heart because he was willing to quickly repent when found in sin, yet he was a man who committed many horrendous sins. We are to learn from these things and we are to work to avoid all sin on both the physical and the spiritual plain.

We are to avoid adultery on the physical plain and we are to avoid spiritual adultery against the Husband of our Baptismal commitment, by not following idols of men, corporate entities or any false traditions and imaginations.

We are to learn from David's mistakes: We are NOT to repeat them or to use them to try and justify our own sins!

When David found himself in sin, what did he do? Did he try to justify himself and defend his actions; or did he immediately admit his sin and repent sincerely and wholeheartedly?

If we also immediately admit our sin, and repent sincerely and wholeheartedly; we will also become a people after God's own heart!

Like David we will become fit to enter eternity and to be the priests of the High Priesthood of Jesus Christ; and to be kings over a kingdom in the family of God the Father.

Visit our Website

theshininglight.info

www.ingramcontent.com/pod-product-compliance
Lightning Source LLC
Chambersburg PA
CBHW081344230426
43667CB00017B/2716